The New
No-Nonsense
Landlord

The New No-Nonsense Landlord

Building Wealth with Rental Properties

Richard H. Jorgensen

Revised and Expanded

McGraw-Hill

New York Chicago San Francisco Lisbon London
Madrid Mexico City Milan New Delhi San Juan
Seoul Singapore Sydney Toronto

The **McGraw·Hill** Companies

1 2 3 4 5 6 7 8 9 0 DOC/DOC 0 9 8 7 6 5 4 3

ISBN 0-07-141793-1

Editorial and production services provided by CWL Publishing Enterprises, Inc., Madison, Wisconsin, www.cwlpub.com.

This publication is designed to provide accurate and authoritative information in regard to the subject matter covered. It is sold with the understanding that neither the author nor the publisher is engaged in rendering legal, accounting, or other professional service. If legal advice or other expert assistance is required, the services of a competent professional person should be sought.

—From a Declaration of Principles jointly adopted by a Committee of the American Bar Association and a Committee of Publishers

McGraw-Hill books are available at special quantity discounts to use as premiums and sales promotions, or for use in corporate training programs. For more information, please write to the Director of Special Sales, McGraw-Hill, 2 Penn Plaza, New York, NY 10121-2298. Or contact your local bookstore.

 This book is printed on recycled, acid-free paper containing a minimum of 50% recycled de-inked fiber.

Contents

The New
No-Nonsense
Landlord

Part One

Getting Started and Getting Motivated

Chapter 1

Profitable Real Estate Investing for the Average Person

16 Key Factors to Consider When Investing Your Hard-Earned Money in Real Estate

Key Factor 1

Thoughtful, intelligent real estate investing is one way the average person, just like you and I, can accumulate wealth by using other people's money, whether it's a loan company's, a bank or savings and loan's, an individual seller's (contract-for-deed financing), the tenant's rent that will be applied to the loan, or tax benefits from the government.

It's not necessary to be rich to get started in the real estate rental business. You'll discover that the common person, the small independent investor who doesn't have the kind of wealth it takes for a large down payment, can invest in rental property. As you go through this book, you'll learn how investment property can be purchased by using other people's money.

This plan for buying, owning, and managing rental property is simply a no-nonsense program with no frills, gimmicks, or tricks. I want to tell you right from the start that, in addition to the fact that I don't have any gimmicks or tricks, I am a small, independent, part-

3

time investor. I write what I know, and what I've experienced, and what has worked for me, and I've added information from other small investors who have also succeeded in this business. These experiences and good advice should help anyone get off to a good start in the rental property business, and I can safely say that it will also help those who already own property.

Key Factor 2

Anyone—regardless of age, education, occupation, or financial status—can invest in real estate.

Let me assure you that I don't possess any special skills or unique talents that might have enabled me to make money. You'll discover that it's not necessary to have any special education, other than the fact that the more you learn from what you read the better off you'll be. But it's not necessary to have a Harvard degree or an MBA or any degree at all, for that matter.

I'll guarantee you that I'm certainly not a financial wizard. I have no more than an average college education, average grades, and an average Bachelor of Arts degree. I have certainly had a much less than average financial background, having spent the first 16 years of my life being poor.

Key Factor 3

A real estate investment can build net worth and wealth by building equity in the property, using tax write-offs, and realizing the increase in the value of the property, which is called "appreciation."

Appreciation, the increased valued of the property, is the key to success in this business. Appreciation comes from the natural flow of the economy, but it also comes from the hard work and dedication you put into your property.

Key Factor 4

Look for seller financing.

In the text we'll discuss at length the contract-for-deed purchase of property.

Key Factor 5

Be cautious when considering urban investment real estate. Look for small communities.

Think about looking for investment property in a rural community, rather than urban real estate. For the most part you can make just as much money with rural property and avoid the hassle and agony of dealing with urban problems. You'll find full coverage on this aspect of investment property in a later chapter.

Key Factor 6

Think "small" duplexes, fourplexes, and sixplexes rather than larger apartment buildings to get started.

A duplex is something anyone can afford as well as being a starter home and investment property.

Key Factor 7

Shop for real estate bargains.

In a recent survey by the Urban Land Institute, low- and middle-income rental properties placed first and second for prospective investment performance. They're still out there, but it takes some intense shopping. Don't be surprised if you have to look at one hundred properties before you find the right one.

Key Factor 8

Learn the art of screening tenants.

Tenants will be the lifeblood of your business and this will be an art
you'll want to learn: screening and getting the "good" tenants.

Key Factor 9

**Be aware of government restrictions. Government agencies and regula-
tors can be your enemy.**

We're going to talk about government intrusion in the real estate business and the effects it can have on your investment property. We'll cover
discrimination laws, equal housing opportunity laws, crime-free and
drug-free housing, proper leases, lead paint and lead-based paint hazards, mold, dealing with eviction, collecting past-due rent, court procedures, rent deposits, and other legal obligations one must endure.

Key Factor 10

Maintaining a positive attitude can lead to a success story.

There has always been, and probably always will be, something about
real estate money and the ownership of property that rings of success
and prestige and is admired by a lot of people. For instance, if a
plumber or a garbage collector becomes rich, you don't notice it, but if a
garbage collector or a plumber buys real estate and becomes rich with
real estate holdings, that individual, as a successful real estate investor,
is looked at with awe.

I suppose part of this mystique can be attributed to the fact that if
you own a garbage-collection service, you've got to work full-time to
take care of the business, no matter how rich you are.

When you own real estate, it's not necessary to work at it all the time.
You don't have to get up in the morning and get in the garbage truck.
You can get up whenever you want. It can be a leisurely business if you
want it that way. However, I don't recommend the laid-back approach.

Key Factor 11

Be prepared to spend time and money on your investment.

The odds are pretty good that most of the income for the first period of time will be reinvested. Where you'll make your money is the time you spend on your property.

What my investment plan does require is a great deal of determination along with a lot of enthusiasm and personal involvement ... and some risk taking. But, remember the risk takers, and I'm certainly not talking about the robber barons of our society, are always the ones who end up with the money. They always have and always will. That's the way things work.

When I say it takes "involvement," I mean that you, the investor, will have to dig in and do some of the menial work in order to succeed. I recommend getting up early in the morning, just like the garbage collector (maybe not that early), and going to work, taking care of the real estate just like any other business, attentively and diligently. A lot of the work will be mental: decision making that will require a higher-than-average intelligence.

Key Factor 12

Get at least one or two good ideas from each book you read.

By taking your time, you can learn how to make wise decisions based on careful analysis. I am confident that, with the basic ingredients of determination and enthusiasm, this plan can and will work. I have invested in real estate for the past 30 years and made money, and I mean good money—money I never dreamed was available to an average, everyday person. And, let me say again: if I can do it, anyone can.

Key Factor 13

Control your own financial destiny.

I imagine by now you've heard of the Enron and World.com executives and all the other corporate thieves. Some time ago most of us were given the "opportunity" to invest our money in these corporations for our savings and retirement. The only trouble is that we weren't a part of the loop. We didn't have control of the money and the benefits that some of the corporate officers, stock brokers, and accountants had. As you well know, they were able to cash in when things weren't going well and just before the corporate structures crashed. There's no sense telling those stories again; you get the idea.

However, as I look back over my career in the real estate business, I realize that I've been able to control my own destiny. I've experienced a great deal of financial success along with a lot of personal satisfaction with my real estate investments and I didn't have to depend on other decision makers. I was my own boss.

Key Factor 14

Real estate is a solid investment.

The primary theme of this book is that ordinary people, just like you and me, can invest in real estate and accumulate wealth. It's very important for all of us to establish financial security without depending on others. That's something we can and should strive for. If the investment business is handled properly, there's convincing evidence in this book that you can achieve financial independence through real estate investing.

Key Factor 15

Be aware of schemes.

You've also probably watched some of the TV hucksters selling tapes and books and ideas about buying investment property. They always seem to have some 19- or 22-year-old kid, an investor, who'll tell you, the TV audience, about how they made $300,000 in 90 days or some such story. It seems to me that their financial success depends on who's counting the money and who's assigning the value to the so-called $300,000 properties.

Frankly, to my knowledge, there aren't any easy or quick ways to real estate wealth, regardless of what's been said by the TV pitchmen. I also believe it's unfair to lead people down the primrose path, making them think they can get rich quickly and easily.

Key Factor 16

If you want to get rich quick, this is not the book for you.

Chapter 2

Success Stories of Ordinary, Everyday People

A Financial Plan for Ordinary People

I don't know of any other system, device, scheme, technique, method, plan, or anything else—short of robbing a bank, hitting a jackpot, or winning a sweepstakes—with which the average, ordinary, everyday person can accumulate substantial wealth and build a solid financial future better or more easily than by investing in real estate.

When I said "the average, ordinary, everyday person," a friend of mine commented, "You'd better not call anyone 'average' because they're going to be turned off and won't be interested in what you have to say. No one wants to be told they're average. Everyone wants to be considered unique."

I guess I can answer that by saying that my friend is partially right because I know all of us are unique in our own way. Those of us who have looked at real estate or who have bought real estate as an investment program are, in fact, quite unique.

The truth, however, is that most of us are average. Very few of us ever become investment geniuses like the very wealthy of our society. In addition, the odds are pretty good that we'll never attain the position of a Bill Gates, the billionaire computer genius. I don't think that many of us, despite our dreams and fantasies, will become rich and famous. The chances of winning the sweepstakes or a lottery are, to say the least, very minimal for most of us. Also, as you and I both know, there aren't many among us who will inherit great sums of money.

That leaves most of us just plain average, ordinary, everyday folks. We dress alike, drive the same kind of cars (with some variations), eat and travel alike, live in an average home with an average mortgage, have an average job and an average income, and a lot of us end up with an average retirement. The sad part is that the retirement, which consists of the proverbial gold watch, an average pension, and a Social Security check, might not cover our needs. All this can and does happen to a million people every day of the week. It also can happen to you and me, unless we make plans to do something about it *now!*

When I make this cautionary observation about retirement, a lot of people don't think it can happen to them. They more or less believe, as I did—and as most of us did when we were younger, that we're immortal and will never grow old and need any security and money. It's something too remote and not worth thinking about—until it's too late.

The plain fact is, though, that no matter how hard we might fight it, we are mortal, and we're all going to grow old. And if we want to grow old gracefully and in comfort, we better have some concern about security and the finances it takes to maintain that security. In fact, security is great, and I recommend it, but we should want more than mere security. We should have a burning desire to have that security, and we should want to go first class, wherever and whenever we want to go.

Building Financial Security for the Future

With the future uncertain and our Social "Security" system insecure, we are left with a question we should all be asking ourselves: "What can I do to provide financial security and some sort of financial growth for my future?"

I don't think any of us want to remain, at least financially speaking, a plain, average, ordinary, everyday person, waiting at the post office for our monthly Social Security check and wondering if there's enough money for a vacation or a trip, … not even being able to consider going first class. But listen, I figure the smart person, the unique person, the one who keeps his or her nose to the grindstone, will think long and hard about this and will want to do something about it *now*. The smart person's going to want more than being in the Social Security post office lineup.

My experience has convinced me that anyone can find a way to escape from this average existence if he or she wants to. And that way, for the average, ordinary, everyday person, is real estate investing, which offers one of the very few opportunities for the average person to accumulate any sort of wealth and build financial security, to maintain a retirement program, and to experience some of the good things in life.

We might not reach the level of the very rich and famous, and we might not make our money as quickly as we would if we won the lottery drawing, but real estate, with its built-in financial components of:

- rental income,
- contract-for-deed or mortgage payments, and
- money in the bank,

represents:

- security,
- freedom from debt,
- independence, and
- first-class accommodations.

For anyone, especially for the entrepreneur who wants to become financially independent, for the average, ordinary, everyday person who wants to make some progress in our free-enterprise economy, *right now is* the best time ever to consider doing something about his or her future. Let me assure you: if I, Joe Average, can do it, anyone can.

Listen, my life certainly was average. I was an average, ordinary, everyday person living in an average neighborhood, raising an average family on an average income ... until I discovered what real estate could do to my average existence. When I bought my first property, I didn't have a lot of money (which is the case for most of us), and that's certainly average. In addition, I had no special education or financial background, other than an average college degree, and that's certainly no more than average. And, believe me, I had no chance of any inheritance. That meant, with an average income and an average education, it was pretty clear that I wasn't going to make a lot of money as a rocket scientist or computer genius, nor was I going to make it big in the business world of pizzas, fast food, cookies, and computers.

The Little Hidden Secret (Which You've Heard Before)

However, I knew, as a restless entrepreneur, that I needed to look for some way to accumulate some sort of financial security. As I searched around, I discovered a "little hidden secret" in the business world, a secret I really hadn't recognized at first. But, once this secret was called to my attention, I could see that there was, in fact, a way for me to accumulate any amount of wealth I wanted and that this method was available to just about anybody who had some initiative, determination, and entrepreneurial spirit. The "little hidden secret" was real estate investing.

Don's Investment Property

Figure 2-1 shows an example of an ideal older investment property. The owner is a college professor who dabbled in rental property. He bought this duplex at a reasonable price, and, as a duplex, it did quite well. However, Don discovered that with a few modifications he was able to have the property approved by the state for residential housing for the mentally handicapped. Because the neighborhood was a mixture of homes and multiunit properties, he had no trouble with the zoning or neighbors. (I might add here that the residents aren't mentally disabled

Figure 2-1. Although this is an older property, it's in reasonably good condition, has a good roof, a solid foundation and basement, and a good location. As you can see, it has many rooms so that it is compatible for multiunit housing. Older properties are usually good investments because their prices are reasonable and, with proper financing, the rents should cover the payments and maintenance.

but are merely mentally handicapped.) A lot of states are currently implementing similar programs through which they house mentally handicapped people in regular residential homes rather than in sanitariums and hospitals.

One thing about renting to the state: you know you're going to get your money. Not only do you get your money, but the state pays all expenses and usually a better-than-average monthly rate. Another thing you'll find when renting to the government is that there are very few landlord responsibilities. When something needs fixing, the tenant usually fixes it. All utilities are paid by the state, and the rent check comes in every month ... right on time.

I have found, and you probably will too, that in a college community the professors are quite active in the real estate investment business. I think one reason for their involvement is that they have some flexibility in scheduling their work hours—class preparation and grading papers, for example, can be done in the evenings.

Randy's Real Estate Investment Career

Here's another real estate story. Randy works in the business office at the college. Several years ago he decided it was time to do something about his future. He was well aware of the fact that his job would provide a good living and a satisfactory retirement, but there would be no way he could accumulate wealth of any consequence. So he looked at real estate investing.

First, he bought a used mobile home, located in a trailer park near the college, for a minimal amount. Because he had a good credit rating, he was able to buy it without a down payment, and it was easily financed, almost like a car, through the bank. He then rented the home to college students. This investment, for the money involved, turned out to be a very good investment. There was steady income from the rent, no great expenses, and not much upkeep and work. So he bought a second mobile home, and then a third.

Because the value of mobile homes isn't all that stable in the real estate market and there is very little appreciation, Randy decided it was time to turn to rental properties that would appreciate more reliably. With the money he acquired by selling the mobile homes—his equity— and having paid off the mortgage with the students' rent, he was able to get together a nice down payment for a duplex.

He purchased the duplex shown in Figure 2-2, and it turned out to be an exceptional investment. It's a large, older home converted into an upper and lower two-unit apartment. It's very rentable and has proven to be a turning point in Randy's investment career. I'm sure as time goes on he'll be buying more investment property.

Figure 2-2. This large old family home was easily converted into a duplex. It's located in a desirable neighborhood, which makes it a good investment property. Maybe one of these won't make you rich, but 10 or 20 of them will. My theory is that if you look at buying 20 all at once, you'll probably not get into the business. However, if you buy one now, and another later, then the odds are in your favor, and you will get started in the business.

Jane's Story of Successful Investing

Jane, age 38 and single, has a good job as a professional photographer, earns an average income, and lives in a big city. Since the time she left college, she has been renting an apartment or a duplex. She told me, "I've paid my rent every month for a number of years and found out that the $615 was going to my landlord, who was buying this property with my money. I ended up each month with nothing more than a receipt. If I am ever going to acquire anything financially, this has to end."

She came to me for some advice about investment real estate. I recommended that she read some real estate investing books, learn about the business, and then start looking around. I told her to look for moderately priced duplexes and find a neighborhood and property that were pleasing to her. The next step, I told her, was to use her savings account for a down payment. She could then live in one-half of the unit she bought, having the comfort of her own home and the security of never being evicted. Most importantly, she could rent out the other half of the property. I told her to be careful in choosing her tenant so that she would have a neighbor who would be compatible with her lifestyle. With the income from the rental unit and the $615 she was currently paying for rent, she could easily make the payment on the mortgage, pay the taxes, insurance, and upkeep, and probably have enough left over to show a profit. There was one more feature that made this a choice move for her: She would have a property that provided a tax deduction.

Jane followed my advice and bought a duplex. It's not the fanciest or the newest, but it is within her financial range. It provides totally adequate living space to meet her needs as well as some financial security as an investment. The property is located in a stable neighborhood where her investment remains secure. It's a two-bedroom duplex with a double garage (Figure 2-3).

She bought the property from an elderly couple who had lived in the unit for over 40 years. The man had died, and his wife was moving into a nursing home, so the property had to be disposed of. After some negotiating, Jane was able to acquire a 10-year contract-for-deed. The payment on this contract was $674.29, which included insurance but not taxes.

Rent for one-half of the duplex brings in $695 per month. She has moved into the other half and maintains homestead rights. With the $695 rent and the $615 she had been paying to put toward the payment on the mortgage, you can see that this obviously is a good investment. She is saving money in addition to building a savings account through equity in the property. She now has investment property for her future, and if she maintains the property, there's no doubt it will increase in value.

I asked her whether she had any difficulties managing the property, and she said, "There's nothing I can't handle. Oh, sure, I've got to be concerned about getting good tenants, and there are a few complaints

Figure 2-3. A low-priced duplex like this can be the ideal starter for someone who wants to get away from renting and is willing to live in an older apartment until he or she can afford something better. This property, if well maintained, will always hold its value and will, with good management, remain occupied. The starter investor, single or married, can move in, get homestead rights, which cuts down the real estate taxes substantially, and start a real estate investment business with a comparatively small investment. In addition, an investor will probably pay less as a resident of the unit than as a renter. Once the mortgage is partially paid off and there's some appreciation and equity built up, the next stop is to buy a better and bigger unit by using that equity for additional investments.

and service calls now and then, but for the time and effort, I feel I'm being well paid. I've really started a little business of my own that I can be proud of. I find it quite exciting."

This story is certainly an average story of real estate investing by an average person, proving my point that

> *Anyone can invest in real estate and earn as much money and become as wealthy as he or she wants to in this business.*

The next step for this investor is to establish some equity in the property, borrow on that equity, and buy another unit, to upgrade her standard of living, and then buy a better and bigger duplex. (I did caution her, however, that if she moved out of the unit, she would lose the homestead rights to it, which could mean an additional $100 more in taxes per month.)

This is a success story. It shows that it doesn't take a lot to get started: this one unit doesn't represent a million dollars, but it's a start.

Ron's Real Estate Story

Ron is a middle-aged handyman, a jack-of-all-trades. He's pretty good at fixing and repairing things, and he makes a good living from it. But Ron has also entered the real estate investment business. You won't see Ron on TV bragging about how well he's done in this business, but let me assure you that he's done quite well.

Ron has a few built-in advantages: he has no children, he is married, and his wife works full-time as an office manager for a large corporation. Ron and his wife have invested in various types of real estate over the years. If it weren't for the tax write-off from the investment property, he and his wife would be in an extremely high income-tax bracket.

Ron's first investment was an older, run-down, single-family home. It was located in a nice middle-class neighborhood and had, when he bought it, great potential for growth and increase in value, through renovation. Figure 2-4 shows the kind of home he started with. This prop-

Figure 2-4. For the brave, innovative, hard-working investor, this kind of property is a classic profit maker. This property was abandoned because of nonpayment on the mortgage and real estate taxes. The property is located in a well-kept, middle-class residential area.

erty has an interesting story, and the story proves that if you keep looking, there's investment property of all kinds out there.

This house had been abandoned for 15 years. The owner suffered a major business failure and wasn't able to pay federal and state payroll taxes, so the federal and state governments filed a tax lien against his home. When a tax lien is filed against an individual, it covers all of that person's property and real estate. Consequently, the government liens plus the mortgage on the property amounted to more than the value of the property, so the owner just walked away from it. As a result, the bank foreclosed on the mortgage. In order for the bank to have recovered their interest in the property, they would have had to pay off the federal and state liens filed against it, so the bank let the property sit, and it sat for 15 years. By the time all the interest and penalties accumulated from the liens and mortgage, there was no way anyone could buy the property. This meant the property was virtually worthless, which was the case for 15 years.

In order to clear the title, the tax liens would have to be satisfied, the bank mortgage would have to be paid off, and the real estate taxes, which hadn't been paid for 15 years, would have to be paid. There was one more catch: the original owner, who had moved to Kansas, still had the title in his name.

Does all this sound impossible? It's not. Here's what happened.

Ron, the buyer, contacted the county officials and told them they'd be better off to get the property cleared up and back on the tax rolls. They agreed. The county attorney then contacted the federal and state lien holders and convinced them that there was no way they could recover anything from the property and that the property was deteriorating to a point of no return. He suggested to them that everyone would be better off if they released the liens and got on with better things. The government agencies involved were convinced they wouldn't recover anything, so they agreed to release the tax liens. In addition, the county agreed to waive all the back taxes. The bank was contacted, and they realized that they weren't going to recover anything, so they agreed to charge off the loan and release the mortgage. The original owner in Kansas was contacted, and for a small fee he agreed to give a warranty deed. All in all, the investor acquired the property for $5,000.

Ron then had to determine whether it was worth investing the work, time, and money necessary to renovate and repair the property. The first and most beneficial observation, of course—something Ron knew when he entered into the negotiation—was the fact that this house was located in a very desirable middle-class residential area. No matter what was done in the way of improvements, the value would pick up and increase. To make a long story short, and a picture is worth a thousand words, Ron went ahead with the project, and Figure 2-5 shows the finished project. He sold the property and made a nice profit for his work, time, and effort.

Ron personally does all the remodeling and renovating of the properties he buys, doing most of the work during off-hours and weekends. This first project, this one-family home, netted him a $9,500 profit. He

Figure 2-5. Here is the finished product, which has become a desirable middle-class home equal in value to the other homes in the neighborhood.

took part of the profit and bought an older, three-story, brick hotel. Yes, I said "hotel."

The hotel was operating marginally as a hotel; there were so many competitive motels that the small hotel business just wasn't profitable. Ron converted the hotel rooms into small, one-bedroom apartments. Each unit had a kitchenette, a bedroom, la iving room, and a bathroom. Once the word was out that this conversion was taking place, there was an avalanche of requests for the apartments. They were filled just as fast as he could convert them. With this project, Ron was able to eliminate the costly management of a hotel operation, yet reap the good income of a smoothly run apartment business … with no vacancies. He operated this business for several years with moderate success and profit, using the income to pay off the mortgage quickly, inasmuch as he didn't need to take anything out of the business for his personal living expenses.

I don't know if he had the mortgage all paid for or not, but he did sell the property, on a contract-for-deed. I also don't know what the selling price was, but I know he made a good profit. Now he has a monthly check that includes interest being earned on the contract-for-deed and the payment on the principal. In fact, I have a feeling that Joe Average could probably live quite comfortably on this check alone. Over the years, Ron has continued to buy and sell fixer-uppers. Now, after about 15 years of investing, he's well off financially owning rental properties and some contracts-for-deed.

Ron is an average person who realized phenomenal success in the real estate business. His is a real-life story, par excellence, of real estate investing. You won't see him on TV, but his is a true success story. Although he and I see one another regularly, the last thing in the world he needs is advice from me. As a matter of fact, there's a lot of his story and information in this book. He, too, knows the business.

Susan's Investment Program

Susan is a 41-year-old, single professional. Her income places her in the highest income-tax bracket. She told me that she was sick and tired of giving all her money to the government. She asked me, "What can I do?"

My advice for her was to use the equity in her personal home as a down payment on a nice, well-maintained duplex ... something that wouldn't create a lot of management problems. I told her to look for something that would come close to cash flow, so that there would be enough rental money to pay the expenses. I also told her that, even if she didn't have enough rental income and she had to use her own money, a duplex was the best place in the world to invest her own money, better than the stock market or low-interest-paying CDs. The fact is that investing money in real estate is a lot better than giving it to the government. The most important thing for her to realize was the fact that all of the real estate losses, if there were any, could be reported on her personal income as tax deductions, just what she was looking for and needed.

She found an excellent duplex (Figure 2-6). The property wasn't available on a contract-for-deed purchase, but she had an excellent cred-

Figure 2-6. Here's a first-rate duplex that takes very little care and management. This property, with each unit having a garage, is very rentable, has good income, and has a good future. A property like this, with two rental incomes, can pay for itself easily in 15 years. And, if there's not too much profit, it can give the investor a nice tax write-off.

it rating, good equity in her personal home, and some cash reserve. The equity from her home was enough for the down payment and closing costs. After managing and caring for this property for a few years, Susan found out it didn't interfere at all with her business career. She decided, after seeing her investment grow and saving on her income taxes, that it was time to buy more properties.

Since this initial investment, she's bought a threeplex, which is in excellent condition and does not take a lot of management. This is a story of an average, everyday, common person investing in real estate. I predict that someday she'll be a real estate millionaire.

Mark's Real Estate Investment

Mark worked for the government as a foreign service officer for 25 years. As a result of starting his career right out of college, he was a young man when he retired. He figured he could easily start another career. At first he looked at various jobs, but all of them meant working from 9 to 5, having a boss to answer to, and no freedom to come and go as he pleased. During the time he worked for the government, he had had a good income. Most of his expenses were paid, so he was able to establish a large savings account.

After I visited with him and we had talked about real estate investments and their advantages, he decided to take some of his savings and buy investment rental properties (Figure 2-7).

Figure 2-7. This property is the next step up for the "passive investor." It's an excellent threeplex, produces steady income, has very few vacancies, and is very rentable. This kind of property will, with time, develop into a real equity builder because it will never decrease in value. By "passive investor," I mean is someone who has a demanding business, profession, or career so that he or she can't devote a lot of time to the real estate business. This kind of investor can either work the property on weekends or vacations or hire a management firm to take care of the property, but a passive investor can still make money in this business.

He has since told me this is one of the best moves he could have made. He started a second career, which developed into a full-time business, giving him the freedom he wished and an excellent income. He works when he wants to and vacations as he pleases.

When he does work, he spends most of his time remodeling and rejuvenating apartments. This work substantially increases the value of the property without increasing his costs much because he does a lot of the work himself: he has been able to build up *sweat equity*. In addition, as he improves each apartment, he can, and does, raise the rents, so he experiences the appreciation in the value of his property and the increase in rents … just like that proverbial money machine. He told me once, "Those rent checks the tenants bring in each month have paid off my mortgages. Now there's enough money that I draw a pretty good salary out of the business. I'd be willing to bet," he said, "that I make about $500 an hour for the time I spend managing and taking care of the property."

Jim and Mary's Investments

When Jim and Mary got married, they bought a nice townhouse in the city. They both worked at regular jobs and both earned a good income. About four years ago, their tax accountant told them they should find a way to protect their income because they were paying too much income tax. (Isn't that the way it is with all of us?) At any rate, they came to me and asked my advice. I knew Jim was a general construction worker, and my thought was that he could handle a small investment property, … something that needed some renovation. I figured he could easily do this kind of work on weekends and during vacations.

We started looking into various properties in their neighborhood where we found a good starter. With very little work, the property could easily be upgraded and show an appreciation in value. It was located in a good neighborhood so it constituted a sound investment. Jim and Mary found what they were looking for: a tax write-off, as well as built-in savings in the form of the equity that accrued. In the short time since they started in this business, they've accumulated a $15,000 increase in value through renovating the property. If they stick with it and continue buying property, this amount will increase with each additional investment, and they will also acquire additional tax write-offs. These are simply average people who have invested in real estate.

Duane: A Self-Employed Businessman Invests in Real Estate

Duane is a self-employed, successful, small business operator living in a rural community (population 16,000). He and his wife own their home and have teenage children. Everything Duane has acquired he's done through his own hard work, ... no inheritance, no gifts. When he was younger, Duane started buying small fixer-upper investment properties. He, his wife, and his children spent long after-business hours upgrading the properties.

His first investment turned out to be a good buy, but it was more of a learning experience than a profit maker. Their next property (Figure 2-8) was much better. This was a sixplex, a large old home converted into three stories of apartments, two on each level. Rental income from this kind of property is usually very good since there are six rent checks that come in each month. In addition, this is an especially wise investment when you consider the basic cost of the property. If you were to build a new sixplex today, it would probably cost (depending on your location) $45,000 to $60,000 per unit. In contrast, the purchase price of most of these older properties will be anywhere from $30,000 to $45,000 per unit (again, depending on where you live). It's a matter of knowing what you're doing, shopping around, and knowing local real estate prices.

With this type of property you're not competing with any other market, either the low-rent housing or the newer middle-class apartments. Most of these converted apartments in older homes consist of one-bedroom units, suited for single working people who don't qualify for low-rent apartments, or don't want them, or can't afford the newer, more

Figure 2-8. This is a large, older three-story home converted into six apartments. This kind of property represents an excellent investment. The apartments are small, usually for single working people—nurses, hospital aides, secretaries, and so on—and the rents can be held within reason. If kept clean and attractive—incidentally, these older homes usually have exquisite ornate woodwork and some stained-glass windows—they make appealing rental units to a lot of people. Most of these old mansions were built in the 1920s and 1930s, and they were built solidly. With good care, they can usually outlast several generations of investors. Ironically, regardless of their age, these older units increase in value each time they're sold.

expensive apartment buildings. A selling feature for those of us who own these older apartment buildings is that, when tenants are looking to rent, we can tell them that, if they take a small unit, they can live alone; on the other hand, if they rent a more expensive apartment, they may have to take in a roommate.

The older properties usually can be purchased at a price the average small independent investor can afford. In most cases, the rental income is sufficient to make the mortgage payment and cover the expenses. Another feature of this kind of investment property is that rents invariably increase, especially at the time of a vacancy. For instance, I've been in this business for over 25 years, and never once during that time have I had to lower rents. In fact, just the opposite is true; every year or each time there's a changeover of tenants, I've had no difficulty in raising the rents $5, $10, or even $15 per month. The nice thing about these gradual rent increases, especially for a sixplex like this one, is that the basic purchase price and the operating cost remain the same. This, just in case you missed it, is called *profit making*.

Since purchasing this sixplex, Duane and his family have continued buying properties. Today his real estate holdings are worth a lot more than his well-managed and successful business. Someday, I predict, he and his family will live on easy street from the investment properties. And I don't think they're going to have to wait until he's 65. The last I heard, he owns three sixplexes, several fourplexes, and several family homes, and his investments are growing yearly.

As he and I visited and talked about real estate, I asked him, "Why did you decide to buy investment property? After all, you were doing pretty well in the business world." He answered, with great pride, "Back some years ago I read a few real estate books that got me thinking. I figured I could do it and thought if I wanted to accumulate and establish any sort of wealth, this is a way it can be done." He further said, "Sure, I was earning a good living, although everything I made was spent and gone at the end of each month." He added, "When I had to make that first decision about buying the first property, there was some reluctance. It was really tough making the decision because it meant more debt and more payments. But as I look back, I can tell you it was one of the smartest and best moves I've ever made."

There's more to Duane's story. He said, "Over the past 12 years I've gained some great experience and learned a lot about the real estate business. I've accumulated, on paper at least, $300,000 in real estate equity, and it's growing with each payment I make. You know, that's money I'd never have had if it weren't for my investing in real estate." Duane also said (this is brought out to let you know that there's work and management involved in this business), "It's not all a bed of roses. There are tenant complaints that have to be taken care of if you're going to keep good tenants; there are vacancies to fill, which is time-consuming; and personal involvement. There are backed-up sewers, leaky sinks, and dirty refrigerators and/or toilets to clean. All these matters need constant attention. However, with my wife and kids (who are in school), we can handle the properties and management pretty well. It's a nice business because all these things, other than the emergency problems, can be taken care of in our spare time."

Why this story? Because Duane is an average person, with an average life, with an average success story in real estate investing. He hasn't made a million, but he's certainly doing very well.

Paul: A Plumber Gets Involved in Real Estate

Paul is a middle-aged plumber. He had worked hard, made a good living in his business, but discovered he wasn't really making any financial progress, ... that is, accumulating savings. His income increased every year, but so did his expenses and standard of living. Paul told me that, before he bought his first property, "I was fixing other people's plumbing, and it seemed to me that, if those people were making money in real estate, there was no reason I couldn't do the same. I figured if I've got to fix other people's plumbing, I might as well be fixing my own. At least I knew I wouldn't have a plumbing bill to pay."

Since then Paul has bought various smaller units, single houses, and duplexes as investment properties. He said, "My wife and I take care of the apartments. We really don't work that hard on it and don't put in that many hours. I do know I'm making money in real estate because every time I make a payment, I see my net worth increasing."

I have a feeling Paul doesn't need any advice from me, and I predict that if he continues and doesn't burn himself out with overwork at his occupation and the real estate business, he'll eventually build a nice secure net worth.

Jim: A Construction Superintendent Buys Real Estate

Jim, middle-aged, over the years has bought a lot of properties, specializing in fixer uppers. I suppose that he has an accumulation of 30 to 35 rental units. He told me once that he acquired and managed these properties on a part-time basis and that he was easily able to invest and fix up real estate without its interfering with his business.

He's talking about retiring from his job in the very near future and taking care of his apartments. He's accumulated equity over the years, his mortgages are paid off so that the rent income is clear profit for him, and he should be able to draw a pretty good salary out of the business.

Jim, too, is no more than an average, everyday, person, working at an average job, who found real estate to his liking. Today, I would be willing to bet Jim's net worth is near $1 million, and that's money he would never have had if it weren't for his real estate investing. The average person working at an average job or business with an average or even an above-average income just can't save that much money in a lifetime.

Harry: A Barber Gets His Cut of the Action

Figure 2-9 shows a property that started Harry, who is a barber in a community of 15,000, in the real estate business. This is an older property, but it has been well cared for over the years. Harry bought the property from a long-time real estate investor who decided to retire. He was able to buy it with a small down payment and on a contract-for-deed. With six apartments in the building, there was sufficient income to take

Figure 2-9. This property was built in 1930. The good condition of the building proves that, if the property is taken care of, it can outlast many owners. There are four one-bedroom apartments on the first floor and two one-bedroom apartments in the basement. There's a commercial coin-operated washer/dryer in the basement that gives the owner another $25 to $30 per month income. The property is located two blocks from the main commercial business district and close to most of the houses of worship in the community, which makes it very rentable. If this property is well taken care of for another 60 years, there's no doubt that its value will increase, the rents will increase, and it will serve the owners well.

care of the mortgage payment and the general maintenance and upkeep.

This is the kind of property that takes a little more care than, let's say, a brand new apartment. But a new sixplex would cost a lot more money, and it no doubt wouldn't be available on a contract-for-deed purchase. The point is that anyone can find properties that are for sale from a previous owner who will finance the project. That's why this business is so available for almost anyone who really wants to get into it.

When you analyze a sale like this one, it's not hard to see that everyone involved is a winner. The buyer was able to get into the real estate business with a small amount of money. The previous owner was able to sell the property and get his price. In addition, by selling and financing the property, the previous owner was able to acquire his equity and appreciation but also able to receive interest on the financing. Once you get into the business of financing your own property, you'll soon discover that interest is a real profit maker. Here's an example of what I mean.

First of all, for the first five years, all that's paid, for the most part, on the loan is interest. Now, if you've got a $90,000 contract for deed at 9 percent, you will make money. Even though interest at the bank might be 7 percent, it's not uncommon for the contract-for-deed seller to charge a little more than the bank rate. At any rate, if you charge 9 percent on a 15-year loan, you'll receive $162,732 for the $90,000 property. And always remember, it was the tenants' money that paid for the original $90,000 property, not your money.

I don't know of any other way, short of stealing, hitting a jackpot, or winning a sweepstakes, that the average person can accumulate wealth and build financial security more easily than by investing in real estate. All of the preceding stories are about common, ordinary, everyday people, just like you meet and know and talk to everyday. Every workplace, every city and community, and every neighborhood has them. I've talked with them, and, without fail, I have yet to find any successful real estate investor who hasn't been totally sold on the idea. It just goes to show you, it takes no special talent, no special training (other than learning some of the basics about real estate), and not a great deal of money to get started in this business.

What it does take, though, is

Some entrepreneurial spirit—you're going to have to want to do it.

Intestinal fortitude (guts)—you're going to have to take some chances.

Determination—you're going to have to have your own driving force to get started, get going, and keep going.

Chapter 3

18 Key Steps to Better Investing

Step 1. Maintain a Positive Attitude

Beyond the financial commitment it takes, the single most important contribution that any individual can make is to start with a positive attitude. The real estate business is a very positive business, so it shouldn't be difficult at all to establish a positive frame of mind in getting started. I guarantee that, if you do, and if you remain positive throughout your involvement, positive things will happen.

In addition to thinking positively, associate and surround yourself with positive thinking, acting, and talking people. These positive people can be used off and on to enhance your feelings, attitudes, and activities because positive attitudes can be downright contagious.

Start your real estate investing career with an optimistic attitude about yourself, about your knowledge as you learn it, and about your ideas and your ability, and know within yourself that you can do it. Whether you're considering a home, a duplex, or an apartment building, don't ever think you can't do it. Remember that it can be done, anyone can do it, and it's a matter of determination. One last word: whatever you do, don't let yourself be dragged down by negative people with negative attitudes and opinions.

Step 2. Get a Good Real Estate Education

The next step in getting started in this dynamic business is to learn about the business. Think of going into the real estate business this way: before you began your present career or profession, whether it was as a teacher, an accountant, a dentist, or something else, you spent a considerable amount of time and money getting the necessary education. The real estate business is no different. It would be ludicrous to go into this business without knowing how it works. Your success or failure, as in any business or profession, can easily depend on how much you learn before you begin. The fact is that it's very risky and not very smart to buy real estate without knowing what you're doing. Obviously, then, the logical thing to do is learn as much about the business as possible.

How does one go about getting a real estate education? First of all, it's not necessary to return to college or classroom work. It's very easy to learn about the business on your own. In fact, you've already started. You're reading this book.

Then, there are other real estate books. Check the business section of your local bookstore or your library. Read as many books as time will permit. You may not agree or accept all of the ideas in every book, but if you only get one good idea out of each book, it's worth your time to read them. Listen: this part of the education, buying books, is comparatively inexpensive.

An important aspect of this business that you should focus on as you learn is the financing of property investment. Know what *interest* means and how it affects your investment. Know about the credit world we live in. Learn how a credit bureau works so that, once you're on the go, you'll know how to get your credit report, the seller's report, and your future tenant's report. I emphasize knowing about your tenant's credit because this information will be important in your dealings with tenants.

Here's a little-known fact about credit that should give you some idea of why you want to know about the credit world: Statistically, we know that in the 1960s about 17 percent of the people were either slow in paying their bills or didn't pay at all. In the 21st century this percentage has increased to over 30 percent who abuse credit. That means that it's conceivable that three out of ten tenants you interview could be credit problems. If you're interested in knowing more about the credit world, I've written a book titled *No-Nonsense Credit* (TAB/McGraw-Hill), which should be available in any library and most bookstores.

Other phases of the real estate business you'll need to learn are fixing, repairing, carpentering, plumbing, and other building trades. It's not necessary that you do the work, but it's important to understand how things work and how they're done, if for no other reason than to be sure that you're not being overcharged for something done by a repairperson.

Step 3. Learn from the Experts

The next learning experience can be an exciting one because you're going to be dealing directly with people who are in the property business. Most of these people, small independent investors, have been quite successful. I'm sure you're going to find that they like to boast about their accomplishments. That's good, because their stories can be a delightful learning experience in themselves.

Generally, you'll find most of these people will be friendly, accommodating, and easy to get along with. I have yet to find one independent investor who isn't willing to sit down and talk about his or her properties and about the business. You can certainly learn a great deal from them. And there's an added benefit in meeting them: once you've built trust between you, there are all sorts of learning and investing possibilities. For instance, there's a good chance of meeting an investor who's willing to talk about selling and financing his or her investment property.

Here's an example of what I mean. I met an investor when I first started in the business. I needed some help and advice about buying a certain property and didn't know where to turn. I established a friendship with this fellow, who, incidentally, was an Internal Revenue agent, and he was more than willing to help me and give me whatever advice he had. Eventually, through our friendship, I bought a fourplex, a duplex, and a single-family house from him. He financed the property on a contract-for-deed. I eventually paid him in full, along with 9 percent interest on the contract. He was happy to get his money, and I was happy to extend my real estate investments substantially.

As you move around in the subculture of independent real estate investors, you'll find all sorts of people you would never have guessed were investors. I know a banker, a barber, an electrician, a dentist, an insurance agent, several teachers, some college professors, and a plumber, just to name a few. These people are all small investors who have, over the years, bought only one property or several properties. Most of them have spent their spare time managing and taking care of their property while holding on to their occupation or business. They've learned their business, and they know their business, and they don't mind passing on their experiences to one another. Incidentally, all of them, without exception, have done very well financially, with one property or with many properties. Almost everyone I have talked to has said that the only regret he or she has is not having bought more property.

By learning the business from people who have experience, and by getting a good real estate education, you can and will avoid problems. Most of these "experts" can tell you what works and what doesn't work, and, by listening, you can avoid learning by trial and error, which is often a painful way to learn. Sometimes, we independent people like to learn through the trial-and-error method rather than asking others, but learning the business from those with actual experience in it can, and will, save you money. This fact alone will make the business more enjoyable for you. The point is, don't try to do everything alone. It just doesn't make sense, and it's not good business. And ignore the "know-it-alls" who seem to have all the answers. Most of them are pseudo-advisors who talk a lot but rarely act.

One more thing, now that we're in changing times and with the economy in turmoil, you've got to do your "homework" in real estate investing or you're not going to succeed.

What about the realtors as teachers of the business? The first thing you should know about realtors is that some are good, and some aren't so good, and some are bad. The second thing to know about realtors is that they're in business to make a sale. The only way they make a living is by making a sale, so their number-one priority is to sell, sell, sell. Some realtors, however, can be helpful. I advise anyone going into this business to meet and establish a friendship with several honest, reliable, and good realtors. They can be an important part of your overall investment career, as well as your educational experience. Once these friendships have been established, let the realtors know that you're a novice and starter investor and not yet ready to buy. Then let them know what you're looking for and what you want. Ask them to help you start looking at properties. Ask about prices and terms, and ask for all the information you can get. Record the information in a three-ring binder notebook for future reference. Keep these notes on a number of properties. This is an excellent learning experience. The information you record will eventually be your encyclopedia, catalog, and guidebook.

Step 4. Start Looking

Now it's time to get down to serious business. Looking for and at properties will be an exciting experience (Figure 3-1). As you travel, keep all the records you can for future reference. There's a good chance you may have to look at 100 properties before the right one comes along that fits your program, but the most important thing is to take your time. There's no rush. Don't think you have to buy the first property you look at.

Start with the realtors. Also check the classified ads in your newspaper, especially Sunday's edition. Look under the columns titled:

• Income Property for Sale

Figure 3-1. This multiple-unit apartment house is the kind of property you should start looking for. There are four apartments on the first floor and two in the basement. Because this apartment building is older and comparatively inexpensive, the rents will remain very reasonable, which means that there's a limited vacancy factor. Being able to fill vacancies quickly is important because this business depends totally on rental income. A property like this can probably be purchased through a seller-financer with as little as $5,000 down plus closing costs.

- Income Property for Trade
- Properties for Sale by Owners

Pick a few of the properties that you would like to consider. Write down the information from the ad in your notebook, using one page per property.

Then start looking at the properties. Keep in mind at this point that you're still learning and not ready to buy. Drive through the various neighborhoods and observe the properties. Also look for for-sale yard signs. Again, write down the addresses and any phone numbers listed on the signs. Later on, call the realtors or owners and get all the information you can about the properties, writing the information in your notebook.

Here's the kind of information you want to keep about the various properties:

- Is the property located in a solid neighborhood?

- What are the neighboring properties like?
- Is this a low-cost property in a high-cost neighborhood?
- Is this a high-cost property in a low-cost neighborhood?
- Is the property located in an industrial area?
- Is the property near an interstate or freeway highway?

Next, cover these items about the property itself:

- How does the roof look?
- What kind of siding is on the building?
- Does it need painting?
- Is there any visible wood rot?
- Are the yard and premises clean and in good condition?
- Is this yard, or any neighboring yard, filled with junked cars?

Junked cars or an assortment of motorcycles or other vehicles in the neighborhood can indicate a seedy and poorly cared for environment. Caution: you don't need this.

The next step, after visiting some of the properties, is to call the realtors. Don't make any commitment at this time because you're only searching for information. Let the realtors or sellers know this, but also let them know you would be interested in hearing about other investment properties as well.

Look beyond the for-sale ads. All investment property for sale isn't necessarily listed. In fact, you will undoubtedly find, as you move about in the real estate subculture, that most of the small independent investors sell their property by word of mouth,... friend to friend, associate to associate, and investor to investor. That's why I stress the point of getting out and meeting other investors, getting yourself established in their subculture club. Most of them know the various properties that are for sale and can give you leads, or they may sell on their own.

Incidentally, let me interject here something important about the real estate investors you'll want to meet. Most of the sellers will finance their properties. You'll see how important this can be for the small independent investor. The subject of seller financing is covered in a later chapter.

Step 5. Think Smart, Think Small

In the real estate business, it's not always true that "bigger is better." We've been led to believe that bigger is better, but that's not the case when it comes to buying investment property, especially the first buy. There's nothing wrong in buying a small one-bedroom rental home as a starter. From there you can buy another, or a duplex, or whatever comes along. The point is, it doesn't make any sense to spend a lot of valuable time looking at property that's not affordable or manageable or property that's impossible to finance. Looking at a 100-unit apartment building, or even a 20-unit apartment building, when we know we're not ready for this kind of a commitment (yet), is a waste of valuable time. The smart-thinking investor will keep it simple and look at a modestly priced duplex rather than a $1,200,000 apartment building.

If you think small, and smart, for properties you can afford, property that will produce enough income to make the payments, property you can manage on a part-time basis, then the chances of your getting involved in this investment business are substantially enhanced ... as are your chances of success. Thinking smart also means knowing and recognizing the fact that it takes time to accumulate wealth through equity and appreciation. In other words, the smart thinker knows an investor doesn't become a millionaire overnight. I'm not saying you can't become a millionaire, because there are a lot of common, ordinary people out there who have become millionaires in this business. What I am saying is that the smart-thinking investor knows it takes time to build a fortune.

Step 6. Eliminate Fears

As I look back to when I started in this business, I have to tell you that I had some apprehension, along with a great deal of anxiety about the debt I was about to enter into and about the regular monthly payments it would take to cover the debt. There's no doubt about it, the fear of going into debt can be thought-provoking, and rightly so because the smart and successful investor is always concerned about the financial involvement. There's always a built-in fear that the investment may not work and it may not be possible to meet the payments. There could be problems with tenants who do not pay the rent or move out prematurely, or something could go wrong in the building and it will be a big expense and there won't be money to fix it.

And, of course, there's a fear of failure … we all have it. Everyone experiences fear when they make a dramatic change in their livelihood or their way of life. Mostly the fears are of the unknown. Fears of the unknown are unfounded. Now, you're going to have to take my word for this, but let me assure you, from my own experience, that about 99 percent of the time we fear something, it's in vain. What we fear usually

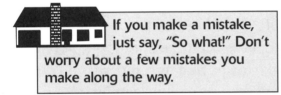
If you make a mistake, just say, "So what!" Don't worry about a few mistakes you make along the way.

never becomes a reality. In fact, just the reverse can happen. What we fear turns out to be a positive experience that works in our favor.

Fear of failure certainly is one of the "seven deadly fears," but you'll find that there's no reason to burden yourself with the fear of failure in the real estate business unless you're careless or unless you haven't learned the business. There's no need to fear failure in the real estate business because there will always be a need for rental housing. There are people out there who don't want to own property—some can't afford a home, single working people aren't ready to buy, and so on—and there's a workforce that moves about that will always remain renters. As housing prices rise, and they will, there will be more of a demand and need for rental properties. The fact is, the need for rental property hasn't changed, and there's as much need now in the 21st century as there was in the 1970s, 1980s, and 1990s.

One last note on fears: I would fear going into this business without the knowledge of how to buy, own, and manage rental properties.

Step 7. Take Your Time

Some investors make poor decisions because they don't have the patience to wait. They want to get rich right now, and they are easy targets for get-rich-quick schemes. The real estate investment business is not a short-term business. It takes time and some long-term thinking. In fact, it took me 15 years to realize the income from my initial investments.

The good money in this business is made by those who take their time, think seriously about how that investment works, and stay ahead of the game. I suppose that's why 10 percent of the people in this country own and control 90 percent of the wealth. This book probably won't get you into the 10 percent category; however, it should get you started in this business and on your way to independent wealth.

In the real estate business, time is on your side. Therefore, patience is a virtue you'll want to develop and nurture. There's no reason to buy the first property you look at. This is especially true when it comes to property that needs to be renovated. Because I waited three years for a purchase to be completed, I was able to buy it at my price. Realtors know there aren't many renovators in the business, so they are usually cooperative and helpful. After all, renovators are a source for them in selling rundown properties.

Some time ago I was contacted by a realtor about an older two-story, three-bedroom family home. The parents who had lived there had died, and the property was being held in an estate. The estate couldn't be settled until the property was sold. The property was located in an excellent neighborhood. Most of the homes were valued in the high five-figure price range. However, the old family home was run down, and it needed a paint job, some rewiring, and a new roof. The yard was unkempt and had a generally shabby appearance. I imagine the neighbors were becoming discouraged with what was happening.

The asking price was $35,000—remember, this was in a neighborhood where homes were selling for $80,000 and $90,000. I declined the offer and told the realtor it was more than I wanted to pay ... and of course called to their attention the various defects in the property. I knew that if the owners had painted the exterior and cleaned up the yard, they would have been able to get $35,000 easily. But they didn't.

Three months later the realtor called again and asked if I'd be interested in making an offer. He said the heirs were pressing to settle the estate so they wanted to get their money. This indicated to me that they were really pushing and it was time to take action on the property. I made an offer of $25,000, knowing full well that I would have to put money into the property to upgrade it. Within a short time the realtor called back and said the owners would take $26,500. I bought the property at this price. I had the building painted and rewired, and I had a new roof put on, all at a cost of $4,000. One year later I sold the property for $39,000. The house was in good condition and qualified for FHA financing. I received my cash and was subsequently able to buy more property, ... which I did.

Step 8. Don't Procrastinate

Most procrastinators will find excuses like:

If only I had bought that property back in 1970 when prices were right, but now they're too high.

Or

I should have bought that 10 acres in Hawaii in 1960.

And,

Do you know that I looked at that apartment building once and could have bought it for $165,000, and now it's selling for $245,000?

Procrastinators don't seem to get going, and they consequently don't make very much money. Procrastinators are hindsight millionaires. Smart-thinking investors don't look back and think of what they could have done 10 or 15 years ago. The smart, good, and successful investor starts *now* and looks ahead.

From what I've seen in the real estate world and from talking to various people over the years, I can safely predict that the average person will not buy investment real estate, other than his or her personal home. The odds are even greater that the average person won't become a millionaire. Do you know why I say this? Because most people just can't make a decision. Despite all the pep talks, regardless of our good intentions, it's hard to take that first step and buy the first property, or the second, or third.

Some people have gone so far as to buy real estate books. They have read them and convinced themselves that they can do it. They truly believe they are going to get started, but then they wait ... just a little. Soon the motivation wears off, and the stall leads to waiting too long. They put the books aside, go back to their daily routine, and forget pretty much everything they've started on. The next thing that happens is that they find out the duplex or apartment they had looked at has been sold.

For procrastinators there are a lot of reasons not to buy investment real estate. All you've got to do is use any one of the following excuses:

- The time just isn't right.
- There's too much financial turmoil in our economic system.
- We're in a recession.
- There's going to be a depression.
- I don't want to lose my money.
- I don't have any money.

These excuses aren't new—they've been around for years. That's good news for the serious investor because it cuts down on the competition. Excuses will eliminate any possibility of having to take a chance. If you find a good enough excuse, then you don't have to make a decision. Those who find excuses don't get in the way and make it difficult for those who want to get things done.

Here's something to think about as you're deciding what to do. There are three types of people. First, there are those who get things done and make things happen. Second, there are those who watch things happen. Third, there are those who sit around and ask, "What happened?" For those of you who want to get things done and make things happen, let's get on with the real estate business and learn more about how it can be done.

Step 9. Learn How to Price Real Estate

I wish I could tell you precisely how to determine a fair and marketable price for real estate ... any real estate, a home or investment property. But I don't have such a formula, and, in all the years I've been in the business, I have never found anyone who does. The only surefire way I know to buy right is to get a good real estate education, take your time, and know what you're doing.

There are some basic questions you might want to look at before starting to buy:

- Can I afford to buy the property?
- Will the income from the rents cover the expenses and payment?
- How can I recognize a good buy?
- Do I like the property?
- Is the property located where it won't deteriorate?
- How can I best deal with the seller?
- Will the seller finance the property?

Step 10. Judging the Affordability of the Property for Your Investment

First and foremost, when dealing with the finances of the property, know your own financial status. Know your precise income and all your expenses. Determine whether or not you can afford the purchase. Don't look at property that's not within your financial means and ability. If you're in a position to buy a duplex or a single-family house, there's no sense in looking at a 24-unit apartment building.

Next, start small. Buy something within your means. Get one property started and making ends meet or a profit. Then go on to the next property.

Know your territory. I'm sure I don't have to tell you that every community has its own values for real estate. Obviously, real estate has a different value in San Francisco, California, than in Clear Lake, Iowa. However, even though prices are different in different locations, there are some basic factors that cover San Francisco, Clear Lake, and every other city or community. For instance:

- No matter what location, is the property overpriced?
- Is there sufficient income to cover the costs of operation?

If the investment doesn't make financial sense, then it's obviously not a good investment.

Step 11. Determining a Good Buy

I can't tell you the prices of property in Clear Lake or San Francisco, but I can tell you about my location, a rural college community, population 12,000. I have bought multiple-dwelling apartments, older buildings for $15,000 up to $25,000 per unit. This means a sixplex in my community will cost about $120,000. From this investment I realize monthly income of $375 per unit. With this income, the property breaks even and is a good investment. Needless to say, $120,000 won't buy a stick in San Francisco, New York, Los Angeles, or other major cities. On the other hand, rental units in any of these cities will probably start at anywhere from $1,000 a month on up. In fact, you probably couldn't get anything in any of these cities for $1,000 a month.

Again, there are some determining factors to analyze before making a financial commitment, such as:

- Is there sufficient income to cover the cost of operation?
- If the income isn't there, can and should I use my own money to keep it going?
- Do I have a personal or business cash reserve that can be used in case of an emergency?

Step 12. Maintaining a Positive Cash Flow

A *positive cash flow* means having enough income to cover the expenses. To help you understand better, here's an illustration of a hypothetical investment property. We'll use a $100,000 investment with a 25-year mortgage at 9 percent interest. Here's the cost of the operation. (Remember, this is an illustration, to show you how to figure cash flow, and not a real investment.)

Mortgage and interest payment	$827
Taxes	150
Utilities	150
Maintenance, repair	120
Advertising	10
Insurance	50
Garbage	15
Soft water	24
Miscellaneous expenses	50

The total expenses are $1,396 per month, so it takes that amount of rental income for the property to have a positive cash flow. If it doesn't have a positive cash flow, the next question for you to answer is: Where does the money come from?

Step 13. Investing Your Own Money

Eventually you'll be faced with the question, should I use my personal money to buy and invest in real estate, or can I depend on being able to borrow money to carry the cost of the operation? I can honestly say I can't answer that question for you. You have to answer it. There is one thing I can say, however, and that is, there's no better place in the world to put your money as an investment and for security than in real estate!

Step 14. Maintaining a Cash Reserve

Sometimes you'll run into situations in which you will need more money. For instance, the property may need a new furnace, a coat of paint, or some major renovation, or, unexpectedly, another property may show up that is a very good buy. When this happens, if you're like most of us, you'll be faced with no reserve cash, insufficient income from the rental property to cover the expenses, and no inheritance in the near future (that near future represents about 400 years for me). These unexpected expenses will require that you spend personal income or take out a loan. The question is, "Should I take money out of my savings or get another loan?" Once again, I can't answer that other than to tell you that this can be a fact of real estate investing and something you should know ahead of time so you don't get caught in a financial trap.

Step 15. Recognizing a Good Deal

Concerns that all of us investors have are these:

- Did I get a good deal?
- Did I pay too much for the property?
- Should I have haggled more about the price?
- Could I have bought the property for less money than I paid?
- Did I act too quickly?
- Was the price right?

Let me tell you something: You'll go crazy worrying about these things. There's only one clear answer to all the questions, and that is:

If it's good for you, then it's a good investment!

Leave it at that. Once you've made the decision, don't look back. Whatever you do, don't worry about what other people may say or think. In fact, make it a point not to discuss any of your business with other people. What you paid for your property is your business. Most importantly, if you think it's a good property and you're comfortable with it, *then it's a good deal!* Regardless of

Life itself is a chance. You really never know what is going to happen. I know this, though: as far as the odds of getting a bad deal in real estate are concerned, real estate far outweighs the next best investment there is for security.

what anyone else says, *if it's good for you, it's good—that's all that matters.* Don't be concerned if someone you know says something like, "You paid too much for the property. It's not a good deal." To be perfectly blunt, tell them it's none of their business. One final word on this subject: If you're the entrepreneurial type, you know that every investment, whether it's in real estate or any other business, is something of a chance. But I guarantee you, you'll have less to worry about with real estate.

Step 16. Controlling Your Investment

There are a number of things you can control when buying investment property. The first, of course, is the location. Buy investment property in a location you like. Second, don't buy high-priced property in a low-priced neighborhood, but do buy low-priced property in a high-priced neighborhood. This only makes sense. The high-priced property in a low-priced neighborhood is going to depreciate, while low-priced property in a high-priced neighborhood (along with good management, good care, and good upkeep) is bound to appreciate in value. That's what makes a good investment.

Step 17. Selecting Your Community

Here's something to think about when you're making plans to buy investment property: if you're going to spend your time and money on real estate, you might as well buy in a community that has a good future. If you can see shortcomings, if the community isn't growing, if industry is failing, if there's not a good employment base, and if the community isn't going to make progress, your chances of success in the rental business diminish.

Step 18. Haggling over the Price

When you get self-confidence and know how to say "no," start looking for the kind of property you'd like to buy. Whatever you do, don't be intimidated by the realtor who'll always tell you "It's a good deal and you'd better buy right away." Wait until *you* think it's a good deal. Thoroughly investigate the properties … lots of them … and find the best one. Even if you miss one that you thought you should have made an offer on, forget it and get on with looking—there are many more out there.

Nobody pays the asking price. Once the seller or realtor establishes the price, then the next move is up to you. Go back and offer at least 25 percent less than the asking price. Don't be embarrassed about doing this. Don't think you'll look foolish if you make this offer, and don't be intimidated by the seller or realtor. You're not in the real estate investment business to make friends; you're in it to make money. If you're going to make money, you're going to have to be an assertive negotiator. I've operated in this business for many years, and I can be classified, when buying property, as being a "cheapskate." The cheapskate buyer is the one who ends up with the good deals. Nice guys, who are afraid to assertively negotiate and haggle about the price, are the ones who end up with high-priced investments, or no investment at all.

Chapter 4

Successful Business People, Not Successful Properties

There are problems, and excuses, and causes and effects, but when you come right down to it—and this is important for anyone considering investing time and money in this business—the investment property itself won't work alone. The fact is, the success of the business depends mostly on the individual person involved. That means the earning power, the profits, and the success of the business are not made from the property. Success is determined by the attitude, the enthusiasm, and the determination of the individual involved.

Using Common Sense

The prime reason for most real estate failures and bad investments can be attributed to the inability of the investor or investors to use common sense. Common sense means having the foresight and knowledge to find the right location, that is, to pick the right neighborhood or community. Common sense means having the knowledge to know how to buy the property correctly. Most importantly, it means that the investor knows how to manage and care for the property in a *no-nonsense* manner.

The success of this business, and any business for that matter, is determined by how well the individual knows the business and how much knowledge of the business is acquired. This book is a part of that learning process. The information is directed to those who are motivated and want to take some action. It is dedicated to those who have aspirations of becoming financially independent and to those who want to start a regular "forced" savings account for their future. It's especially directed to those who have not found any other method of achieving that financial independence.

> Come what may, land was wealth to count on.
> —David McCullough, *Truman* (1993), pp. 963–964

The American Dream

The real estate investment business is exciting because *it's one business that gives each and every one of us, no matter how much or how little money we have, the opportunity to participate in our free-enterprise economic system to the fullest.* It's also exciting because anyone, and I mean *anyone*, with initiative, drive, desire, and determination can strike out on his or her own. Investors can reach any financial goal they desire and can become totally independent.

Let me tell you, those opportunities, the opportunities to achieve financial independence and security, are few and far between for the average person. If we do no more than look squarely at reality, we pretty much know that most of us aren't going to share in the kind of wealth that, let's say, a major league baseball player or a brain surgeon or even a corporate CEO can enjoy. Those positions, and the kind of wealth that goes with them, are beyond the realm of possibility for most of us.

On the other hand, the American Dream is available to anyone who enters into the real estate investment business. We acquire total independence and can acquire as much wealth as we desire by buying, owning, and managing as many rental properties as we want. There's no limit. The only limits on how much we can make in the real estate investment business are the limits we put on ourselves. Each of us individually has complete control over our own destiny and future in this business.

And, for all practical purposes, this business is comparatively free of strong competitive forces. In fact, you'll find a subculture of real estate investors, especially among the small independent investors, who are more friendly than competitive.

Determination

There's another factor that makes this business exciting for the small independent part time investor: we can set our own goals and work at whatever pace we want. Success and failure are in our own hands, and the only restrictions are our own abilities, enthusiasm, performance, action, and determination.

I want to point out here that you're going to see a lot of the word *determination* in this book. It's an important word and a trait that can be the driving force to the success of real estate investing. With that in mind, there's another exciting part of this business: we can individually take on a project, our own project, work with it, fix it, and coddle it, all to our own liking. Then we can stand back, see the end result, and look with pride at our successful venture and say to ourselves: I did it, and it's all mine!

Working for Yourself

I've said this before, but it bears repeating, over and over and over again: real estate is the only way I know in our free-enterprise system that enables average people to accumulate wealth … any amount of wealth they desire, up into and through the millions. The only restrictions to entering this business are self-restrictions of our own design. As I've said before, I've been successfully investing in rental properties in the 70s, 80s, 90s, and now into the 21st century, and I intend to continue in this business.

You can take my word for it: it works now, has worked in the past, and I'm sure it will continue to work in the future. The only thing that has changed are the times, the conditions, and the people involved. The fact is, and you can quote me when I say:

This business is just too good to pass up!

A Repeated Message

There's an important message here that bears repeating, and that message is the primary purpose and thrust of this book. Take another look.

As we look for sources of wealth, it's interesting to see where the rich people got their money. Some have inherited great sums of money. Some are super athletes, super musicians, and movie stars. Some doctors and attorneys have done very well. Then there are "superhuman" computer geniuses who have made millions, and the corporate CEOs have also made out pretty well.

So where does that leave us, the average people? It leaves us looking, but we don't have to look too far if we're really serious. That wealth is right there in front of us if we want to take advantage of it. It's called "rental property," "investment property," "duplexes," "fourplexes," and whatever else fits in the category of real estate. Real estate, then, can provide the average person with the means to be able to earn great amounts of money.

Think of this. An investor can buy one property with as little as $5,000 for the down payment and closing costs. With the income from the property, equity is acquired as the mortgage is paid off. That equity and savings can be used to borrow more money, which can be used for another down payment, ... ad infinitum.

Chapter 5

How to Avoid the Pitfalls in Real Estate Investing

Potential Problems in Real Estate Investing

It would be foolish for me to tell you that there aren't failures and set-backs, financial losses, and, yes, even bankruptcies in the rental prop-erty business. There's no doubt that many investors make bad decisions about buying properties, about managing their properties, and some don't watch their financial commitments. All these things can cause great anguish and create financial dilemmas for some investors.

I don't want to scare you, but I imagine about now you're asking something like:

If real estate is such a good deal, how come I hear about all these people who have bought property and have then gone broke and lost everything?

That, of course, is a good question and obviously calls for an answer, especially since I've presented this business in such a favorable light (which I will continue to do). But I don't want to mislead you into thinking that every property is a bed of roses.

There is an answer—and I speak from personal experience and observation—that real estate itself isn't the cause of these failures. Most of the failures have been self-inflicted, caused by the individuals involved with the property. Let's take a look at some of these individual mistakes, bad investments, and various problems related to unsuccessful investments.

The Causes of Depreciation

Whatever you do, don't get involved with investment property that is going to depreciate before you get a chance to make your move. All one has to do to find the causes of property depreciation is to look at the growth pattern of the communities where depreciation has taken place. Usually neighborhoods decay because of neglected individual properties or environmental circumstances, and these factors force prices down.

But the most important element in real estate depreciation is the sheer lack of good management practices on the part of owners: either they don't know enough about the business, or they have a lackadaisical attitude about an important aspect of protecting their investment—the sound management of their properties.

I find that most of the investors who have paid attention to the management of their property have not only succeeded financially but have substantially increased the value of their real estate. The point is, real estate management is an important ingredient of success ... and "success" is synonymous with profits.

Overzealousness

Many real estate investors become overzealous and get involved with real estate when they don't know about the business, don't know how to finance the property, and don't understand that rental property takes astute management. This is especially so when inexperienced investors become involved with property. They buy at inflated prices, don't understand the financial consequences, and then don't take the time to see if there's sufficient income to cover the costs of the operation, in addition to the mortgage payment.

Real Estate Taxes

Oftentimes, careless investors will forget that twice a year real estate taxes have to be paid. They neglect to put aside the money on a monthly basis, so that, when the tax comes due, there's no money and, consequently, a financial urgency. Other investors overlook various costs that lead to a situation in which the money needed for the tax and mortgage payments is used for other expenses. Eventually the mortgage payments aren't met, which leads to financial anxiety, distress, and possible failure.

If ever you feel you're being overtaxed, it's a good time to meet with the county or city tax assessor.

Over-Renovating

Here's a case of a 49-year-old general contractor-investor. You would think that a general contractor would have enough knowledge about real estate costs that he could avoid financial failure, but that's not the case. As I wrote this story, I found what I perceived to be a flaw in the character of this person. You might take heed. This man was a "know-it-all"; he thought he was just a little better than everyone else, and his arrogance was overbearing. He never asked for anyone's advice and went into things entirely on his own.

For the first 10 years in business as a contractor, he did well, building and selling houses. However, he then got the idea he could invest in real estate on his own. He bought some older apartment buildings that needed renovating, which wasn't a bad move, especially for a contractor, but he made some mistakes. For instance, he put in the best of everything. Rather than installing inexpensive cupboards, bathrooms, airconditioners, and so on, he bought the best and most expensive of everything. What happened was that he ended up with a new "old" apartment building. With the original purchase price of the building and the cost of renovation, he could easily have bought a brand new apartment complex. Instead, he ended up with an old building and had to charge the same rents as if it were a new building in order to recover his costs. He did this with several properties. Ultimately he went into debt, owing more money than the properties were worth, which led to bankruptcy. The fault was not in the real property; the fault was in the fact that, as an investor, he didn't use common sense. And, of course, I couldn't advise this investor, nor would he have taken my advice anyway. However, I can tell you about the mistakes he made and show you how to avoid them in the future.

If you buy older property that needs renovating, don't over-renovate. For example, find inexpensive kitchen cupboards, rather than expensive wood cupboards. I have found some excellent metal cupboards in the Sears catalog (which doesn't exist anymore) that were comparatively inexpensive and certainly worked well in my apartments. Metal cabinets saved money because the wood cupboards were, and are, considerably more expensive. Another item that can be a money-saver is carpeting. When it comes to carpeting in an apartment, color isn't all that important, but price is. Shop around, and get the best deal you can. Of course, do this with all materials you use.

Watch the costs of all materials and products carefully so you don't overspend and find you've got more money in the property than it's worth or than it will earn from rent. Also, when taking on any renovation work in a property, it's a good idea to stay in close touch with the lumberyard manager who can help cut costs (this is especially so in a smaller community) and to contact other investors who have done similar work. Ask questions of carpenters and others you know who have had experience with real estate renovation. Get their opinions and advice.

Burnout

I know a part-time investor who works for the U.S. government. He has an average job, an average lifestyle, and lives in an average middle-class home. He has a better-than-average mind and, by using his mind, he thought it out and knew that he could enhance his finances by buying investment real estate.

For 15 years he bought and sold fixer-upper properties. Most of the work he was able to do on his own during vacations, on weekends, evenings, and whenever he could find time. He did very well for several of those 15 years. However, he overdid it. He didn't take the needed vacations he had coming to him, he was gone from his home and family on weekends and nights, and pretty soon he had more than he could handle with the real estate, while still working a full-time job. He overdid it, and burned himself out.

As his property began to deteriorate, he came to me for some advice and consultation. He told me outright that he was getting tired of working at the property—and let me interject here that the property has to be cared for on an ongoing basis. He said he had accumulated all this property and now didn't know what to do. He came to me for advice, and I gave it to him. I suggested that he either hire a firm that specializes in property management or put the property up for sale. I suggested that he make this decision as soon as possible so that the property wouldn't deteriorate to the point of no return. The fact is, by the time he got to me, it was almost too late.

Deterioration only takes a short time with neglected property. I noticed that my friend became more distraught with the tenant problems, fixing this and fixing that, handling complaints, and filling vacancies, and then things began to go downhill. At first he lost some good tenants, and then he couldn't get good tenants to replace those he lost. He ended up with some slow-paying and no-paying tenants, which only added to his dilemma. What he got into is what I call a *real estate sinkhole*.

After a couple of years of steady deterioration, he finally sold the property. He was only able to get market value because the properties needed some rehabilitation, which he didn't care to do. As a result, he lost the appreciation he had gained over the years. However, he did end up in pretty good condition financially because he was able to recover all of the equity he had built up, so it wasn't a total disaster.

The point of the story is that anyone in this business must also realize their own limitations. It's like any other business: you can't overdo it. This story also illustrates the fact that it isn't the real estate but rather the individual involved with the property that can make the difference. Despite this sad story of real estate, I still believe the rewards far outweigh the liabilities and trouble.

Absentee Ownership

This is the story of an individual who bought an older fourplex in a city located 100 miles from where he lived. Although he knew me, he didn't come to me and seek advice before he bought the property. Probably he knew what the advice would be. I would have told him right out that absentee ownership is dangerous and not a good investment program, especially that far away. Nevertheless, he bought a property with the expectation of being able to manage it from 100 miles away.

The first mistake he made was renting with no control over the tenants. He had no idea how they paid their bills, and this started him on the first of a series of problems. Next, driving 100 miles to handle complaints and fix plumbing problems turned out to be very expensive and time-consuming. Ultimately he had to hire someone to make all the repairs. This led to the next problem: being at the mercy of servicepeople. He had to pay whatever they charged. That meant when a sewer was backed up, it had to be cleaned out right away. There was no time to bargain-shop for these quick repairs. To make this story short, the property turned sour for this investor and he lost it on a mortgage foreclosure, and now he's back working at his job, waiting for a pension.

I believe the investment idea was good, but the property was just too far away. Had he bought a property within, let's say, 40 miles of where he lived, within commuting distance, I think it could have worked.

Personal Overspending

Here's the story of a couple who started out investing in rental properties at a fairly early age in their careers. They bought their first property with very little down with a mortgage for almost the full value.

However, working together as a couple (they owned their own small business—real estate was a separate venture), they were successful, right from the purchase of their first property. They gave excellent service to their tenants and had clean, well-maintained apartments so that there was never a loss of income due to vacancies. In fact, there was usually a waiting list for their apartments.

They continued their operation for a number of years, bought more properties, worked on them, increased their values, and maintained the good service to their tenants. Their cash flow was tremendous, as were the expenses and mortgage payments. But during the first few years both the income and the outgo worked out well so they didn't have to dig into their own pockets to make things go.

Actually things may have worked too well because they started living an expensive lifestyle. They bought things they didn't need, expensive new cars and the like. Then they bought new furniture for their home, and a plush summer home, and they took several exotic vacations. To support this spending binge, they started dipping into the monthly rent checks. This uncontrolled spending went on for about a year, and then the problems started setting in. From that point it was downhill. First, there wasn't money to pay the taxes, and upkeep and maintenance were ignored.

Ultimately they lost the properties, all of their investment, and this excellent business they had built up because they couldn't make the payments on the mortgages and contracts. In addition, because of the strain and stress this caused, the husband lost his health. The sad part of this story is that it shouldn't have happened. It was a case of getting caught up in a "status symbol" lifestyle and living beyond their means.

The answer: be constantly alert to the financial affairs of your personal life and business. Don't merge these things and lose sight of the needs of your investments.

Cynicism Toward Real Estate Investors

Real estate investing often gets a bad name from a number of sources. One of these has been the corporate executives who dabble in real estate. Some of the reports of massive failed real estate investments that have come out of cities like Houston and Chicago and Los Angeles are testaments to the mismanagement of self-serving, incompetent corporate executives. These widely publicized failures have given a bad name to real estate investing. They have even crashed the market in some places.

Some of these failures have created a general skepticism about real estate investments. Media coverage on the nightly TV news has scared people out of buying property and has created the impression that real estate is a questionable, risky investment.

> Greed can be as devastating as cheating. Quick bucks, easy money, and get-rich-quick schemes all represent questionable business tactics. How often have we heard about someone who has been taken in by some slick salesperson: hot stocks, oil wells, "nothing-to-lose" deals, and "you-can't-go-wrong" gimmicks? All in the name of profit, … which means caution!

As an example of this phenomenon, all we have to do is take a look at Sears. The corporate executives of Sears built a massive corporate symbol called the Sears Tower. On completion, the tower was only half-filled with upper-level, highly paid Sears executives. Sears had intended to rent out the other half, but they were unable to do so, and it remained vacant. This, along with their other failed business ventures, placed Sears in financial straits. Now what do we have? Irony. In the 1990s the catalog business was among the flourishing businesses. Sears, the company that introduced catalog buying to the American public, now has the Sears Tower, but no catalog. The point is that greed got in the way of logical, smart thinking and created business and financial disasters.

Of course, these kinds of investments, the Sears Tower or the Houston overbuilding of investment property, are beyond the realm of reality for the average, everyday small investor, but the story makes a point: an investment failure, even one caused by sheer incompetence, can give an unfairly negative impression of this otherwise excellent business.

It's amazing how, within the past 10 to 12 years, business greed has crept into our social structure. Greed seems to have become more acceptable and commonplace, and the real estate business is certainly no exception. Take a look at what the savings and loan, banking, and insurance businesses have done to us with their corporate greed and get-rich-quick schemes.

Greed has certainly become a pitfall in the real estate investing business. For the last decade, investors have often bought property at highly inflated prices, got heavily in debt, couldn't make the payments, and ultimately lost everything. Some investors, including some of the so-called rich and famous (no longer so rich anymore), became overzealous and kept buying property regardless of the circumstances. Others invested, mismanaged their property, didn't pay attention to the costs of their operation, got into severe financial difficulty, and ended up with mortgage payments they couldn't meet.

Most of the get-rich-quick schemes simply don't work. The real estate business, like every other business, is a practical business. Successful real estate investors, on whatever financial level they operate, aren't suckers or dummies who are ready to be fleeced out of their money.

Chapter 6

The Myths About
Real Estate Investing

I n addition to the pitfalls of real estate investing, the overzealous investors, the careless operators, and greedy investors, there are some real estate myths that I call to your attention.

Myth: You Can Trust the Owner

Real estate owners who are selling their property can be trusted and they'll always give you the complete truth about the value and condition of their property.

Hmm. Now I don't want to come down hard on owners, especially owners of investment properties, because they can be the lifeblood of the business as the seller-financer for the small independent investor. However, the fact is that the seller, whoever it may be, isn't going to tell you about all the defects in the property. Instead, he or she will tell you about all the highlights of the property. And you're going to get the price ... and be sure you note, I said "price," not the value.

Sellers most often will not point out the flaws and scars about the property. If there's wood rot any place in the building, you're not going to hear about it from the owner. You're going to have to find it. If there's a defect in the plumbing, the owner-seller isn't going to point it out. If the roof leaks, the owner will avoid taking *you* to any place in the building where the leak is conspicuous. Therefore, when you negotiate with an owner-seller, don't depend on the individual to give you factual information about the property. It's up to you to know what you're looking for and to search out any defects. It's also up to you to know the prevailing market prices.

While I'm on the subject, let me mention that the defects of the property are an important negotiating tool. Point them out very explicitly, and use these defects in negotiating the price to your advantage. Don't be bashful about it—the seller certainly isn't.

But listen, I don't want to paint such a bleak picture about real estate and real estate sellers that you'll lose all interest. The main point here is to let you know that, as the buyer, you should be aware that the prime motive of the owner is to get as much money as possible from the sale. To protect yourself, learn the business so you can recognize the various property defects. Check everything out. Know what you're doing. And remember that, no matter how friendly and courteous the seller or realtor might be, this is a "buyer beware" business.

Myth: You Can Get Rich Quickly

I haven't attended any of the real estate "get rich" seminars, but from what I've seen and heard about most of them, I think they are all about the same. They get $299 or so for the seminar, and for that $299 they'll teach you how to "get rich quick" in this business. They pretty much operate on the premise that they'll teach you how to get something for nothing ... that is, once they get your $299.

Here's an example of what you might learn for the $299. Their proposal goes something like this. You find a property for, let's say, $150,000. You then offer the seller $100,000. Assuming the offer is accepted, you go to the bank. You tell the banker you're buying a $150,000 property and you want a loan of $125,000. Assuming the banker accepts this, you then leave the bank with $125,000. You pay the seller $100,000 and put the $25,000 cash in your pocket.

Do you think any part of this plan can or will work? I know this business, and I don't think there are many investors who are going to sell a $150,000 property for $100,000, and I doubt that any banker is gullible enough to advance $125,000 on this kind of proposal. An owner who has a $150,000 property and can get a loan for $125,000 is not going to be snookered into selling the property for $100,000. It doesn't take a brain surgeon to figure this out.

Another scheme taught in these seminars is this. The pitchman will have someone in the audience who claims to have made hundreds of thousands of dollars in a short period of time. What probably has happened is this. The investor may have bought a $150,000 property. Then the day of the seminar she personally appraises the property at $200,000 so that, according to her calculations, she's made $50,000 in a short period of time.

Another tactic they sometimes teach seminar participants is that government foreclosure properties are easily available and great money-makers. Theoretically, if you buy that kind of property, you're sure to make money and you can't go wrong. Well, that too isn't the way the "real" real estate business works. Government properties that have been foreclosed on usually are distressed properties and are located in some pretty questionable areas. Going into this kind of business takes some special talents, along with guts and know-how.

Myth: You Can Trust the Realtor

All buyers eventually will end up dealing with a realtor, so a part of learning about the real estate investment business is learning how realtors work. Let's take a look:

Politicians, attorneys, used-car dealers, and realtors are trustworthy, and you can believe everything they say. They'll always stand by their word.

For the time being we'll forget the politicians, attorneys, and used-car dealers. But let's see what motivates realtors to do what they do.

First of all, remember that realtors work for sellers, which means they're going to back up what a seller says about a property. In addition, the odds are pretty good that the realtor is going to tell the seller that he or she can get $84,000 for a $74,000 property. Next, realtors, like the owner-seller, will tend to hide as many of the defects about the property as possible, and you can be assured that they'll accentuate the positive and ignore the negative.

When the realtors strike the hardest, though, is when they're going for the "kill," that is, when they're closing the sale. It's at this point that a lot of realtors, even honest ones, lose their credibility. When realtors make their closing "pitch," they come up with all sorts of misstatements, half-truths, and tricks.

Here are some of what we might even call "scare tactics" used by almost all of them. In my mind they are demeaning. Most of us recognize them, don't like them, but live with them. A sarcastic comeback often works, but, then again, you don't want to lose the relationship you've already established. Here are some typical closing pitches:

- They've already turned down an offer for more money.
- There's somebody who's made an offer so you're going to have to make a decision.
- It'll be gone tomorrow if you're not ready to make a deal.
- I've got a signed contract from a buyer who's made an offer, but if you want to pay the going price, I think I can get it for you.
- If you'll sign an earnest-money contract, I'll take it to my supervisor and see if I can get your deal through.
- You can't go wrong because it's a good deal. It's too good to pass up.
- This is really a good deal that's going to make money.
- This deal isn't going to last so it's a good idea to sign a contract right away.
- Why don't you give me $1,000 to hold the property, and we'll put in a bid? I'm not promising that they'll take it, but at least we can make an offer.
- You'd better buy now, or someone else will grab it.

- If you don't sign a purchase agreement, I don't know if I can get it past at this low price.

It's not necessary to listen to, act on, or pay attention to these shallow warnings. Cut off the communication right from the start, and let the realtor-seller know that you want the truth. Don't be intimidated by the realtor or seller, but do keep the door open for negotiations. Life is too short to go through these hassles.

Myth: You Can Trust Yourself to Make the Right Decision

Getting involved in the real estate investment business is a highly charged and emotional event in anyone's life. It's a new business, it's a self-employed business, it's a family business, and it's a financial commitment business. Buying things gives all of us an emotional high. Real estate is no different. However, the best way to get the best buy and the only way to buy real estate is to try and remain calm and not become emotionally involved.

Sometimes the first property people are interested in becomes so enticing that they act before they think. Don't fall into that trap. Take your time. Be aware of the dangers of thinking under the influence of anxiety, excitement, and enthusiasm, all of which can set in and cause a new investor's emotions to "run wild." That first investment can take your breath away and can cause your brain to run amuck. When this happens, it's time to take a break. Get away from it all. Find some quiet place to think things over. In your mind run through all the phases of the project, how you'll finance the property, what you'll need to fix up the property, whether or not you can handle the management, what you'll do when the first tenant calls and says the toilet's plugged, or what you'll do when you have your first vacancy. Then think of how good it will be to deposit the first rent checks, how you'll be able to make the first payment, what it will be like to drive by the property for the first time when you'll be able to say:

I did it. I'm on my way!

Myth: The Lending Agency Will Be on Your Side

Bankers are friendly, kind, considerate, and community-oriented, but bankers are motivated by profit. Profit is made through loans when they receive their payments as agreed. Bankers want to give loans to people who are stable and have a good income. Bankers don't like to take chances. Bankers like to finance homes. Bankers don't like to finance rental properties. In short, as a small independent investor, search for your own financing. Learn as much as you can about financing.

Part Two

Buying Rental Property

Chapter 7

Don't Be Afraid to Start Buying Income Property

(Even if You Think Prices Are Too High)

Before we get ahead of ourselves, let's take a look at the real estate business during the mid-1990s to the 21st century, and see if we can predict what's in store for those of us who are interested in this business in this century. In this way we should be able to see whether or not real estate will remain the enticing and profitable business it has always had a reputation for being in past years.

Throughout this chapter we'll examine the general trends and attitudes that affect the real estate market. Looking at the attitudes and reasoning of the people involved in this business should help you to avoid the pitfalls others have stumbled into. You will also be able to see why the real estate business is a business that can withstand some turmoil and remain fairly stable.

In order to accumulate any sort of wealth in our lifetime, it's necessary to have more than one source of income. Real estate investing can provide that source.

Building Wealth with Rental Properties

I've been asked a number of times, especially during tumultuous and turbulent times, the following questions:

- Does real estate investing still work?
- Can money be made in this business?
- Have a lot of the benefits of real estate investing been eliminated?
- Isn't the quick and easy money gone for the investor?

Let me answer these questions by saying this: I've been in the business of buying investment real estate since the 1960s. Since that time, year after year, during the 1970s, 1980s, 1990s, and now, in the 21st century, I've been a strong advocate of investment property as a money-maker. As the old saying goes, "The proof is in the pudding," by which I mean that I've continued buying property year after year with no hesitation or qualms, and I have every intention of continuing in this business in the future.

As I travel about the "real estate world" and talk to real estate people, I find that there are some advisors out there who tell us that it's not a good time to buy investment property. Their reasoning is that there just aren't many sales of investment property. Maybe that's so, although I personally see properties sold all the time. But I figure it this way. You don't buy property when everyone else is buying and forcing prices up. You buy when it's a down market, when the real estate people are looking for buyers. That's when you can "strike a deal."

What I found to be the case, in the mid-1990s, was that everyone was holding back. They were discouraged from buying investment property. They'd been told, "It's not a good time to buy because investment real estate isn't selling." That, in my opinion, is a myth, but the widespread belief in this myth opens the doors for aggressive investors.

I've been around for a long time, and I've heard negative stories for the past 35 years. If I had listened to the doomsayers, I would never have gone into this business, I would never have made the money I made, and I would still be sitting around procrastinating ... and thinking the only thing I had to look forward to was a monthly Social Security check.

It took me a little time, but eventually I came to the conclusion—and you should too—that I wasn't getting all the truth.

Cyclical Changes in the Market

There are, of course, definite factors that have an effect on the market. For instance, there are daily reports of how the Department of Housing and Urban Development (HUD) and the Federal Housing Administration (FHA) have bungled real estate projects. Both agencies are constantly being criticized for their bungling, and justly so. These agencies have become a part of the problem rather than part of the solution. What has happened at HUD and FHA is that they've been consistently overzealous in building and financing rental properties. Then they end up with bad investments, which lead to uncollectible loans, past-due rents, and mortgage payments. These agencies have often built apartment buildings and then, because of a lack of good management, have torn them down almost as soon as they were constructed.

I mention this about HUD and FHA because what they've done in the real estate investment business hasn't helped the image or public perception of real estate and good real estate practices. Their business activities are part of the cause of the public's present belief that real estate is a poor investment.

Then, of course, consider what those wonderful folks from the savings and loan business have done to the reputation of the real estate business. It's not necessary to go into the details about their binge because we've all heard about the destruction they have done, and now we just don't want to hear any more or know any more.

The Trendsetters

The perception—that is, what we think is happening in the real estate market—can make all the difference in the world as we decide which course we should take in our investment career. As an example, some apartment owners and landlords complain that there's an overabundance of apartments—just too many units and not enough tenants. Some say that the market is saturated and the government has subsidized some landlords who are lining their pockets at the expense of all real estate investors. Some landlords complain about decaying neighborhoods, and that the tenants now have all the rights and there are none left for the owners. "Taxes have become such a burden for property owners," some say, "that it's almost impossible to buy real estate and come out ahead on the investment."

There are other complaints and complainers, but you get the idea. For the cautious investors, all of these complaints ring with a certain amount of truth and should be recognized, but they should not be a deterrent. What this means is that, for any investor, it's a matter of taking the time, searching for the right property and the right location, and then buying the property in the right way.

Overcoming the Burdens

There's no doubt that, in some areas, apartments and apartment buildings have been overbuilt. However, remember: there are still tenants out there who are always looking for good rentals. Listen: what tenants want, and good investors can provide, is an apartment at a reasonable rent, clean living conditions, and good service. And I can tell you, good service doesn't necessarily mean new buildings. Good service means good management. The fact is, good operators who provide reliable service usually have a waiting list of people to take their apartments.

The Influence of Contractors, Realtors, and Bankers

Contractors

Building contractors certainly play an influential role in what happens to real estate prices, rents, and the overall market. Here's why: when there's a slight indication that there's a demand for apartments, building contractors and speculators will start building, and then build and build. That's fine, when there's a need, but, for some reason or another, contractors will all build at the same time and ultimately glut the market. When this happens, of course, prices and rents drop, and sometimes properties depreciate in value. It's a vicious cycle.

Once that cycle of surplus housing is completed, the market levels off again. This cycle is often hard, but not impossible, to determine. It's important to know your market when you're investing in rental properties. I know the prudent, sensible manager can and will watch and know these trends and be prepared. Being prepared means having good service and good management of the properties.

Realtors

Realtors not only influence what happens in real estate, they also establish the public perception of the real estate investment business. What they say, whether it's true or not, can set a pattern of thought. Here are some of the comments I've heard from realtors about what's happening in the real estate business:

- There's very little good news about the real estate investment business right now.
- Prices have plunged.
- It's a down market, and there's very little property moving right now. Prices are too high.
- It doesn't seem to be a good time to buy.
- Sales are slow, and there just aren't any buyers out there.

Does that sound fickle? It is, and I know that if those same realtors had investment property for sale, there would be a different tune and story.

One advantage the investor has, when realtors say there aren't any buyers out there, is that the myth forces the seller into talking terms, and those terms, as advocated in this book, involve seller financing. Chapter 10, "How to Get Real Estate Financing," covers seller financing extensively.

Bankers and Loan Officers

Here are representative remarks from bank and savings and loan real estate officers:

- There are too many properties and not enough renters.
- There are many foreclosures and bankruptcies in the real estate business.
- I believe investors should listen to these professionals with reservations.

A lot of people are telling us the gloom-and-doom stories about real estate investing … and this includes bankers, realtors, and, especially, media people. Ironically, most of these people don't even own investment property and probably never will. They just don't know (or, to resort to an overused cliché, "they just don't get it").

Here's an example of what I mean. The only people I know who are saying, "The tax benefits are gone for the real estate investor, and it's not a good time to buy," are people who don't know and don't understand how real estate tax benefits work. The tax benefits do work, and work wonderfully well for the investor. This is covered in full detail in Chapter 12, "Taxes and Real Estate."

Procrastinating

Well, we've heard a multitude of reasons not to invest in real estate. There's no doubt that in some areas the market is saturated with too many apartments, and there are also decaying neighborhoods, and taxes are getting out of control. I also hear some potential investors saying things like:

- The times just aren't right for buying.
- The tax laws aren't good for the investor.
- I could have made a fortune if I had started buying real estate back in the 1970s.

There's no doubt that the real estate investing business is a constantly changing business, but it's important to realize that these changes, for the most part, are cyclical rather than unchanging. This means that the market and the prices of real estate can and will vary through the various low and high cycles. For instance, in the late 1980s and 1990s, real estate was experiencing a low cycle in most parts of the country. Investment properties hadn't been moving as readily as they had in the past. Prices, for the most part (and there certainly were exceptions and variations to this, depending on location), held steady, and most investors found that their properties hadn't appreciated as strongly as they had in the past. In fact, in some cases values depreciated. (We don't buy investment property for the sake of depreciation of value.)

Now, however, as the 21st century begins, this situation has been changing. Interest in investment property, especially since the stock market took such a tumble, has increased. Is real estate still a good investment?

Yes, money can be made in this business. And, no, the benefits haven't disappeared. Maybe some of the "easy money" is gone ... but good money can still be made.

There are a lot of people out there who think that real estate was much easier to buy in the past because the prices were lower. I hear comments like:

Yeah, when you bought property back then, you could buy a house for $50,000, $60,000. You were lucky.

But remember, back then when houses were selling for that price, everything else was less—wages, and lumber, and service calls, and even a loaf of bread. It's all relative.

As you look into this business, you should know right from the start that, despite the ups and downs of the real estate market and prices, regardless of all the unpredictability of our economic system, and notwithstanding all the foreclosures and bankruptcies we hear and read about, the real estate investment business is a moneymaker.

Positive Outlook

The people who think positively, the successful investors, the real estate entrepreneurs, and the real estate authors all will say:

The time to invest and buy real estate is now!

The best time to invest in real estate is now—not last year, 10 years ago, not next year or the year after, but now.

The majority of real estate investing, when done in a *no-nonsense* manner, can be great and profitable. The fact is, despite all the "ups and downs" of the market, real estate has remained comparatively secure and stable ... and I don't see that changing. Why do I say this with such confidence? Here's why. Because I've been in this business for the past 35 years, and I've heard the same old negative stories about real estate. I've never found them to be true, and what I've done is turn those negative stories into positive investments.

All one has to do is look back to the late 1940s, when the military people were returning from World War II. Here's what they were told:

Whatever you do, don't buy a house now because prices are too high. Wait, prices will go down.

Back then those homes were selling for $5,000.

The point is that real estate in itself is about as stable a business and investment as you can find. The majority of real estate investing is great and profitable. I know this, and if I had listened to all the naysayers over the past 35 years, I would never have bought investment property. I would be one of those people who sit around and wait for the right market.

But I did go into the business ... and I am still in the business today. I went into the business, remained in the business, and experienced nothing but success. I was able to turn all those negative stories into positive investments. I discovered, and you will too, that all those negative stories about real estate have been exaggerated and compounded, either through misinformed sources or through the news media. The true story is a positive story. That story, as told in this book, will show that real estate investing is not only a very viable and lucrative business, but one that's very much alive and doing well for those who have kept investing through thick and thin. I will have to tell you that now, as we enter the 21st century, it will take a lot more "homework" and managerial skills than it did in the past. But that should be of no concern if you're paying attention.

Incidentally, if you do go into the business, don't panic if you find that real estate is going into a down cycle. Stick it out because it will bounce back up again. We've been through this before. Every time we have a real estate recession and then prices start going up again, some of the "should-have" investors end up saying:

Gosh, I should have bought that duplex (or fourplex) back then, and I could have bought it for $10,000 less than it is today.

Then it's too late.

But let me add to that. Whether prices are low or high, now or in the future, they will ultimately increase. To verify this, all you have to do is look at the past history of real estate in this country.

Sunny-Side Real Estate Economics

In the present market, real estate prices are so high that the average young couple can't afford to buy a home. So what do they do? They rent. What does this mean? It means there's going to be an ongoing demand for apartments and rental property. In the real world of real estate, when there's a high demand for rental property, rents go up. And I have a feeling, as things are going, rents will continue to increase as time passes. Again, history has proven this to be the case. What this means then is that the time is right for the investor.

A Once-in-a-Lifetime Opportunity

It might be a good time to ask:

How many times will I have an opportunity to start anything on my own?

or

I wish now that I had bought that investment property back then. I wonder why I didn't.... Now it's too late.

How easy it is to put off our plans until next week or next month or even next year. Many would-be investors sit around and wait for better times. I've got some news for them. Better times aren't coming. Waiting for them is a form of procrastination. Doing nothing is easy. I can't help those who want to wait for better times, but to those who do want to get going, I can say this: there's only one way to get going, and that's to do it. If you don't start now, you will not acquire rental properties.

The fact is, nothing is going to happen at all if you don't make it happen. The "right time" or the "right property" or the "right location" may never materialize. I've been in this business, as I've said, for 35 years, and I've never found the perfect time or the perfect property. Despite that fact, I've always made money. The point is that if anyone is serious about getting started in this business, there's only one answer: start. Don't talk about it, don't think about it, and don't figure you can wait until the right deal comes along.

If you're willing to accept the fact that real estate investing in the 21st century is for you and you think that this may be your once-in-a-lifetime chance, the next step is to find out the best way to make those investments. Here's some advice that can help.

Making the Most of Today's Opportunities

Only you can make the decision about the kind of investment program that fits your needs. The rental needs will always be there. They are there now, and they'll be there in the future. I'm convinced that, if the property is bought in the right way, if it is in the right location, and if it is managed astutely and with common sense, it's practically impossible to fail ... in the 21st century or any other time. This means that real estate investing is as viable and stable a business as there is, or ever has been. It's too good a business to pass up.

One of the secrets to successful investing, in addition to determination, is patience. Take time to ride out the fluctuation of the market. You'll be well rewarded. Here's what I mean. If an investor had bought a house back in, let's say, 1970, the price would have been about $15,000 to $20,000. Now that house is probably selling for $160,000 to $170,000, or more. Similarly, an investment property that was selling in the mid-1990s for $100,000 will probably be worth $285,000 today.

Value appreciation is the history of real estate, almost since the beginning of time. It's true that, during the Great Depression, real estate prices decreased dramatically, but soon after the Depression, prices started to rise, and that trend hasn't changed since. But, of course, it's easy to be a hindsight millionaire.

No Magic Wand

Now that you know that real estate investing can and will work, the next question is, "What's the best way to get started?" It would be easy if you could wave a magic wand and there would appear before you your initial investment property, all set up with financing, filled with outstanding tenants, and enough rental income to pay the taxes, insurance, maintenance, and the mortgage. All you would have to do is deposit the rent checks each month and make out the check for the payments on the mortgages.

That certainly would be a start. However, as most of us know, that's not quite the way this business works. What really happens is this. Someone we know tells us about a real estate success story. This creates a great deal of interest, especially if we've thought about buying investment property at one time or another ... and most of us have. The next thing we know we're reading some books about investment property, and, as our enthusiasm grows, we get excited, especially after we've heard about those who have prospered in this business. We then begin to think it's time to take some action.

Getting off to a Good Start

But that first step, making the first contact with a seller, looking at the first property, whatever it may be or whatever it leads to, is not all that easy. After all, we don't just go out and buy property in the way that we buy groceries. As a matter of fact, this is probably a once-in-a-lifetime experience. So, that first look, the first excitement about thinking of this business, or maybe even walking into the first duplex, fourplex, or apartment, becomes a challenge that is thought-provoking. We become especially cautious about jumping in too quickly and buying the first property we look at.

Despite all our enthusiasm, despite the fact that we know all the financial benefits of real estate ownership, and regardless of the many success stories we've heard about, taking that first step can be somewhat daunting. Let me stop here so I can assure you that, although this may be a scary experience, it can and will be very rewarding.

Taking Risks

The risk takers in our society are the achievers. The risk takers are also the people who control most of the wealth. Therefore, to gain anything, it's necessary to take some risks. For instance, there are some personal and financial commitments necessary to make a real estate business work. There's no doubt that it takes some money. Not a lot, but most real estate purchases require a down payment, and there are closing costs. I'm sure, if you're like most of us, you don't have that kind of money sitting around that can be used to "gamble." Of course, the last thing in the world that anyone wants to do is invest hard-earned money into something that's foolish. Let me stop here again and assure you that real estate is the last thing in the world that could be called foolish.

It's easy, of course, for someone to sit on the sidelines and tell you that you should buy this or buy that. Most of these well-wishers are probably sincere, but they are not the ones taking the risks. Therefore, in ore.

As you take the initial steps, and the first should be learning the business thoroughly, you should also learn some things about yourself: what you want, where you're going in the business, what motivational forces you respond to, and whether or not you have the temperament to handle the real estate rental business. Here, then, are some questions you might want to ask yourself:

A Personal Inventory

1. Does the thrill and excitement of the thought of owning rental property get me motivated enough that I want to get going?

2. Do I get excited thinking about owning my own business, establishing my own destiny and future?

3. Can I foresee the financial rewards and benefits that real estate has to offer?

4. Am I highly motivated after seeing what real estate has done for others, so that I can hardly wait to get started?

5. Do I have the ability to regulate my time so that I can manage the property successfully, yet remain secure with my current work and business status?

6. Do I have the temperament to handle problems, complaints, and service calls in a positive, sensible manner?

7. Have I sufficiently motivated my family so they, too, will be an asset to the investment business?

8. Are there any business-work conflicts that can't be settled before I make my first investment?

9. Once the "glow" and excitement of ownership subsides, will I still be as enthusiastic and follow through with my investment program?

10. Can I make "crack" decisions?

11. Does the mere mention of real estate get me excited and on the go?

Understand the Money Game

In addition to your personal inventory, you want to know if you can handle the financial aspect of investment property. With that in mind, there are some personal financial questions you should ask yourself:

1. Do I have the financial backing it takes to buy investment property?

2. If I go into this business and don't make it, can I survive?

3. Do I have the ability to make a commitment to use my own money, if necessary, to help the investment survive?

4. What have I earned and saved, so far, that would be in jeopardy if I needed cash to help pay bills for the investment property?

5. If there were vacancies, would I have sufficient income to pay the expenses until new tenants were brought in?

6. What if something breaks? Can I afford to fix it in case there isn't enough reserve cash?

7. Do I really want to establish my own financial independence?

8. Can I live the way I want to live, do I have enough money in a pension or retirement fund that I can lead a life of leisure, travel as much as I want, and have total financial freedom without going into the rental property business?

9. Can I find another business or career, either on a part-time or full-time basis, that will provide me with the kind of income that real estate can?

10. Can I hold on to my current employment, job, business, or profession and invest in real estate on a part-time basis?

11. Do I have a good credit rating?

Chapter 8

The First Property

Duplexes

Unless you've inherited a great deal of money or solid financial backing or reserve wealth, the best way to get into the real estate investment business is by starting with a duplex. For the first-time investor with limited funds, no matter what kind of job status, no matter what age, if you're looking for something you can afford, something within your means, if you need personal housing for yourself, if you're looking for rental and investment income, and if you've made up your mind that now is the right time to start an investment program, then without a doubt, the best starter investment property is a *duplex.* There are many benefits and advantages of owning, buying, and managing a duplex. Let's take a look.

First of all, a duplex is readily available to purchase. Not only can you buy one comparatively easily, but when it's time to sell, there's a market. A duplex is less expensive to buy than an apartment complex. Oftentimes, a duplex can be purchased for about the same price as a one-family home. Second, the duplex provides the buyer with his or her own personal housing, and you can maintain your full-time occupation or business.

With a duplex you can live in one unit and rent out the other. The tenant's rent helps pay off the mortgage. You won't be able to pay the full mortgage payment from the rent, but think of it this way. If you're buying your own home, you're going to have payments. Take the money you'd be using to pay off your personal mortgage and add it to that of the tenant's rent. The two combined will pay off the mortgage on the duplex. Don't worry about that payment because it's going to be building equity and it's equity that increases your net worth. Also, making that payment is a lot better than paying rent. I want to point out that it's all-important that, as you interview for a tenant, and next-door neighbor, you want to be sure that you have a good one … one that pays the rent.

If you start investing by buying a duplex, you'll have a wide variety of learning experiences, such as managing a real estate investment, dealing with tenants, and working on your own property. With your own duplex, you can do all the repair and maintenance work yourself, nights or weekends, thereby avoiding the expense of paying other people to do the work. This also includes mowing your lawn, shoveling snow, repairing a broken window, and painting. It's called sweat equity.

If you own a duplex, rather than a twelve-plex, for example, and you charge your tenant too low an initial rent, it'll only be one mistake and one rent to raise rather than 12. If you live in the duplex, 50 percent of the property expenses are totally tax-deductible. One more thing: by buying and living in a duplex, you have complete control over your investment … and your tenants. If they should cause you any trouble, you're right there to make the adjustment.

My daughter rented an apartment in a large city for a number of years. One day we made some calculations and discovered that, if we bought a duplex for her and if she rented out half of it and lived in the other half, she would pay less than she was paying renting the apartment. Not only that, but after buying the duplex, we realized that the unit was larger than her apartment and that there was a garage, which she hadn't had before. Buying made financial, as well as practical, sense.

What to Look for in a Duplex

Looking for a duplex is no different than looking for a home. Find a good stable property and neighborhood. As an investor who has the ability to work on the property, find a unit that needs some general maintenance and repair work. That way, the work you put in will enhance the value. The value added by your work is called sweat equity.

Figure 8-1 is an example of an investment property that has good potential for financial growth. From the general appearance you can see that the building is in good condition. It's located in an excellent neighborhood, so there are no detracting factors. The property is very rentable, which means it has a steady and stable income. The interior has good oak woodwork throughout, the carpet is in good condition, and the kitchens and bathrooms are in good order. Each unit has a garage, which is a good selling point for potential tenants. Some cosmetic repairs need to be made to make the property a high quality value. For instance, you can see there's one shutter missing. Also, the small garage doors are shabby and need to be repaired or replaced.

Figure 8-1. A duplex is an excellent starter investment. This duplex is relatively small, which makes it affordable, and it is compact, with a garage for each unit. Some minor renovation will upgrade and enhance the property with minimal cost.

Eventually the entire building will have to be painted, but in the mean-time the front entry needs to be touched up. These repairs can be done by anyone, and they aren't costly or time-consuming.

This unit is for sale. The owner probably has ignored the minor defects, which is easy to do, or perhaps has dismissed them as insignificant. (As the old saying goes, "If it works, why fix it?") With a few dollars and a few hours invested by an owner, this property could easily increase in value substantially. This is a good potential starter. The financial aspect of the property is very good. The annual income from the property is $9,480. Expenses are minimal because the tenants pay for almost everything: utilities, garbage, soft water, and lawn service. After deducting the insurance, taxes, and minimal maintenance costs, there's a net gross profit after making the mortgage payment, and this profit figure doesn't take into consideration the tax write-off for depreciation.

Figure 8-2 shows a slightly different kind of investment property. This is a small, fairly inexpensive, compact duplex, and an excellent starter investment. It's stable but needs some work, which, again, will enhance its value.

A friend of mine, living in a metropolitan area, had been renting an apartment for a number of years. She could see that there was no financial gain in paying someone else rent each month, so she decided it was time to do something. She came to me for advice, and I could see that she had plenty of anxiety about buying real estate. We sat down and discussed her financial situation. She had a limited income, so I knew there would be a limited number of properties she could look at. She was paying $415 per month for an apartment, and for that amount renters don't get anything to brag about in a big city. I told her to think about a duplex and to start shopping.

She took my advice and found a duplex located in a blue-collar neighborhood, all older single-family homes and converted duplexes. An elderly lady who had lived there for 45 years owned this duplex. Her husband had died, and she could no longer care for the property.

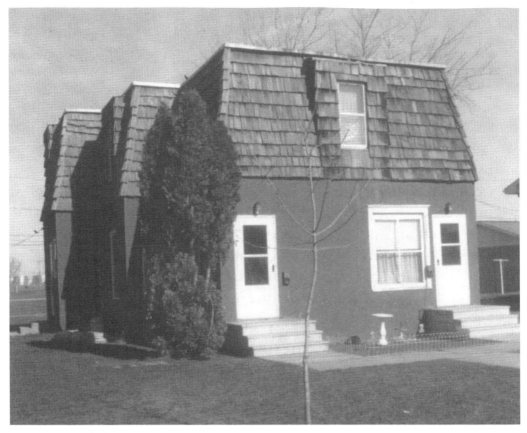

Figure 8-2. This duplex is a good property for renovation. Because it's stucco, the exterior will remain basically maintenance free. The property has two two-bedroom units, and it is small but very compact. Because of its size, the rents can remain fairly reasonable. Therefore, the investor should have few vacancies, along with a profitable investment, if it is purchased on the right terms.

She wanted the money so she could go into a retirement home. Through the negotiations my friend was able to get financing and bought the property very reasonably. She ended up paying off the mortgage with her own money, plus the rental income from the other unit. She made money, and this turned out to be a good investment for her. This building was probably 50 years old, and I would recommend similar older properties if they're well kept and in a reasonably clean and stable neighborhood.

Counting the Savings

Take a look at this. Let's say you're 32 years old. You've got a good job and are living within your means as a middle-class homeowner. You've been putting some money away in a pension fund—that is, as much as you can. You also have a good credit record. Now, let's say you decide to buy an $80,000 duplex as an investment property. Just one property. That duplex will, on average, pay for itself easily in 15 years. That means you'll have an $80,000 savings account when you're 47, and an income of anywhere from $900 to $1,400 per month, which is the net profit after expenses from the rents. You can either sell and get the $80,000 at 47 or continue to collect the rents. Or, you could buy one duplex a year, and at the end of each 15-year payoff period … well, you can imagine how much savings you can accumulate.

It's important here for me to point out that the prices I've quoted obviously will not apply to properties everywhere. But, as you look at properties, remember that the more you pay the higher the rents will be.

Chapter 9

Why You Should Consider Rental Properties

An Investment Plan That Works

Here's an excellent, manageable, and readily available real estate investment plan that can work for anyone who's really interested in buying rental property. This plan is especially applicable for those who are living in communities or cities where investment real estate is unaffordable, unavailable, unmanageable, or heavily taxed.

Before we get to the dynamics of this very special investment plan, keep in mind that, if there's a choice of where to buy investment property, the ideal location is to have the property as close to your home as possible—down the street, down the block, or within a mile or so from where you live. Close proximity means that you can see the property on a daily basis. It also means that you can manage the property easily and solve problems immediately. However, I know—and you'll see as we go along with this plan—that finding property close to where you're currently living isn't possible for a lot of investors ... especially urban beginners who're out there trying to get started or who want to expand their investment.

Restrictive Urban and Suburban RE Prices

As I see it, one of the principal deterrents to buying suburban and urban rental properties is that prices are simply out of reach for the average person. Let me give you an example of what I mean. I recently received a call from an investor who had read my first book. He wanted to know what I was talking about when I said, "If I can do it (meaning buy investment real estate), anyone can." He said, "It can't be done here in Los Angeles because you can't even look at a duplex for less than $1,000,000."

I have to tell you that until then I wasn't all that aware of how high some of the metropolitan real estate prices were. I hadn't realized that there were probably a lot of urban and suburban areas where investment property was so costly that it would be impossible for a lot of people to buy. Once I thought this over, I came to the conclusion that there are also other factors that would be downright discouraging for anyone looking and wanting to buy urban property.

Depreciation

In some urban areas there are decaying neighborhoods where property doesn't have a chance to appreciate. One of the main reasons for buying investment property is to be able to take advantage of appreciation because appreciation is money in the bank. However, I found that a lot of these urban property areas are depreciating, losing their value.

Unmanageable Property

In addition to the high cost of property, decaying neighborhoods, and the lack of appreciation in some areas, there are some urban properties that are just plain unmanageable for other reasons. I can assure you of this: in order to succeed in this business, the investment property must be manageable. The last thing anyone needs is unmanageable property—property filled with tenants who are past due on their rents, tenants who are feuding and fighting, tenants who are using or dealing drugs, or tenants who are destroying the property because of their careless living habits.

Unmanageable real estate is a certain route to "real estate burnout." Once anyone has gone through real estate burnout—when an investor becomes sick and tired of the whole thing—he or she will probably never again want to look at another apartment or rental unit. An unmanageable property can, in fact, become the end of an investment career.

High Taxes

In some cities and communities—and not just urban and suburban areas—taxes have become so destructive that it's virtually impossible to realize any profit in real estate investing. High taxes eat up the profits and eliminate any incentive to invest. As you probably know too well, these tax-burdened communities are fairly commonplace in our country. I'm sure I don't have to tell you that there are communities where government bureaucrats have overspent to the point of creating a tax crisis.

Unless the "tax spenders"—whoever they are or wherever they might govern—recognize the problem and awaken to the reality that it's got to be stopped, they will find that people won't want to buy property in their communities. Unsold properties will ultimately be boarded up, and there will be no tax income at all from them. Real estate will no longer be a viable business, and the communities will end up with slums and deteriorating neighborhoods.

The Bright Side of the Picture

I don't want to paint a gloomy picture about this business, because real estate investing right now is still one of the greatest ways I know of that enables the average person to accumulate any sort of wealth. Therefore, it seems to me that there's got to be a workable alternative plan that will enable those of us who are eager to buy investment property to do so without those burdens that make investing difficult, if not impossible. What I propose to you is a plan that can work, a plan that is within the reach of almost anyone interested in investing, and a plan that's positive and filled with exciting experiences.

Becoming a Commuter Investor

What I've come up with is a new look at buying property. Think of investing this way: there's nothing in the world that says you've got to buy real estate in the city or community in which you live, especially if negative factors, such as decaying neighborhoods, unmanageable properties, and high taxes and high prices, work against you.

Here's how this plan works. The first step is to start looking elsewhere. Look outside your community. Look in neighboring towns and cities. Examine a map of the area surrounding your home base. Do you see any interesting communities that are within, let's say, 50 to 70 miles of where you live? When I say "interesting communities," I mean strong, viable, *growing* communities. The reason I say 50 to 70 miles is that, as you start moving outside a metropolitan area, prices start dropping. For instance, a $150,000 property in the city proper can be a $90,000 or $100,000 property located 50 to 70 miles away. In addition to the price, this distance of 50 to 70 miles is easily accessible and within driving distance for the commuter investor. That means it's easy to get there in an hour or so.

Choosing a Community

After identifying one or several communities within commuting distance, the next step is to write to the chambers of commerce and ask for whatever information is available about each community. This organization will send you all sorts of material describing and promoting their industrial park, educational and medical facilities, and demographic and growth potential information. From this material, you should be able to determine the community's viability and whether or not it's a suitable community for real estate investing.

Community Vitality

The next step is to visit some of the communities. When you reach one of the communities you are interested in, drive through the various neighborhoods. Look at apartments, and look at for-sale signs. The small independent investor should especially look for large older homes that have been converted into apartments (Figure 9-1). These properties oftentimes are the most affordable as well as the most easily financed by the seller. Seller financing in a rural community is a common practice. Maybe it's based on local trust.

Next, drive through the main business district. Many vacant downtown stores, boarded-up storefronts, and shabby buildings can be a sign of a dying community. On the other hand, if most of the stores are full

Figure 9-1. Here is a perfect example of an older, larger home that's been converted into a sixplex. This is a good structure, built back in the 1920s and converted in the 1940s, and it will provide great investment profits in years to come. This kind of property is usually reasonably priced and seller-financed, which makes it a good investment property.

and it appears to be a lively business community, there may be economic stability and growth ... that's what you're looking for.

Commercial Downtown Property

Let's take a minute here and consider the advisability of investing in downtown commercial storefront properties. Let me preface my remarks by telling you that I'm an apartment investor. The apartment business has been very good, and there's no reason to change something that works. I do know this, however: in many viable rural communities commercial downtown property is, to say the least, reasonably priced. I see storefront buildings in some of these communities selling anywhere from $25,000 to $55,000. I've noticed that hasn't changed much in the 21st century. However, I'm just not sold on investing in commercial property, regardless of the price. The commercial property business seems highly volatile and vulnerable, and I say this for several reasons. I see nothing happening in the downtown commercial areas other than consistent depreciation of values, and I see nothing in the foreseeable future that's going to change that. That means the dollar invested today may not be returned in the near future.

One reason for this instability is that it's not easy to get and keep dependable retail downtown tenants. The small retail business is a dying business, with retailers going out of business almost daily. In many communities we're seeing J. C. Penney and Sears stores closing their downtown operations. The cause, of course, can be attributed to the new competitors: Target, Wal-Mart, and others are literally killing the downtown business areas.

What is happening then is that those downtown buildings are being converted to rental units for small businesses such as beauty parlors, barber shops, and specialty shops. The problem is that these retailers and specialty shops just don't have the volume of business to pay the rent it takes to support the buildings. Add one more factor to that scenario: 95 percent of those downtown buildings have flat roofs. When it comes to flat roofs, it's not a matter of whether or not they're going to leak … it's just a matter of when. And when it comes time to fix a leaky roof, it means major problems, both inside the building and out. This means major repairs and major, major expenses. To repair a flat roof on an average downtown commercial building can cost between $15,000 and $25,000. If you look at that in terms of apartment rents, that expenditure comes to almost half the purchase price of a duplex.

So, as long as the apartment business is good and comparatively easy, both in financing and managing, why bother with something that can mean financial disaster? I believe this is especially good advice for the small, independent, part-time investor.

Now, getting back to my plan…. As you're viewing your potential investment community, check the industrial park to see what kinds of permanent and stable industries are doing business in the community. Keep in mind that it's not necessary to look for a General Motors or IBM plant. The way things are going for "big business," you may not want one anyway. What I would look for would be some small basic industry that's been around for a long time.

To give you an idea of what I mean, take a look at Figure 9.2, a map showing London, Ohio. This is a community of 8,000 people located near Columbus and Dayton and Springfield. If I lived in any one of those urban communities, I would certainly consider London as a potential small community for real estate investing, because London has the kind of industry that represents stability and longevity. For instance, London is the home of Brillo pads, and Brillo pads have been around for a long time. The odds are that they'll be here for years to come. It's also interesting to point out that the new Honda plant is located 30 miles from London in Marysville, OH. Add one more feature: London is the home of a large Ohio State University agriculture farm. Now, listen, this is only an illustration—I hope that a couple of thousand people don't converge on London, Ohio, looking for investment real estate.

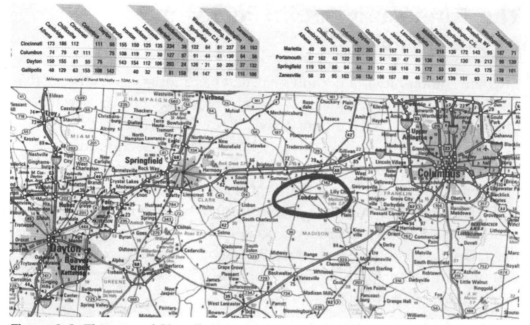

Figure 9-2. This map of Ohio illustrates the availability of a small community within commuting distance of larger cities.

Once again, returning to my plan for checking out rural communities.... The next step is to find out what kind of medical facilities are located in your potential investment community. Is there a good hospital? If so, it will attract doctors, and most doctors settle only in growth communities. Another very important part of the investigation should be finding out what educational facilities are located in the community. If there's a college or vocational-technical school, then there usually is good potential for rental property, since students are tenants. We'll get to more on student tenants in Chapter 15, "Tenants: The Lifeblood of the Real Estate Business." Of course, while you're checking the community, find out from realtors how high taxes are on investment property.

Take several trips to communities in various directions. Maybe you'll find a community in which a relative lives. I have a feeling that eventually you'll find something that looks good in a community that you will have a good feeling about.

The Formula for Profit: Equity and Appreciation

My own community is alive and vital, and has a four-year college and a good industrial base. It's the home of Schwan's Sales Enterprises, the manufacturer and distributor of Tony's Pizza, Red Baron Pizza, Schwan's Ice Cream, and many other home-delivery food products. As the home office, it employs secretaries, computer operators, plant employees, and executives, and they all are potential renters. A college and a large multinational corporation are all it takes to provide the tenants necessary to keep apartments occupied, and occupied apartments mean cash to pay off the mortgage. Paying off the mortgage represents equity; equity, and appreciation are the two main sources of real estate profitability. That's what we're looking for.

The Success Record of the Community's Real Estate

There are others I know who've made good money in small rural communities. In my community of 12,000, one investor owns over 300 rental units. I figure they were worth at least $25,000 to $35,000 per unit when he bought them. Each unit brings in enough income per month to make the mortgage payment. The units are full all the time, and the rents are paid on time, which means the mortgage is being paid off. Paying off the mortgage brings about the second wonderful benefit of the real estate investment business: *equity.* Equity is the money difference between the value of the property and what's owed on it. Incidentally, let me tell you that the above-mentioned investor is doing very well. I admire him. No, I envy him.

I also know an investor who owns an eight-plex in a town of 340 people. These apartments are government subsidized, but I've been told that there's a waiting list of people who want an apartment in this complex, mostly retirees. The only possible negative factor of this kind of investment that I can see is that in this size community there may not be the kind of appreciation one could possibly gain in a larger community. But then, you never know in this business. When it comes time to sell, the appreciation just might be there. Even if the appreciation isn't there, the rents are paying off the mortgage, and that, again, represents equity.

The only work involved in building equity is collecting the rent, depositing the money, and making the mortgage payment. Each check reduces the balance on the mortgage, and, as the balance is reduced, the equity builds. Equity is truly money you can put in your pocket, your net worth. You can use equity to borrow more money to buy more property to build more equity.

Community Size

No community is too small for investment real estate (Figure 9-3).

Figure 9-3. Small-community investing that works. This apartment building is located in a small village, population 340. The apartments are filled from a waiting list. With a farm and an open field in the background, this small community has some beneficial assets in that it is quiet, peaceful, and relaxing.

Keep this in mind. Since the beginning of time, there have been people who don't want to own their own home or who can't afford to buy a home. These are renters, and they represent the people who will be giving you, the owner of the property, their rent each month, which you can take and use to pay off the mortgage. This part of real estate investing, the availability of tenants, is never going to change.

The Commuter Investor

This, then, investing in rural communities, becoming a commuter investor, is the plan that can be highly productive and is available for anyone who wants to get into the real estate business if they really want to invest. With this plan there's no doubt that there's as much profit (appreciation and equity) in most stable rural communities as there is in any metropolitan area. With this plan, when it comes time to sell the property, the rural market is just as good as the urban market.

I know a lot of people who have bought investment real estate in small rural communities, and they've made good money doing it. They have been able to do so because in these rural communities they have been able to find affordable property. On the other hand, I don't know of anyone in my financial peer group who could even consider buying real estate in New York, San Francisco, Los Angeles, or other urban centers. The prices are simply out of reach for the average person, and that's not going to change.

The Benefits of Investing in Small Communities

When you analyze any potential investment community, keep in mind that you're not buying the town. All you'll be looking for is a viable community where you can buy a duplex, fourplex, or any other investment property. As you look at these communities, it's nice to know there are some additional small-community features, besides the fact that the prices are more reasonable. For instance, the quality of life in some of these communities can be less stressful and ultimately more enjoyable. The pace of life is much slower and easier-going. There are no traffic jams, and there's no smog or any of the other irritable conditions that go along with big-city living.

Another feature of small rural investing is that, for the most part, you'll find that plumbers and electricians are more readily available. You'll also be able to develop a closer and better relationship with carpenters and other servicepeople, especially if you're going to take on a renovation project. In a small community you'll be able to establish a close business relationship with the lumberyard manager, who can be a center point for any remodeling and renovating you want to undertake. That manager oftentimes is a jack-of-all-trades. He or she spends a lot of time with carpenters, contractors, architects, and others in the building trades. From these associations the manager has been able to learn most phases of building and remodeling. That means that this yard manager can be in a good position to give you solid advice. There are times when, if asked, he or she may go right out to the property and help directly with your project, helping you save time or money. This information may seem insignificant right now, but down the line, as you get involved in the business of remodeling and renovating, a lumberyard manager can be very helpful.

Comparing Urban and Rural Areas for Investments

I'm not interested in starting any conflict between urban and rural areas, but I feel that these special kinds of services aren't so easily available in some of the urban centers. Do you think an urban lumberyard manager would go out on the job with you and give advice on a project? Do you think you'd even get a chance to meet the urban lumberyard manager, let alone get personal service? Living in an urban area while investing in a rural area offers the best of both worlds: the economic advantages of the big city, where you make a living, and the availability of affordable investment real estate and the special personal services of the rural area.

Investments in Rural Areas: A Concept That Works

This plan of investing in rural American real estate works. If I lived in a big city and couldn't find affordable properties, I'd be heading out to the countryside right now, looking and buying. It's not a difficult plan, and it's one that anyone can implement. It's a matter of finding the right community. Let's take a look at some communities where this plan might work. Remember that these illustrations are only illustrations and not necessarily prescribed or recommended locations for investing. You make that decision.

The 100 Best Small Towns in America

The 100 Best Small Towns in America (1993), by Norman Crampton, is an excellent guide to the 100 best small towns in America. I highly recommend it, especially for the independent investor who might be looking for a small rural community.

As an example, here's what the author has to say about Crawfordsville, Indiana:

CRAWFORDSVILLE, IN, Population 13,584 (1990). Economic base diversified manufacturing, agriculture, county seat.

Another community of interest might be Geneva, New York:

GENEVA, NY, Population 14,143 (1990). 53 miles southwest of Syracuse, 46 miles southeast of Rochester. ... Rich agricultural production ... fruits and vegetables. New York State Agricultural Experiment Station, Hobart and William Smith Colleges.*

*Norman Crampton, The 100 Best Small Towns in America, Simon & Schuster, New York, 1993. Reprinted by permission of the publisher, Prentice Hall General Reference/a Division of Simon & Schuster, New York.

The Sleeper Community

To further illustrate my point, I've picked an interesting small community: Waconia, Minnesota (Figure 9-4). I bring this community to your

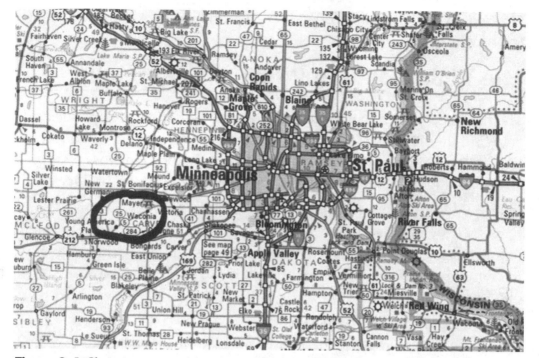

Figure 9-4. Sleeper communities are usually located near a large metropolitan area and have great potential for future growth.

attention because it's what I call a "sleeper" investment community. Located near the Minneapolis-St. Paul area, it is close enough to have the advantages of the big city yet far away enough so that it doesn't have the disadvantages of the big city. Waconia is located in a hilly and wooded terrain, and, because it's located on a lake, the real estate around this community will become very expensive indeed someday.

One of the main reasons that this community (and the idea is to look at reasons a community has the potential for investing) is going to survive and grow is because Waconia has a population of only 3,000, but there are 145 doctors practicing medicine in this town. It's becoming a medical center for the urban area. Remember, I said most doctors settle only in growth communities. In addition, hospitals and doctors attract nurses, nurse's aides, hospital workers, and medical assistants. These people make up a group of highly recommended tenants.

Well, by now I'm sure you get the idea and can look for a community on your own.

The Right Location Within a Community

The next step of this plan, once the choice community has been selected, is to find the right location within that community. Picking a bad location, in any community, can be a contributing factor to the loss of appreciation. Remember, appreciation is one of our main wealth builders, so we want to protect the property from depreciation.

As we look *in* the community (not *at* the community), it's important to know some of the details about the locations where we intend to buy the rental property. For instance, to help make the right choice, check out these things:

- Is it a quality neighborhood?
- Is the neighborhood zoned for business, industry, or multi-dwelling property?
- Are there traffic and/or freeway problems that could create a noise factor?
- Is the property near an airport (noise)?
- Are there streets, curbs, and gutters, and are they in good repair? If not, this could mean costly expenses in the future.
- Is there a crime and/or drug factor in the neighborhood?
- Could there be any problem with flooding?

The next step is to analyze the property itself by asking the following questions:

- Is this a low-priced property in a high-priced neighborhood? (This situation is an ideal investment because the high-priced property will bring up the value of the low-priced property in Figure 9-5.)
- Or, is this a high-priced property in a low-priced neighborhood? (This works against the property.)
- Is the building solid and stable?
- Are there any tax assessments or judgments filed against the build-

Figure 9.5. Here is a perfect example of a lower-priced investment property (a duplex) located in a high-priced neighborhood. Note the middle- to upper-middle-class homes in the neighborhood.

ing and/or land? (Be sure and check this out before making the purchase. You don't want to get stuck paying someone else's bills.)

Once the community, neighborhood, and property have been sufficiently scrutinized, there's no need to scrutinize any further. You're ready. Next is taking that first step: getting started. Determination will take you to the next stage of investing. Your plans should not include sitting around and telling everybody how you've found the right community and the right property, but you're not quite ready.

Self-Satisfaction from Making a Good Choice

Over the years, I have found—and I'm sure you will too—that success in this business provides a great deal of self-satisfaction. Self-satisfaction enhances one's ego, one's ability to think well of oneself. Feeling good gives one more energy, and that energy can be put to work to produce more profitable ventures, which leads to more self-satisfaction, which leads to the next challenge, the next great project, or the next great buy.

A Critical Factor: Management

Don't become complacent and overlook an all-important ingredient of successful real estate investing: management. The money I've made in the real estate business can be attributed to the fact that I managed my properties with great concern and solicitude—all the time. Without good management there's an overwhelming possibility that failure will be more dominant than success.

Incidentally, one of the reasons for the 50- to 70-mile commuting range for investment property (discussed earlier in this chapter) is that the property will be close enough to you for careful management. With consistent and good management of my property, I've been able to experience the "gem" of my investment business, that is, where I've made my best profits: *appreciation.* Appreciation means the property can be sold for more than it was bought for. Appreciation is one of the best ways in the world for the average, common, everyday person to make money. It's truly a wonderful benefit of the real estate business.

Looking Toward a Bright, Exciting Future

Now, if it's your intention to work for someone all your life, making a living, building a pension fund, but never accumulating any wealth, then this plan isn't for you. On the other hand, if you want to start a program that can build a great future, now's the time. Next year, or even next month, may be too late. Your enthusiasm can subside, and then you're back to excuses and procrastination.

Everything's there. It's your choice. No one else can do it for you.

Chapter 10

How to Get Real Estate Financing

One of the most frequently asked questions, and probably the number-one problem for most small independent investors is: How can I buy real estate if I don't have the money?

In answer to that, I can tell you that there's money and property out there, but you've got to search it out. Let me put it this way: if you've made up your mind that you want to get into this business and you're willing to make sacrifices and adjustments in your life, you'll find many sources of money for investing. It's been done by many others before, and it can be and will be done again. The first step is to start looking.

The Availability of Financing Money

There's no doubt about it—anyone who is gainfully employed and earning even a modest, but regular income can find money. Where there's a will, there's a way. The first step is to find the will. Then it's a matter of looking in the right places for the way.

Here's an example of what I mean. This idea I'm passing on to you is very practical. It won't cost anything, and it won't entail any additional mortgage payments. This source of money won't cause any family hardships and shouldn't diminish your standard of living or affect your general lifestyle. It may take a little more time and planning than just walking into the bank and getting a loan, but the money's there if you're willing to make the commitment.

A Plan That Works

Did you ever stop and think about how much work, time, money, and effort are required to own and operate a "status symbol" car? Most cars represent the biggest drain on our financial well-being there is. Furthermore, the return on the investment is the worst of all investments we make. A home costs more, but the mortgage payment is like a savings account as we build equity. In addition, most homes appreciate in value. On the other hand, the car payment is mostly down the drain, and the car depreciates in value immediately, the day we drive it away from the lot.

There's no doubt about it, we all need a car. But the expensive cars are the ones that keep us broke and out of the real estate investment business. For some reason or another, we've been led to believe that we've got to have just a little bigger and better car than the Joneses down the street. So we put a lot of time and effort into buying a fancy automobile with all the gimmicks, perhaps just to impress someone, but we get nothing in return other than transportation. It just isn't worth it.

So, where does real estate enter this pathetic picture? First, take a look at the car you now drive. Is it a status symbol, or is it down-to-earth practical transportation? If it's a status symbol, consider trading it in and using the money for investing in real estate. The money you're spending foolishly on this car could be used as a down payment on a house, a duplex, or any investment property.

The next time you need to buy a car, don't look for a status symbol. Look for a less expensive model, one that gives good transportation but doesn't keep you perpetually broke with the payments. (And there's certainly nothing wrong with a good used car.) Then use the leftover money that it would have taken to finance an expensive car, and use it to buy real estate.

This source of money for financing real estate purchases is simple to activate. It's possible, and it can work if you're determined to make that simple sacrifice. It is certainly a practical way to answer the question: How can I buy real estate if I don't have the money?

There are other methods of finding money for investment property. For example, check with relatives. Are you in a position that you can borrow enough for the down payment from a parent or parent-in-law? If you've maintained a good family relationship, this can be a source of money to get started. Partnerships are another source of financing, although you must be careful. Sometimes you can find someone who's willing to put up the money for the investment property while you do the management and work.

Most of the investors I know, including myself, started in this business on a shoestring. Having no money to start meant it took some searching to get financing. For instance, I had to borrow against my personal home in order to get started.

Common sense tells us that it takes some money to buy real estate (or anything else for that matter), but it is possible to find the money you will need.

Using Home Equity or Insurance Cash Value for Financing

At the time I financed my home to buy investment property, my first thought was that I might be jeopardizing the roof over my head. However, it turned out to be one of the best moves I've ever made. It's something I've never regretted for one minute, and, in fact, since that first time, I've used my home equity for many other investments.

I'm convinced that, if you see a good property, if you're ready to make the move and become involved in rental properties, if you can get a home improvement loan or second mortgage on your home equity, if you don't have to pay exorbitant fees and points, and if the extra payment for this loan doesn't put a burden on your lifestyle, then there's no reason not to use this source of money for investment property.

For some reason we view the equity in our home as a security blanket that we hate to give up, and we want our home paid for in full. I suppose it's part of the American Dream, but it doesn't, in actuality, provide that much security. For one thing, you can't use the equity unless you borrow against it. There's no way to spend equity, and it doesn't do that much for your well-being. I'd rather have a large loan on my home, and use the money to buy investment property. That arrangement would make me feel more secure than having my home paid for and no investments.

Another source of financing is life insurance, that is, the cash value of the policy. Check with your agent. You'll be surprised at how this can accumulate. A benefit of using the cash value of a life insurance policy is that the interest rate with most insurance companies is much less than with a bank or conventional loan. I have a friend who borrowed on his life insurance cash value and was able to get enough money to make a down payment on a nice fourplex.

Incidentally, when you do borrow against your life insurance policy, there usually isn't a set plan for repayment. In this way, it's possible to get the property going well and making a profit before you start making payments on the insurance policy loan. If you feel uncomfortable about using your life insurance cash value for loans, then do this: buy a term life insurance policy covering the amount of the loan. This new insurance policy can be a tax deduction as part of the cost of the real estate.

After watching some of the television investment programs, you might be led to believe that getting financing for investment property is easy. But I can tell you, no matter how many of these get-rich-quick schemes you see, there's no such thing as easy financing and easy money for real estate investment property. As a matter of fact, I don't think anyone should give you the impression that buying real estate and financing it is an easy proposition. I make this statement because, in my experience, obtaining financing is an integral, serious, and important part of the real estate investment business, and it should be fully understood.

I know that if you don't take this important part of the real estate business seriously, you can become easily discouraged. I've seen more people disheartened about buying real estate because they thought it was a matter of walking into the bank, getting the money, and closing the deal the same day. It just doesn't work that way. On the other hand, there isn't any reason to discourage anyone from seeking financing and buying real estate, despite the inconveniences, which I'll point out as we go along. There's money out there; it's just a matter of finding the best deal and the best source.

Seller Financing

To give you an idea of how to find seller-financed properties, let's first take a look at the various reasons why investors sell their properties. We'll start with the owners who are most likely to finance their property. First, some investors want to sell their property and have a regular monthly income afterward. This, for the seller, represents a nice way to retire and have a steady income of principal and interest. This kind of purchase can be good for the seller who wants the income and for the buyer who wants the investment property.

Then there are investors who have bought on a contract-for-deed or assumable mortgage and will resell and transfer that contract or mortgage, take a profit, and move on to bigger and better things by buying larger rental units. This is a way for investors to upgrade their investment and improve their financial future. Other investors just plain get burned out and tired and want to get away from real estate. They no longer want to deal with tenants, tenant complaints and problems, the financial obligations of real estate, and the work that goes with management of the property. Most of these investors have spent a number of years in the business, and now they want to reap the harvest, so to speak; that is, they want to spend their money on the luxuries of life. This kind of seller is quite common in the real estate business. Age plays a part in deciding when it's time to quit. Some investors, as they get older, are no longer interested in taking on the responsibilities of management and believe it's a good time to find a reliable buyer. This kind of seller is usually very good for the buyer because, for the most part, the seller doesn't want to give up total interest and so will work with the buyer to enhance the property.

The Real Estate Subculture

All of the preceding potential sellers are often hidden. They represent the kinds of sellers who will sell if the "right deal" comes along, but they're somewhat covert about revealing the fact that their property is actually for sale. Most of these sellers don't list their property, and they know pretty well that they can sell on their own without paying a realtor's fee. These investor-sellers are able to get the word out to other associates in the business through a network of acquaintances that is almost a real estate subculture. Part of the vernacular of this subculture is the word *interested*, which means that, if the "right buyer" comes along—and it's got to be the right buyer—and all things look good, then they're "interested."

Oftentimes, dealing with this subculture of investors can be a slow process. You'll hear comments like "I'll let you know" a lot of times because the seller will investigate thoroughly, think it out completely, and then make a decision. You can be assured that the seller-financer is going to want to know everything about the buyer before making a commitment and handing over the property. When dealing with these investors, remember that seller financing is very much to the advantage of the buyer because the seller will not only finance but will help oversee the operation. The seller definitely will not want to see the property become run down and lose its value, so he or she is going to keep an eye on it.

Cash Purchases

There's another group of investor-sellers who are open to selling their property but are not in a position to finance. Because they're forced for one reason or another to sell, the properties are often good buys. The first of these are investors who want to get out from a mortgage. They have probably run into some financial difficulties, other than their investment property, and can't carry the burden of the property along with other financial commitments. So, if the mortgage is assumable, this property can be a good buy and a way to get into the business, although it may take a little more than a down payment.

Then there are sellers—and this may seem rather mercenary—who have to sell because of sickness or death. Cynical or not, this is a fact of life … and death. In many cases the heirs are anxious to get their hands on the money. They don't care how much work, time, and effort went into building the investment property, so the value sometimes is not a significant factor. They're not interested in waiting around for any long-term negotiations or even for the best price. What they want is the money, so they may take the first offer, which may be their only offer. I've seen some tremendous real estate buys become available under these circumstances, but, in most of these cases, the buyer has to come up with all the money in order to acquire the property from the estate.

Liquidating Property

There are other sources of real estate sales that represent good buys. Some of these include single-family homes as well as investment property. Because we live in a mobile society, people are frequently changing jobs and relocating. In these situations, sellers have to dispose of their property as soon as possible so they can buy at their new locations. Oftentimes they cannot wait for the best price and will take a reasonable offer. Then there are cases of divorce. In a divorce, often the property has to be sold in order to settle the finances. This may not be a common occurrence, but you should nevertheless be aware of it.

There are times when property has to be liquidated because of a failed real estate partnership. Under these circumstances the purchase money must be paid at the closing, and there's little chance of seller financing.

The Word-of-Mouth Sale

Of course, there are many other reasons for forced sales. The best sources of leads to any sale are realtors and other investors. Let them know, especially the realtors, that you're interested in seller-financed properties. The word-of-mouth network on the availability of property is one of the best markets there is. Once you're in the swing of things and people know you're serious about buying investment properties, the word gets out, and all sorts of things will happen.

During the 35 years that I've been in this business, over 90 percent of the properties I bought were brought to my attention through the word-of-mouth network—somebody called or talked to me and gave me the lead. Getting my name out was a good move. The next best thing that occurred was that I was able to buy almost all of the property by seller financing. That, to say the least, is a marvelous way to get into this highly lucrative and exciting business.

Let me add something else here, for your consideration: the reason I've been able to get seller financing is the reputation for trustworthiness that I've developed over the years. Realtors and investors know they can depend on me. They know they will get their payment, and they know I won't renege and turn back the property. They can count on it. And something else: the worst fear of every seller–financer is that they will get the property back in a rundown, dilapidated condition.

Recognizing the Good Terms of Seller Financing

There are some distinct advantages to buying real estate through seller financing, and they're important enough to look at. First, in dealing with a seller, there's no hassle and jumping through hoops as there is with banks and financing institutions. Also, with seller financing, there are no points to pay, and often there are considerably lower closing costs. Some of these points and closing costs can be exasperating. Another advantage to seller financing is that the terms of the contract aren't as rigid. The buyer can tell the seller, right up front, that he or she has only a limited amount of money for a down payment. When dealing with a bank or financial institution and trying to buy investment property, often you're going to have to come up with 20 to 30 percent as the down payment. In contrast, when negotiating with a seller–financer, there's a possibility of having to come up with as little as 5 or 10 percent down.

Another benefit of seller financing is that the other terms of the contract such as rate of interest, amount of the payment, and longevity of the contract are all negotiable. The amount of the payment can work both for the seller and the buyer. Because an investment property that is a financial burden can lead to investment failure, the seller wants to make sure that the investment works for the buyer so the seller will want to keep the payment within reason and within the income of the buyer and the property itself. The buyer's payment then will be low enough so that it doesn't put a strain on his or her standard of living and income status.

Being able to negotiate with the seller-financer on the length of time of the contract can be important. Some seller-financers want a short-time payoff—five, seven, or nine years. Thus, at the end of that period, the buyer will have to come up with the balance of the contract. If, in the eyes of the seller-financer, he or she is getting payments as agreed, if the property has been kept in good condition, then the odds are pretty good that the contract length of time can be renegotiated and extended. As a matter of fact, if you meet your obligations in the contract by making the payments and taking care of the property, there's no reason this relationship with the seller can't continue until the property is paid for.

The Disadvantages of Seller Financing

As a buyer, you should know there are some disadvantages and negative features to seller financing. As an example, if the seller has a mortgage on the property, that payment must be made as agreed. The first mortgage holder has the first rights to the property. So, if the former owner and seller doesn't keep up the payments as agreed, the mortgage holder can foreclose on the property. The buyer on contract-for-deed could end up with a *zero value*, … or a lawsuit.

Knowing Whom You're Dealing With

It's very important to know who the seller-financer is if you're going to become involved financially. Casual acquaintance knowledge isn't enough. The seller might "look" good and may be the nicest person in the world, but it's what's under the surface that's important. What you don't see is what can ruin you. So you want to look for a solid citizen. One way to get information about the seller-financer is to ask for and check out references. Also, request a credit report. If the seller has a questionable credit file, and what I mean is collections, judgments, and a slow-paying record, you want to stay clear. Don't get involved; people who abuse credit also abuse people.

Nothing-Down Sales

I wish I could tell you that I have a plan by which you can buy all the property you want with no money down and no closing costs. I don't. It takes money to get into the real estate business. Think about it. If there were an unlimited number of nothing-down deals out there, everybody would be in the investment real estate business. Most bankers and sellers expect money to change hands—and this means from the buyer's hand to the seller's.

As a buyer, it's important to have a good financial status, good credit rating, some equity in your home, life insurance cash value, bonds, stocks, or other assets. All these assets help in negotiating with the banker and seller. It only makes sense that lenders are going to be more willing to take a chance on somebody who has built up a good financial record.

Let me make this important statement here: a good credit rating will provide one of the best financing vehicles there is for a contract-for-deed purchase. With a good credit rating, some equity in property, and a respectable reputation, there's no end to what you can do in this business.

The amount of money it takes to complete a purchase can vary. Regardless of how much we would like to buy real estate with nothing down, there's money involved that must be paid. Here's a list of expenses involved in most real estate transactions that are usually paid by the buyer:

- attorney fees for title opinion
- deed preparation
- appraisal fee
- title search
- title registration
- mortgage tax
- credit report
- title insurance
- down payment

We've been bombarded on television and in some books about how easy it is to buy real estate with no down payment. I'm not saying it can't be done; however, I've been in this business for years and have yet to find a quality investment property that I could consider a good nothing-down deal. Most banks and lending institutions demand at least 20 percent down for investment property. Foreclosures, government sales, and abandoned properties for sale do exist; however, I'm not encouraged to invest in these kinds of properties. I caution you to know exactly what you're doing before you get into this type of investment.

Let me tell you of an experience I had with a nothing-down real estate purchase. This happened a number of years ago, and, I have to admit, I was rather naive at the time and didn't know too much about the business. I had the experience of having had a couple of successful real estate transactions and thought I was pretty smart and knew what I was doing. I figured I could do no wrong. Well, let me tell you, I wasn't smart enough, and the investment did go sour. It turned out to be a lot of work and frustration. Here's what happened.

A local church group contacted me, a word-of-mouth transaction. One of their members had a Veterans Administration (VA) mortgage on their home. He had lost his job and couldn't continue making the payments. The church group was trying to help him out and save his credit and avoid a foreclosure. I was assured that I could purchase the property, nothing down, and all I had to do was take over the payments.

Sounds good? Nothing down ... a simple and easy transaction, and I own the property. On the surface it looked like a no-lose situation. Remember, I was pretty smart about this business and could not go wrong. Well, I did go wrong. The deal was nowhere near as easy and simple as I had been led to believe. By the time the title was cleared, the abstract brought up to date, documents filed, and deed taxes and fees paid, I had to come up with about $1,000. And that's before one payment was made. That wasn't the end of it. The next thing I discovered was that the furnace was out of commission, the bathroom and kitchen needed repairs, and there was a load of garbage and junk that had to be hauled away. By the time this work was completed, I had to spend another $5,000.

How did I come out on the deal? Well, as you can see, it was by no means a nothing-down deal. However, with time, that great and wonderful ally of the real estate business, I was able to wait it out. The rents made the payments so I gained some equity and covered some inflation. For the most part, I was able to recover my financial investment.

The point of this story is to let you know what I found out, and that is: *There's no such thing as something for nothing.* From this experience I was able to learn that the nothing-down deals are more of a myth than a reality. I also learned that I wasn't as smart as I thought; I didn't know it all, and I had a lot to learn.

Because I'm writing this book to help you the best I can, I'd like to make it as easy as possible to buy investment real estate. However, from my years of investing experience, I've learned that "slick" deals just don't work. There's no doubt that there are some good real estate deals out there. I'm sure that most of the sellers will negotiate all the terms, including the down payment. However, there's going to be some money involved. I know this business, and when sellers sell property, they're not going to pay money out of their pocket to sell it.

Gimmicks and Tricks

I have heard various gimmicks and tricks presented to potential investors for making purchases with no down payment. One of these suggestions was to use a personal credit card for the down payment. It's true that some credit cards grant sizable limits, up to $5,000, or even $10,000. The problem with this idea, however, is that the credit card is a loan that must be paid back. That certainly doesn't constitute a nothing-down deal. Not only does the money have to be paid back, but the rate of interest on most credit cards is 18 percent.

Another suggestion I've heard for buying a nothing-down property is this. Run an apartments-for-rent ad in the paper. Collect the rent deposits, asking each of the potential tenants for three months' advance rent as the deposit, and using that money for the down payment on the apartment or investment property. Do you think you can make this plan work? I can't believe any seller would go along with this idea, and I can't imagine any potential tenant who would lay out three months' advance rent as the deposit unless they're dumber than a board.

There's something else to say about gimmicks and tricks. Banks and lending institutions, as well as most real estate sellers on contract-for-deed, aren't interested in the gimmicks and trick deals. Banks and others expect you to be totally honest and up-front. Real estate investing is a serious business. It seems to me that, if you're interested in getting into this business, you're not going to rely on gimmicks or tricks. You're going into a business to make money and invest in your future.

Federal Housing Administration Government-Guaranteed Loans

Let me start by telling you there is no such thing as a "government loan," per se. The mortgage money comes from banks and lending institutions. The government guarantees the loan, and if the borrower defaults on payments, the government pays off the mortgage holder. Applications for government-guaranteed loans are made through the banks and lending institutions, not through the government.

Getting a government-guaranteed loan involves a lot of red tape. If you have ever applied for a government-guaranteed loan, you know it's not all that easy. It can take some extra energy, a lot of time, and plenty of patience. To quality for a government-guaranteed loan, it's necessary to fill out many forms. Some information takes time to search out, so it's best to start early. Here's what's needed:

- Two years' employment history is required, verified by your employer. The two years must be in a related field: one year as a banker and one year as an insurance salesperson wll not qualify.
- Two years of income statements are required, verified by your employer, along with two years of W-2 forms. Self-employed applicants must provide two years of income-tax returns.
- A complete financial statement, including all bills and obligations, loans, and credit card debts with current balances, is required. The financial report must include all assets, liabilities, and obligations.
- Copies of your driver's license and Social Security card are required.
- A professional property appraisal is necessary.
- A credit bureau report must be provided.

Snags to Expect

If you expect snags in the process, you can save yourself headaches. About the time you think your application is going along fairly well, suddenly something turns up and takes more time and work. Here's an example of what I mean. A friend of mine applied for a government-guaranteed loan through his local bank. Included on the application was the fact that he owned some limited-partnership oil stock. Before the loan could be processed and completed, he had to acquire a financial statement from the oil company, despite the fact that he had no legal financial obligation.

Things like that take time. If you learn to expect this kind of red tape, you can save yourself a lot of irritation. You'll also learn the value of time, good or bad, in the real estate business. Most Federal Housing Administration (FHA) applications will take from 90 to 120 days to complete, and sometimes longer. Be prepared. Now that you know time is involved—and most loan applications, no matter whom you are working with, do take time—here's some advice: stipulate in the purchase agreement that, if there are unsolvable difficulties and circumstances, you can get out of the agreement without losing your money.

Unforeseen Costs

In order to qualify for a government-guaranteed loan, the property must be appraised. The cost of this appraisal is $300, and in some cases more. What's important to know is, if the appraiser indicates repairs need to be made on the property before the loan can be approved, who pays for these repairs? In all probability, the loan will not include the cost of these repairs. Therefore, it's necessary to have a stipulation in writing and in the purchase agreement regarding who pays any additional costs.

Another restriction is that, if you own five or more properties in one community, including a personal home, the government will not approve a guaranteed loan. Don't ask me why.

Some restrictions can depend on your financial status; others depend on the property itself. Be aware of the various inconveniences and problems you might encounter. It's a lot easier to tolerate the government red tape if you know it's there. I think it's safe to say you'll receive competent help from your banker in getting the application for a government loan. Bankers know the procedure and problems.

Now it's time to get back to the actual source of the money: bankers, savings and loans, financial lending institutions, and sellers. From now on I'll refer to all lending institutions as "bankers" for the sake of brevity.

Confronting the Banker for Money

Over the years I've had a pretty good relationship with bankers, and as you get into the business and establish a relationship with a bank, you too should develop the same type of relationship, a good one. The basis of that relationship is the understanding of what the bank is there for: it's there to make profits. Most bankers aren't different from you and me, and they aren't difficult to get along with. Bankers are pretty much down-to-earth people, just like you and me, and some are even our neighbors. However, the fact is that the banker has one job to do, and that is to make a good loan, make sure the payments on that loan are made as agreed, and make sure the loan results in a profit.

This much you can be assured of: the banker is going to ask for as much security as possible on any loan he or she makes. You will discover, quite early, that banks aren't all that eager to loan out money on distressed and renovatable property, simply because banks survive on security.

Checking on Your Borrowing Power

The first step in establishing security is to know what borrowing power you have. If you're reading this book, you probably have more security and borrowing power than you realize. The following is a list of assets that can be considered money power:

- a good credit rating
- equity in real estate
- stocks, savings, and bonds
- life insurance equity or cash value
- pension funds
- personal property
- job longevity
- earning power and income

All of these items represent security, net worth, and borrowing power. There's one ironic thing about security, summed up in the old saying:

If you've got money, you can make money.

The important question for most of us is: Which comes first, the chicken or the egg? How do we get that money in the first place?

Your Credit Record

A good credit record is very important, and it must be one of the first assets for the investor to protect. I think it's safe to say that if you're overloaded with debt, if you don't have sufficient income to make the payments, and if you have a bad credit rating, you're not going to get the bankers' attention, or anyone else's for that matter. Credit is part of the lifeblood of the real estate business.

A good credit record represents borrowing power. If we go on the assumption that you have some stability, some security, and a good credit rating, we can start looking for financing at the bank. Any one of the previously mentioned assets should be enough to get an open door to the loan officer at the bank. Security impresses bankers. You can also enhance the impression you make on the banker by being well prepared before the initial interview. The banker likes to deal with people who are well organized. So prepare your financial statement with vigor.

The following is an inventory of potential assets for inclusion on a financial statement:

- home
- investment real estate
- cabin, summer home, winter home, or condominium
- savings and/or retirement funds
- stocks
- bonds
- insurance cash value
- household goods
- cars
- personal property

The following is an inventory of liabilities and payments:

- home mortgage
- car loan
- credit card balances
- personal loan balances
- insurance loan balances
- all outstanding debts and obligations

This is a list of potential earning power:

- salary and commissions
- additional family income
- investment income
- financial gifts
- future inheritances

Prepare a complete report of property you own, with the following information included:

- location and description
- type of property (duplex, fourplex, and so on)
- price paid
- value in today's market
- rental income

- taxes, insurance, and upkeep

If the property has sufficient income to ensure cash flow, that is, if the rents cover the mortgage payment, taxes, insurance, and maintenance, be sure to cover this fact in full detail in your financial statement. In fact, make a point to verbally call this to the attention of the bank loan officer.

The next step then is to let the banker know how much and what kind of a loan you want:

- amount of the loan
- length of time and other terms of the loan
- payment schedule
- estimated interest

Although the banker will most likely order a credit report, it might be a good idea to go to the credit bureau and have a copy of your own report ready for the banker. This action will indicate to the banker that you know what you're doing and that you really mean business.

Present yourself, with all your information, in a very businesslike manner. The day you make your presentation, dress up. Look sharp, act sharp, and be sharp. This presentation is almost like a job interview in that you're about to enter into one of the most dynamic businesses there is: real estate. Real estate investing could be your job, either on a part-time basis or eventually full-time, possibly for the rest of your life.

One last word of advice: be positive and assertive; don't be wishy-washy.

Avoiding Paying Points and Higher Interest

Being assertive in the real estate business is important. You can use this assertiveness in dealing with the banker, especially when he or she asks you to pay points, and in dealing with the amount of interest the banker wants to charge. All banks don't charge points, and all customers of the banks don't pay points. Does this surprise you? It shouldn't, because it's a fact. Wealthy people don't pay points. People with a lot of borrowing power don't pay points. I don't pay points. Small-town banks some-times don't charge points.

There's one other way of not paying points, and that is by paying a higher rate of interest on the loan. Sometimes this can be the best way, especially when you're dealing with investment property. I say this because, if you're buying property all the time, usually you're constant-ly going through refinancing. For example, a friend of mine bought a property and financed it with a long-term mortgage. He made the pay-ments for about five years and then decided to buy more property. He had some equity in his first property, so the old mortgage was scrapped and a new mortgage written covering the two properties. As you get involved in this business, you'll find you're constantly making new loans and paying off old ones. In analyzing the loans, pay the higher rate of interest right from the start so you don't have to come up with the cash to pay points. Incidentally, interest rates, like points, vary from bank to bank and customer to customer. Wealthy people don't pay high interest rates, and people with borrowing power don't pay high interest rates. Poor people do pay high interest rates. Shop for interest. Check with all the various lending institutions before making a final decision.

Tell your banker you're interested in a loan without points and the best rate of interest available. When dealing with these two issues, it pays to be assertive. Come right out and tell the banker you want a loan to fit your needs. Tell each and every banker that you would like to do business with him or her, and then work one against the other. Tell them you've got a better deal down the street or out of town. Use whatever money power you have to negotiate your loan. And don't beg or grovel.

Contract-for-Deed Financing

This completes the overview on real estate financing other than the con-tract-for-deed. Because the contract-for-deed (seller financing) is so important to the small, independent, part-time investor, this subject is covered thoroughly in its own chapter.

Chapter 11

The Legal Aspects of Owning Real Estate

Don't Eat the Paint

It appears as though one of the next big "scares," which can be costly to a property owner, is eliminating lead paint and mold. Remember how the government took us through the asbestos scare, which naturally was followed up with all sorts of costly law suits filed by attorneys in every corner of the country? That episode cost everyone. And it seems that there have been mixed reviews about whether asbestos was that dangerous. The scare was there, but was there danger? Could they really prove that it was the asbestos that caused lung cancer, or did the cancer come from smoking or other factors? Maybe under intense conditions asbestos could do this, but then again how many of us have lived in buildings, gone to schools, attended church, or whatever where there has been asbestos? Our office building has a furnace covered with asbestos. Most of us would have been dead or we'd have acquired cancer years ago if it was so dangerous. Some say that it wasn't as bad as the scare made it seem. Some say it was just another way to transfer our money to trial attorneys.

All this could mean that if "they," and I speak here of government bureaucracies, find that there's lead paint on windows, windowsills, doors, door frames, stairs, railings, banisters, porches, and fences in or around a building, that paint may have to be peeled off and everything repainted. You can imagine the cost. Even some of those older toys and old furniture were painted with lead paint. There's also lead pipe and lead solder in some of the old buildings.

Be aware of the fact that bureaucracies are always looking for ways and means to justify their jobs. It appears they are in the process of taking on lead paint or mold just as they did asbestos. And, once a government agency gets on to something they are relentless ... and will never admit they were wrong.

So, provide a warning to your tenants. Put up a sign: "Don't Eat the Paint."

The U.S. Environmental Protection Agency in Washington, DC has published a bulletin entitled *Protect Your Family from Lead in Your Home*. Incidentally, they have a phone number, 1-800-424-LEAD, for those of you who want more information.

Is there really a danger? Many of those houses built before 1978 were painted with lead paint. In fact, I was raised in a small rural community where we'd paint the entire interior of our house every spring, with lead paint. If any of you remember, the lead paint had a horrendous odor. My grandmother would use pig fat, called lard, and fry onions and potatoes oftentimes when we were going through the painting stage of keeping our house up. To be honest, keeping our home clean and painted was about the only things we could afford in upgrading our home. We just didn't have the money to do any remodeling or renovating. At any rate, the smell of lead paint and lard/fried onions was something we had to put up with. It was usually too cold in the spring of the Minnesota year to open the windows, so we lived with the smell for several days.

Everything in our house contained lead: the water pipes were lead, all the walls and woodwork were covered with lead paint, and most of the wooden toys were covered with it as well. My bedroom was small, so the bed was pushed right up against the lead-painted wall, and I lived in that room for 14 years. If lead paint was all this dangerous I should have been dead 20 years ago.

Government bureaucracies say that people can get lead in their bodies by swallowing lead dust or eating paint chips. They say that lead can cause damage to the brain or nervous system, hearing problems, difficulties during pregnancy, high blood pressure—well, let's put it this way, they say it affects almost everything concerned with our health. Can you imagine the attorneys getting onto this?

There is a "disclosure form" regarding lead-based paint. Here's what you can use as a part of your lease contract if you are concerned:

LEAD WARNING: Housing built before 1978 may contain lead-based paint. Lead from paint can pose health hazards if not taken care of properly. Before renting pre-1978 housing, landlords must disclose the presence of known lead-based paint and lead-based paint hazards in the dwelling. Tenants must also receive a federally approved pamphlet, titled *Protect Your Family from Lead in Your Home*, published by the United States Environmental Protection Agency, form number EPA747-K-94-001.

Then, you, the owner–manager, and the resident both sign the form and keep it with the lease. Again, post a sign to caution your tenants and their family: Don't Eat the Paint.

Insurance

Coverage

Scrutinize your insurance policy. Go over it with your agent, and ask the agent to tell you what everything means. If you own single-family rental units or duplexes, you can add these properties onto your homeowner's liability policy. However, you do need a separate policy for fire and extended coverage. If you need coverage for more than two units, look into a type of policy called "special multi-peril insurance." You should also investigate another type of policy called "owner's, landlord's, and tenant's liability."

The following is a list of concerns that you should include in whatever insurance coverage you have:

- fire
- lightning
- windstorm or hail
- explosion
- riot
- vehicle
- vandalism
- theft
- smoke from faulty operation of heating and cooking
- damage from steam or hot water
- accidental leakage from plumbing, heating, or appliances
- freezing of plumbing, heating, and air conditioning
- damage to electrical appliances
- falling objects
- snow, ice, sleet, or collapse of building
- glass breakage
- physical loss to building
- liability, medical, and accidental death

Endorsements are available for most policies and can cover personal liability and loss of income. Again, be sure you consult with your agent, and make sure you have adequate coverage.

What all does your policy cover?

Will it cover the costs of defending against a discrimination claim? Take your time and shop for the best buy in insurance. Contact several agents and get estimates. This doesn't take that much time but it can pay off in savings on your premium.

Watch for premium changes. Every time you get a billing notice, make sure they haven't increased the price of your coverage. If so, contact the agent, and tell him you're going to have to go out and get bids again.

Be sure that you include the cost of insurance (and other overhead expenses) in determining what to charge for rent. Notify each renter personally, and also have it written in the lease, that each renter is responsible for insuring his or her own property.

Beware of attorneys who are eagerly waiting for anything and anyone to sue. They like people with assets.

You might consider, and ask about, a $1 million dollar personal liability policy.

A recent law was passed stipulating that, if a tenant discovers mold in their housing unit, he or she can break the lease. The attorneys are going to love that law.

Chapter 12

Taxes and
Real Estate

Anyone involved in the real estate investment business knows that one of the great benefits of buying investment property is the *tax incentive* (or the *tax write-off*, the *tax loophole,* or whatever else you might want to call it). The fact is that the tax benefit of real estate investing amounts to using the government's money to purchase and maintain investment property. The great benefit is that the tax write-off not only applies to the actual property itself but also to any tax losses on the property since they can be charged back to the investor's individual income tax, as a deduction from that tax. That means that if there are losses in your investment property—after deducting the cost of operation, insurance, real estate taxes, maintenance and upkeep, improvements, and depreciation—the amount can be shown as a loss on your Form 1040 individual income-tax return. Therefore, by investing in real estate, the government won't receive as much income tax from you as it would if you didn't have the real estate tax deduction.

Everyone—and I mean everyone—in the business of investment property knows about this tax break and considers it to be one of the best incentives there is for buying property.

The Tax Write-Off

A tax write-off means money in the bank. Tax write-offs are such an integral part of the real estate business that none of them should be overlooked. Let's examine this tax advantage and see how it works.

Some people don't understand that an investment tax write-off is a profit because they can't really see the money; it's not a visible asset. It's not like having cash that can be deposited directly into a bank, but it is there, and let there be no doubt about it. I know. It took me some time to fully understand and realize just how it worked because I was too busy negotiating, buying, and managing properties. But once my accountant told me and showed me directly how much money I didn't have to pay the government when my tax bill came due, I realized what a benefit for the investor write-offs were.

Tax Depreciation

Real estate depreciation, that is, deducting so much of the value of the property each year, is the best part of investing in rental property. This is a clear-cut gift to the investor. Here's a hypothetical example to illustrate how it works:

> *An investor owns a $100,000 investment property. This property has a depreciation period of 27.5 years. Let's say the investor pays 28 percent income tax on his total income. This means, then, that each year for 27.5 years the investor will have a $1,018.18 tax deduction. This deduction can be used and filed as a deduction directly from his or her personal income tax.*

The government is saying, for 27.5 years you can deduct the value of the building, down to zero value. The irony here is the fact that rarely does property ever depreciate! In fact, it usually appreciates. What a benefit!

> For the small investor, the future in real estate is indeed bright. There's always going to be a need for housing, and regardless of any Internal Revenue Service (IRS) tax mazes, the housing business is a growing and lucrative investment.

Depreciation is great, but it's not the only benefit. In addition to appreciation and equity, other benefits exist, and, for this reason, people should be optimistic about buying, owning, and investing in property. In fact, the small independent investor, like you and me, should continue doing just what has always worked: buying real estate. If you've started, there's no reason to hesitate; if you haven't started yet, there's no reason to wait.

The 1986 Tax Reform Law

For some reason or another, we've been given a distorted view of the 1986 tax reform law as it applies to real estate investment. In listening to some of the "reliable news reports," one would think that the tax benefits of investing had been totally demolished. As a matter of fact, I have been asked a number of times, "What are you going to do now that you've lost all the tax benefits of owning investment real estate?" The answer is simple. I have not, nor have any investors, lost any of the tax benefits.

Let's set the record straight about the 1986 tax reform law. When this law was enacted, it was said that all of the benefits of buying investment property would be gone. In reality, the only people in real estate who really were affected by these new laws were some wealthy investors who had been buying real estate in limited partnerships or had been investing in overpriced or inflated real estate. Before the 1986 law, real estate was a method, at least on paper, by which the wealthy investor expected the real estate he or she purchased to be a losing proposition, and the plan was to use this loss to offset his or her personal income.

The tax reform law did not affect the small independent investor, the one who's out there to make money in real estate itself, the one who knows that there are many other benefits in this business. For that person, the tax benefits are still there. The majority of investors I know are in the real estate business for the right reasons. They are in it for the long haul, to buy, to own, and to manage real estate and to make money doing it. These investors know that real estate is an independent business in which you use other people's money—the banker's, the seller's, and the tenant's—to build equity and pay off the mortgage and, ultimately, to develop a sizable savings account. For most of the investors I know, the tax benefits are simply an added feature of the business.

As I've mentioned, *depreciation is* the wear and tear on the property. As the 1986 law reads, all properties owned up to and through the year 1986 can continue using the old depreciation schedules, which are for a period of 19 years. Under the new law, rental investment properties purchased after December 31, 1986, must be depreciated over 27.5 years, rather than 19 years. Depreciation over 27.5 years isn't all that bad, especially for the small independent investors who are in this business for the long term. The way I see it, many of the big-time investors will discontinue building large apartment complexes for tax write-off purposes. This could increase the demand for existing apartments, which in turn will increase rents.

Another benefit for the small independent investor is the new clause in the 1986 tax law that states that any individual or business that does not materially participate in the property cannot use the property for a tax write-off. The 1986 tax law also states that if an investor earns less than $100,000 yearly adjusted gross income, that investor can deduct up to $25,000 of annual losses from the properties. Any unused losses can be carried forward to a future tax year or can become a deduction at the time the property is sold.

These are basically the only changes that affect the small independent real estate investor. However, if you're not sure about these laws, you might want to contact your accountant. At the same time, have the accountant analyze what effect real estate investing can have on your overall income tax.

An Honest Tax Plan

Here's a list of policies to consider regarding your investment business and taxes:

1. Take advantage of all legal tax benefits available.
2. Pay every penny of personal and investment income tax that's due.
3. Operate the real estate business with complete and total honesty.
4. Take every deduction the law allows.
5. Be sure you take into account the mileage on your vehicle.

The rate you can go by, which is accepted by the IRS is .365, 36 cents a mile. You can also deduct the interest expense related to financing the vehicle, and you can deduct depreciation on the vehicle at the rate of 15 cents a mile. You might want to keep a daily log showing the time, place, and purpose of the miles traveled in conducting your business affairs.

The reason I say you should pay every penny of personal and investment income tax due is because there's no sense asking for trouble. The last thing anyone needs is to deal with an IRS audit. It's usually a situation that raises the anxiety level to bursting proportions, it's time-consuming, and it's costly.

I also said that you should operate your real estate business with total honesty. I say this because there are plenty of benefits available in this business without having to operate dishonestly. An important feature of owning and operating your own business is being able to deduct expenses for operating that business. This means that, as an investor, it's legal to deduct everything that has to do with the business. If you operate a business and use shoe leather in so doing, then take the shoe repair bill as a deduction. Don't let a single penny slip through the cracks because, if you do, it's money out of your pocket; it's profit lost.

To make a profit in this business, or any business for that matter, you have to count the pennies. From there, the dollars will add up. So that no deductions are missed, I've made up a list of all items that are deductible. I didn't include this list just to fill space but to remind you that nothing should be overlooked.

> Real estate investing is a form of forced savings. We're forced to save other people's money, the bank's or seller's, the tenants', and the government's.

Every item, and I've probably missed some, is used in one way or another in the real estate investment business. Use all of them.

Let's go back a little about being honest and not cheating: don't. Life is too short. Let me give you some examples of what I mean about cheating. For instance, some things aren't deductible. It would be difficult to justify buying 12 boxes of shotgun shells in the fall of the year and charging this expenditure to the security of your real estate. Also, don't charge your personal garbage or electric bill to your real estate property. However, if you legitimately attend a real estate seminar, for the benefit of your business investment, let's say in Tahiti or Hawaii, this trip and all the expenses can be charged to your real estate investment.

If you're self-employed in the real estate business and have an office in your home where you conduct business, part of your home expense can be deducted. Check this with your accountant.

Here is the list of items that constitute legitimate real estate deductions:

- tools: hammers, saws, screwdrivers, pliers, flashlight, screws, nuts, bolts
- lawn mowers
- soap and cleaners, cleaning materials, brooms, brushes
- car: gas and oil, car repairs and other car expenses
- business machines: typewriter and typewriter ribbons, adding machine, copier, personal computer and printer, machine repairs
- books and magazine subscriptions (related to real estate investing)
- telephones and telephone bills
- newspapers and advertisements for vacancies

- postage
- insurance premiums
- stationery and other office supplies
- utilities (heat, electricity, garbage collection)
- interest on mortgages
- payroll taxes (if you have employees)
- Social Security (yours and employees')
- taxes (federal and state, property)
- capital investment
- legal fees
- accounting cost
- fees
- business-related entertainment and travel
- meetings, conventions, seminars
- charitable donations
- building repairs (plumbing, etc.)
- depreciation
- clothing
- salaries (yours and employees')

On the other hand, I know an investor who put new carpeting in his personal home and did other repairs and then charged all these expenditures against the investment property. All that's too obvious: the IRS auditor is no dummy. They'll find this kind of thing in a second.

The sad part of this scenario is this: I wonder if Mr. Big-Time Investor, who owns apartment buildings and other investments, uses employees from the investment company to take care of his personal and recreational homes (including yard work, painting, repairs, and general upkeep), keeps these records separate when paying the bills, and doesn't take the deduction. I also wonder if the plumber who comes to one of those personal homes to fix a leaky faucet or the painter who does work in one of the personal homes gets paid out of Mr. Big-Time Investor's personal checkbook instead of the business checkbook. Well, that's not up to me, that's up to the IRS.

The Financial Benefits of Repair Versus Improvements

In this business, where tax deductions are very important, know and understand the difference between a repair and an improvement. A *repair* is charged off as an expense. *Improvements* are capital investments and are tax-deducted on a five-year basis. To better understand how these deductions work, let's see how they differ.

First, here's what the IRS says about repairs and improvements:

- You may deduct the cost of repairs that you make to your rental property. You may not deduct the cost of improvements. You recover those costs by taking depreciation.
- A repair keeps your property in good operating condition. It does not materially add to the value of the property or substantially prolong its life.
- An improvement adds to the value of the property, prolongs its useful life, or adapts it to new uses.

To be more specific, here's how it works. A $200 repair becomes a $56 tax deduction. However, a $200 improvement represents a deduction of $11.20 per year for five years.

When it comes to declaring a repair versus an improvement, my recommendation is to be as aggressive as possible, but don't overdo it. If you do, you could be subject to an audit, and, if an auditor finds that you owe taxes, you could also owe a penalty and interest.

Chapter 13

Government Regulations and Your Investment Property

It's going to be important that you know the state and federal laws covering real estate, ownership, management, construction, and renovation.

Fair Housing and Discrimination Laws

By all means have a complete understanding about fair housing and discrimination.

Some disgruntled tenant or potential tenant may report you for discrimination, whether you're guilty or not. What do you do? Be constantly aware and be sure that you don't break the law.

If you have a feeling you might be treading on unsafe ground, take notes the minute any trouble seems imminent. Write everything down about any conversation you've had with that potential tenant. This includes any complaint you might have received or dispute that might have occurred. Again, write it down, the date and time and word for word what's been said between the two of you. Keep this information in a secure file. And especially keep a file on any tenant you may have turned down and the reason for the turndown. The odds are pretty good that the potential tenant won't have kept records. On the other hand, you'll have your records in order and this can be invaluable before a judge ... if the case gets that far. Whatever you've said can always be held against you in a court of law.

Laws Regarding Accessibility for the Handicapped

Do you need to have handicap accessibility on your property? Know what this can entail if you have to convert your building. There are laws specifying the kind of accessibility you must provide. Be aware of them.

Smoke-Free Property

What laws protect you if you demand that your property be smoke-free? One thing you can be assured of is that, if you do have smoke-free property, you're going to get better tenants. In addition, most people are willing to pay a little more for their rental unit if they know they're living in a smoke-free environment. For the most part you'll have less turnover if those tenants know they are living in a smoke-free unit. In addition, having smoke-free apartments will decrease the work and cost of cleanup in preparation for the next tenant.

Abandoned Property

You also may eventually have to deal with furniture or personal property that's been left in an apartment. If so, and if you can, notify that tenant to remove his or her property immediately. If you get no response, the next step is to find a place where you can store the furniture. Get it out of the apartment as quickly as possible so you can rent it right away. After the property has been stored you'll have 45 days (in most states) to make contact with the tenant and insist that the property be picked up. Once again, if you have to go to court over a sticky issue like this, the tenant probably will tell the judge that you ruined his or her property or it got soaking wet or it got broken or some of the things were missing. Take pictures for evidence. From my experience the judge will most likely be more responsive to the "poor" tenant than the "rich" landlord. It's just one of those human things we have to live with.

If the ex-tenant doesn't pick up the property, the next step is to get rid of it. Keep receipts of the costs involved in storing and moving so that you can either deduct this from their rent deposit or, if it becomes a legal matter, file a claim in conciliation court.

Be sure that you or your management representative inspects the apartment at the time of notification of vacancy before making any arrangements to return any rent deposit.

All this is said to emphasize the need for thorough screening of tenants. These are also good examples of why you'll want to demand a full month's rent as a security deposit.

Chapter 14

The Contract-for-Deed and Other Contracts

U sing a contract-for-deed is probably one of the most significant procedures there is for the small, independent, part-time investor to acquire investment real estate. The contract-for-deed represents the easiest, least expensive, and most reliable instrument for the average person to get into this business. In fact, it is, in my mind, the key to starting for most small investors. The contract-for-deed is the lifeblood of the investment business for anyone who doesn't have a lot of start-up money for buying real estate.

For one thing, the down payment can be negotiated with the seller and can be much less than would be required by a traditional lending agency. Banks are tough to deal with when it comes to financing investment property. They usually want 20 to 30 percent down. So, if the investor doesn't have the borrowing power to get bank or savings and loan money, the contract-for-deed certainly can be an answer.

The Document Name

There are various names given to the contract-for-deed, and they vary from one location to another. Here's a list of some of them:

- agreement for sale

- land contract
- installment land sale contract
- contract for sale of real estate
- installment contract
- conditional sales contract

There may be others, but for the sake of our communication, I'll use only "contract-for-deed" when referring to this procedure and document.

The Definition

The contract-for-deed is a simple legal agreement between a seller and buyer for the purchase and transfer of a parcel of real estate. The buyer agrees to pay a certain amount for the property. Let's say, using a hypothetical case, a property is selling for $100,000. If the contract is written for 25 years, no down payment, and a 9 percent interest rate, the buyer will pay $827.98 per month for 25 years. After 25 years, when the contract has been paid in full, the title of the property will be transferred to the buyer.

The Benefits of a Contract-for-Deed

With the purchase of property on a contract-for-deed, there's usually less money involved, especially for the down payment. The amount of the down payment is totally negotiable between the buyer and seller. In addition, the contract establishes immediate financing once it is drawn up. There's no bank or financial institution to go through. The seller-financer becomes the bank, so to speak. Oftentimes, when there's a good relationship between the seller-financer and the buyer, and when substantial equity has built up on the contract, the seller *will* issue a warranty deed and cancel the contract-for-deed. In contrast, with a traditional mortgage the deed to the property is transferred at the time of the purchase rather than at the end of the payment time period.

The contract-for-deed is a comparatively easy document to negotiate. It's quick and inexpensive. Once completed, the buyer can take over operations of the property immediately. There is no waiting or forms to fill out, and the entire transaction can be completed in a short time. There are no points to be paid on a contract-for-deed as there are with banks and lending agencies. And the interest, like the down payment, is totally negotiable.

Negotiating a Contract-for-Deed Purchase

Obviously, the first thing in negotiating a contract-for-deed is to find a seller who is willing to negotiate a contract. This search can be done through real estate agents as well as through direct contact with sellers. Let your real estate agents know you're interested in buying on a contract-for-deed so they can start looking for properties. You might want to consider going to several agencies. Call the agents periodically because sometimes they can overlook you and forget your interests. In fact, I've made it a point to become casual friends with several agents, and I have coffee with them periodically. In this way, they look after my interests.

In addition to real estate agents, of course, there's the individual seller. Watch the newspaper advertisements and yard signs for these sellers. Also, contact other investors. If there's an apartment owners' association in your community, you might join it and meet other investors. I've bought 80 or 90 percent of my holdings from other investors, and most of this property was never listed with a real estate agency.

The next step, of course, is to ask the seller if he or she is interested in a contract-for-deed. I'm convinced a lot of sellers are interested in a contract-for-deed if the right person with the right credentials asks them. At first you'll probably hear, "No, I want a cash sale," but once communication is established and the seller finds you to be dependable, there will often be a change of mind.

Usually the contract-for-deed sellers are just ordinary people who have probably been in the real estate business for a number of years and now want out. They want to sell to an investor who's going to take care of the property and make the monthly payment. I have found that most sellers have their property paid off. Therefore, if they sell on a contract-for-deed, they receive a number of benefits, such as:

- eliminating management problems,
- earning interest on their investment,
- receiving a regular monthly income, and
- becoming financially independent.

Not a bad combination.

Most sellers like to get their price for the property. It's kind of a pride thing. When negotiating a contract-for-deed sale, I'll usually accept the selling price if it's within reason, but then I like to negotiate the interest and down payment. Let's take a case in point. A seller has a $100,000 property, and he offers it for sale. He asks $100,000 and wants $5,000 down with 11 percent interest on a 15-year contract. The monthly payment on this contract would be $1,022.67. I make a counteroffer on this purchase, leaving the $100,000 price but offering no down payment and 9 percent interest. The payment on this purchase would be $1,004.52. If the seller won't take the no-down-payment term, then offer the $5,000 if you have it and the $95,000 at 9 percent interest (or some interest rate slightly above the market). The payment on the balance at 9 percent would be $954.30 per month for 15 years. One more option: if you don't have the $5,000 down payment, offer $5,000 at the rate of $158.62 per month, 9 percent (or some other reasonable rate) interest and payments for three years. This is an optional method of buying investment property if you don't have the down payment.

As you can see, negotiating the interest on a contract purchase can sometimes be a better bargaining chip than negotiating the actual price of the property, unless the price of the property is way out of line. Remember, too, that on a contract-for-deed purchase there are no closing costs, which can be as high as $3,000 on some mortgage loans, and points, fees, appraisals, and so on are all eliminated, thus giving the buyer some leeway with the price.

Here's another benefit of the contract-for-deed compared with the mortgage. Let's say the buyer gets into financial trouble and can't make a payment. By contacting the seller and holder of the contract, this problem usually can be worked out either by extending the payment or by establishing smaller payments. The seller will try to negotiate something to save the contract and not have to take the property back. I doubt that this kind of thing can be worked out with a conventional bank loan.

I've been contacted by buyers of my contracts-for-deed and have negotiated terms to take care of their various temporary problems, and you can anticipate that this will happen. I might add that during this time I have charged interest on the contract. However, often this action can solve a problem that would otherwise become a disaster.

There's one more advantage of a contract-for-deed: it is a more flexible instrument than a bank mortgage. Let's say the buyer has paid on a contract-for-deed for a number of years, and there's a balance of $35,000 on the contract. The buyer often can negotiate a payoff on this contract for, let's say, $30,000 or $32,000. Discounting contract-for-deeds is a common occurrence. I'm not saying all contract holders will take this discount, but it's certainly something worth pursuing. This negotiated payoff can take place at a time of refinancing. If the buyer has paid off the contract, there's a chance the property has enough equity to qualify for a conventional loan.

Also, when buying property without a down payment, it's possible to negotiate a contract-for-deed with the seller for the down payment. Some sellers are more happy to do this financing so they can close a sale. If you consider going this route, be sure to contact the bank before getting involved. Also, make certain there's enough cash flow to pay the contract and mortgage payments.

Preparation

Once you've found a property that can be purchased on a contract-for-deed, the next step is setting up a plan of action. Of course, the first and most important transaction is to have agreed with the seller on the price, down payment, interest, length of contract, and any other terms. Then provide a good financial report to the seller to establish your own credibility. After all, he's turning his property over to you and has a right to know if he's going to get paid. You can bet the seller isn't going to be interested in dealing with an unreliable buyer—one who misrepresents, mismanages the property, or is financially irresponsible. It's not only wise to have a well-prepared financial statement for the seller to establish this credibility, but it also serves as a reference for future purchases.

Legal Representation

Always have an attorney represent your interests when transacting a contract-for-deed purchase, or any other real estate deed, for that matter. Have the attorney explain to you in complete detail the various aspects of the contract. Make certain you understand and know (not guess) your responsibilities and liabilities as well as the seller's responsibilities and liabilities. If the seller isn't there at the time, be sure to let the seller know what you've learned.

Some people are afraid of contracts-for-deed, and certainly there is cause for concern if you're dealing with someone you can't trust. However, for the most part, the contract-for-deed is a financial obligation just like a car loan, a personal home loan, a credit loan, or whatever credit transaction we take on. The main thing is to understand and know the obligations involved.

Buyer Protection

The seller obviously needs protection, but it's equally important for you, the buyer, to have the same protection. When dealing with the seller, ask permission, in writing, to get a credit report. With this authorization and the seller's Social Security number, you can request a report from a credit bureau. When requesting the credit report, ask them to check for suits and judgments on file at the courthouse. It is very important in any real estate transaction to know about lawsuits and/or judgments that have been filed against a buyer or seller.

One reason you want to know everything you can about the seller is that after, before, or during the time of the contract-for-deed sale, that owner can have a mortgage on the property. If the payments on the mortgage aren't met as agreed, the mortgage holder, bank, savings and loan, or even an individual can foreclose on the property and the new mortgage holder has absolutely no responsibility to the contract-for-deed holder.

Here's a case in point. Let's say you're in the process of buying a $75,000 property. You offer $5,000 down, and the owner-seller finances $70,000 on a contract-for-deed. In the meantime that owner-seller has a $55,000 mortgage to a bank on the property. If the owner-seller takes your payment for two years but doesn't make payments on the mortgage as agreed, the bank can foreclose on the real estate, take it back, and you—the contract-for-deed holder—receive nothing. The only recourse would be to go back, through legal action, and sue the owner-seller.

Well, that's an extreme case, and if you know whom you're dealing with, it isn't going to occur. However, there are several ways for you, the buyer, to protect yourself if this is a concern. First, and foremost, know the seller. Second, have written into the contract-for-deed that the mortgage payments will be made directly to the mortgage holder by the contract-for-deed buyer. Third, have the mortgage holder notify you, the contract-for-deed buyer, whenever a payment is missed.

Record Keeping

If and when you buy real estate on a contract-for-deed, you will have monthly payments. Usually these contract-for-deed sales are written for many years. During that time it's possible that the payment records could get mixed up, so that, for example, you don't receive credit on a payment. To avoid any confusion or conflict, it's a good idea, when you make out the monthly payment check, that you write the balance of the contract on the check.

Here's an example of what I mean. Let's say you have a $40,000, 9 percent, 10-year contract-for-deed. The monthly payment on this contract is $500.28. On the 30th payment, the interest is $246.82, the principal is $253.46, and the balance is $32,656.03. This information is important for you to know each month. All of these figures are included on an amortization schedule, which the buyer and the seller have. When making out the check each month, put this information on the check so there's no misunderstanding later and so that the contract-for-deed holder cannot come back and insist that you have missed a payment.

Foreclosure Time and Conditions

As a buyer on a contract-for-deed, as I've said before, you need to have a complete understanding of the terms. For example, most contracts-for-deed stipulate that if a payment is in default for as little as 30 days, the holder of that contract can take possession of the property and void the contract. In other words, you could pay on a contract for five or even 10 years, and then find it difficult to meet a payment or two for some reason or another. At that point the seller—financer could take back the property and keep all the money that had been paid during that five or 10 years. Not only would you lose the equity but also the hard work and the appreciation built into the property. However, if this should happen, I have a feeling that a court would rule in favor of the buyer, who would then be able to recover some of the equity that was built up over five or 10 years. Let's put it this way: if I've paid for 10 years and built up a profit, I'm going to put up a pretty good fight to keep at least a portion of my investment. I'd take my case to court and recover whatever was possible.

Here's another concern for the contract-for-deed buyer. If the holder of the contract-for-deed—the seller—files for bankruptcy, the bankruptcy attorney can claim the property. The equity in that property becomes an asset of the bankruptcy. That means that, if you've paid off $5,000 in equity, that equity is no longer yours. In order to recover the property, you might have to come up with another $5,000 or just give the property back to the seller. In addition, all the rents accumulated during the period of the bankruptcy become assets of the bankruptcy. Creditors can collect the rent and not make the payments on the contract-for-deed.

Very little protection exists in a bankruptcy case. Therefore, to protect your assets, *know the seller and holder of your contract-for-deed.* Also, once again, have an attorney present when entering into the contract negotiation. Also, you should know that no lending agency or bank will give a mortgage on a property you purchased on a contract-for-deed. The title must be clear of the contract first.

When purchasing any property with a contract-for-deed or any other contract, be sure to have your attorney check for any mortgages on the property or judgments against the owner. Your attorney should advise you that those judgments must be paid before a clear title is issued on the property. And, while I'm on the subject of attorneys, make sure your attorney knows real estate. Make sure that your deed and purchase agreement contains a full legal description of the property. If it doesn't, it can become costly and troublesome to clear up the title.

The Contract-for-Deed with a Balloon Payment

Usually, sellers of property on a contract-for-deed want their money as quickly as possible, Most of the time the contract seller wants a five- or seven-year payoff, or what is known as a *balloon payment.* This balloon payment is great for the seller but not for the buyer. The reason it isn't advantageous for the buyer is that in five years all that has been paid is interest on the loan; very little has been paid on the principal and, therefore, very little equity has accumulated.

Here's an example of what this kind of contract means. I sold a property on a contract-for-deed at a price of $31,701, amortized over 25 years, at 9½ percent interest with a balloon payment in five years. The buyer is paying $295.50 per month, or a total of $17,700 in five years. However, only $3,332 of that $17,700 is equity, which means the buyer will have to come up with $28,369 at the end of five years.

As you can see, the balloon payment deal isn't all that great for the buyer. The alternatives are to ask for a 10-year balloon or, if the seller insists on five years, to find a way to make a high enough monthly payment so that equity will have built up in that five-year period. After all, the main reason anyone is in the real estate business is to gain equity.

The preceding information pretty much covers the basics of the contract-for-deed. Mainly, you need to have an understanding of how it works. Even though there are some negative aspects of the contract-for-deed, I'm totally convinced it's a great way to buy investment property. For some of us, it's the only way. I can add only this bit of advice: when entering into a contract-for-deed purchase, *be sure you know whom you're dealing with and what you're doing, and have it in writing and have good legal advice.*

The Earnest-Money Contract

Basically, the contract for sale, purchase agreement, and earnest-money contract are one and the same agreement. These terms mean that there's a buyer and a seller and that the two agree with the terms in this document to buy and sell a piece of real estate.

When transacting a purchase agreement, it is imperative that you get everything in writing. The following is a list of important items you should not overlook when you are drawing up the contract:

- a complete description of the property
- a statement of personal property
- the purchase price
- encumbrances and mortgages against the property
- assessments

When negotiating a purchase agreement, make sure there's an understanding, right from the start, of who pays what taxes. Here's the way I work it. The owner of the property pays all taxes due for the time of possession. The buyer then pays the taxes effective the day he takes over the property.

Also, when drawing up a contract for sale for rental property, stipulate who collects the rents between the time the contract is being drawn up and the completion date. In addition, spell out if there's any interest due on the contract in the interim, and who pays for the insurance during this time. Some other payments that must be accounted for during the transition period are:

- utilities
- water
- sewer tax
- assessments

In the contract, make sure it's understood who assumes any existing mortgage payments. Once again, have legal representation.

The Quitclaim Deed

The quitclaim deed is a fairly simple deed in which the seller gives up his or her interest in the property. Of course, there could be other interested parties to that real estate. Have legal representation when dealing with a quitclaim deed.

The General Warranty Deed

Several different warranty deeds can be used. As you transact real estate deals, your legal representative will make certain the proper deed is completed. In general, the warranty deed is the most secure. It means that the owner is guaranteeing the title from defects and previous owners. As with anything else, however, there can be exceptions. Therefore, as with all other real estate transactions, make sure you have good legal advice in getting a clear title.

The Right to Rescind

The Consumer Credit Protection Act gives the buyer the right to rescind the purchase up to midnight of the third business day following the transaction date. This right gives the buyer time to think it over and back out if desired.

Getting Clear Title

Getting clear title is something that can't be overlooked. Not getting it done right the first time can be costly and time-consuming. Therefore, get an attorney who knows titles. Here's why. I know a case in which an individual bought a piece of property from an estate. The title of the property had been transferred several times since the original owners had first sold it out of the estate. However, it was later discovered that no one had transferred the grandchildren's interest in this title. That meant it was necessary to go back to each grandchild to have him or her sign off on the deed. Fortunately, they were cooperative, and eventually the title was cleared, but it could have been costly.

A lot of stories could be told about titles. As an example, I know of one title that couldn't be cleared until 42 different parties had signed off interest on the property! It was, again, one of those titles that had never been cleared.

The point is, have good representation to clear that title. Do not try to make up deeds, clear titles, or read abstracts on your own. The legal work required to clear property titles costs money. Know well ahead who pays for what.

The Abstract

Reading the abstract means getting a title opinion. This opinion is given by an attorney or abstract company. It is the buyer's responsibility to make sure the abstract is updated; however, it's usually the seller's obligation to pay the necessary fees. You should know who will pay these fees ahead of time.

The Deed Tax

One last item on deeds: most states have a deed tax that must be paid when the mortgage and deed are registered. Have in writing who will pay this tax.

Hiring an Appraiser

A real estate appraiser charges from $300 to $400 to examine a single-family home. An independent appraiser will usually give the fair and marketable value of the property. This appraisal is usually based on the valuation of other similar properties, along with other relevant information regarding the property.

It is not necessary to have an appraisal done if you feel comfortable with the price, but if you're not quite sure, an appraisal might be a good investment. This step is optional unless you are taking out a bank, VA, or FHA mortgage. These institutions demand an appraised valuation. At any rate, it might contribute to your own peace of mind to have an appraisal done before completing your real estate purchase.

The Real Estate Contract

If you have a contract with a real estate agent, make sure the contract clearly states who pays for what. This contract sometimes can and will go along with the purchase agreement, but some agents have their own contract.

Property Transfer Expense Summary

The following are some expenses incurred that should be spelled out before everything is completed:

- lender inspection fee
- advance commitment fee
- loan processing fee
- FHA mortgage fund fee
- prepaid interest
- mortgage insurance reserve
- credit report fee
- settlement escrow fee
- document preparation
- attorney fee
- state tax stamps
- pest inspection
- mortgage insurance premium
- appraisal report fee
- appraiser inspection fee
- title examination
- notary fee
- title insurance fee
- state tax
- survey

Obviously, all these charges do not apply to all real estate transfers, and most of them are not incurred in a contract-for-deed sale. However, a lot of them are a part of real estate sales. It's best to at least have some awareness of all the expenses involved when buying property.

Finding a Contract-for-Deed Seller

When most people think about financing property, they seem to have it in their heads that it takes a bank and that it's usually a 30-year mortgage. This is a fallacy and one of the real estate myths. I have bought property regularly and consistently using a contract-for-deed. In fact, very few properties that I've bought were financed through a bank. I've bought one-bedroom houses, three-bedroom houses, and up to sixplexes with contracts-for-deed. That being the case, you're probably asking:

Where are they?

There are literally thousands of seller-lenders out there, and, of course, as I said before, this is the best market for the small, independent, part-time—and starter—investor.

The kinds of sellers who are selling their investment properties are usually those who have had investment properties for a number of years and now want to be relieved of their management duties. I'm one of them. I bought property for a number of years, and then I decided it was time to get on with other things, including writing books. So I sold a number of my properties with contracts-for-deed. I've never regretted this decision.

A good benefit of buying property on a contract-for-deed is the fact that the seller financing the property is going to go all out to make sure the property succeeds. The seller will watch over your operation with a keen eye and oftentimes help out, if it's no more than verbal advice that's needed.

Part Three

Dealing with Tenants

Chapter 15

Tenants:
The Lifeblood of
the Real Estate
Business

Certainly the majority of real estate investors will tell you that good tenants are the most important ingredient of a profitable, smooth-operating, real estate business. Whether you select your tenants or hire someone to do it for you, make certain it's done right so you get the best. You do want the best tenants, tenants who aren't on the move.

Tenants can make or break an investment business. This fact applies not only to how they pay their rent but also how they take care of the property. They are, in fact, the *lifeblood of the real estate investment business.*

Think of it this way. Tenants pay for your investment. Their rent pays all the bills, which includes interest, taxes, utilities, upkeep, maintenance, and the payment on your mortgage. That mortgage payment builds equity, and equity is your savings and your security. It's not hard, then, to see that the better the tenant, the more profitable the venture and the better the operation. With a good operation, you eliminate most of the problems of the business and almost all of the headaches. As I've said before, eliminating headaches is one of the goals of this book.

I wish I could tell you that you could rent apartments at random to anyone who comes along and there would be no problems or nuisances.

Of course, that's not the real world of real estate. Problems and nuisances do exist, but they can be avoided if you take your time and screen and select tenants with the utmost care and concern.

Make sure your apartment or rental unit is always in A-1 condition, clean and freshly painted, with all utilities working properly, a clean carpet, clean bathroom and kitchen, and a well-kept clean exterior, yard, and garbage service units. This will attract good tenants.

It doesn't hurt to maintain good public relations with your tenants. Treat them with dignity. However, don't get too personal or neighborly with them. It sets you up for them expecting more from a "friend" when it comes to fixing up this or that.

Once you develop a reputation for being a *first-class landlord*, the word gets out. When it does, the *first-class tenants* will call you.

Screening Tenants

Probably one of the most important managerial duties for the small independent investor is selecting and screening tenants. Screening tenants isn't that difficult, but it takes some assertiveness to get the job done correctly. Assertiveness is a necessary part of the real estate rental business, and you'll find it to be one of your most important, and reliable, attributes.

Here's what can happen by *not* being assertive. Some of the "nice-guy" managers I've known take the first tenant who calls for an apartment. They seem to want to keep this image of the "nice guy" so they don't want to turn anyone down. Needless to say, this is the beginning of a series of mistakes. The first mistake is not taking the time to screen and check the credit and references of the potential tenant. What happens? The second mistake. An unreliable tenant gets into the apartment, doesn't pay the rent, and is slovenly in taking care of the apartment and housekeeping. The next thing you know, Joe Nice Guy is out there cleaning up and repairing a vacant apartment and trying to collect past-due rent. Oftentimes he ends up digging into the profits of the business, or even his own pocket for that matter, to cover the expenses, all because he didn't select and screen tenants. He remains a nice guy, but the tenant got away with his money. That kind of a business operation just doesn't make sense, and I will guarantee you that it definitely won't make money.

Advertising

My theory about running newspaper advertisements for apartment or rental unit vacancies is to make the ad as simple as possible. For instance, use this:

Two-bedroom apartment for rent. Call (phone number).

If you put too much information in the ad, some good potential tenant might not call. If you leave out information, more people will call, and, in this way, you can screen them accordingly and eliminate as you go.

Wording your advertisement is something you as an investor can experiment with and learn as you go. Your community, city, or neighborhood will determine just what to say in the ad.

Some Rules for Screening Tenants

The following is a list of some basic rules to follow when handling the screening of tenants:

Rule 1: Be Thorough. Check and screen the tenants. Do not accept a tenant without knowing as much information as you can. Eliminate the problem tenants before they get settled into your apartment.

Rule 2: Take Your Time. Most of us in the rental business have a tendency to take the first caller in response to our ad … like Joe Nice Guy. I suppose we just don't seem to have the ability to say "no" when the first call comes in. In addition, we're probably a little afraid that if we don't rent to the first caller we may not get the apartment rented. In our haste, we make a commitment before mak-

One of the greatest invisible assets of the real estate investment business is time. No matter what happens with your investment, time is on your side.

ing a sound, common-sense, rational judgment. I repeat, *take your time.* Keep in mind that the ad will remain in the paper, and there will be other callers. The vacancy will be filled—it's simply a matter of time.

Rule 3: Investigate Credit and Personal Histories. Proceed with a thorough investigation of the potential tenant. Investigating that potential tenant isn't time-consuming, is comparatively inexpensive, and pays in the long run. I'll give you more details on how to do this as we go along.

Rule 4: Conduct a Thorough Telephone Interview. You'll gather a tremendous amount of information over the telephone. Here's how. Start by being assertive. Be in charge of the call, and the caller, right from the start. Don't let the caller get ahead of you with his or her questions. Handle it this way. The person calling will invariably ask, "Can you tell me about the apartment?" or "How much is the rent?" or any number of similar questions. Before giving an answer, give your name but no information—especially no information—at this time about the apartment. Once you give your name, ask, "May I have your name, please?" At this point expect and wait for an answer. Now, if that person doesn't want to give his or her name to you, my advice is to eliminate the caller and wait for the next call. If that person isn't willing to give his or her name, there's a good possibility he or she is trying to hide something.

If, on the other hand, the caller freely gives his or her name, write it down and proceed to the next question, which should be "How many people is it for?" Some typical answers include "It's for my husband and me," or "It's for my husband and small baby," or "It's for my buddy and me," or "It's for my girlfriend and me." You can thus quickly determine if you are speaking with a single person or married person with or without children. Remember, you're still in charge, you're still asking the questions, and up to this point you still don't have to and don't want to give out any information about the apartment.

Next, ask the caller, "Whom do you work for?" Be insistent on getting an answer. The answer can and will determine a great deal of information about the person. Sometimes you'll get an answer like "What difference does that make about renting the apartment?" Just answer by telling the caller, "I'm sure you understand that I want to know whom I'm renting to and who's going to be living in my apartment." Sometimes in this process the caller will just hang up. If so, it may be for any number of reasons, but usually it's because he or she doesn't want to give you some negative information. You're usually better off without the "hanger-uppers" anyway.

At about this time in the telephone interview—and again stay in charge of the call—you want to make the following statement: "I don't allow any loud parties, loud stereos, or mismanaged pets." Then add, "If you think this policy doesn't fit your lifestyle, then maybe it would be better for you to look elsewhere." 99 percent of the time, making this statement at the outset works out for both you and the potential tenant. If the person is reliable, he or she usually says something like "That's fine. I'm looking for a quiet place to live and don't want to be where there are loud parties."

Along about here in the interview, you'll want to know if the potential tenant wants a long-term or short-term lease. From the information you've collected so far, you should be able to determine whether you want to pursue the interview. The information you have gathered tells you who the tenant is, where he or she works, the number of occupants, and how long he or she intends to stay.

Pursuing the Good Tenant

If the information you have collected thus far reveals a good potential tenant, the next step is to give your best sales pitch, along with complete details about the apartment, including its size, location, and the amount

of the rent. Tell the tenant you will have to get a credit report on him or
her, and, in order to do so, you'll need his or her written permission.
Make arrangements for this to be done.

Every time a tenant moves out of an apartment, it costs money to prepare it for the next tenant. Therefore, long-term leases make sense and are moneymakers.

The next step is to set up an
interview at the apartment, at which
time you can have the prospective
tenant sign the document needed to
obtain the credit report. After the
apartment interview, go back to
your office and call for a credit report. If the prospective tenant checks
out as a good credit risk, then you're on your way.

When setting up an appointment at the apartment, do it on your
terms. If you don't, you can spend a lot of time waiting. Some people
will tell you they'll meet you at 4:30 and not show up until 5:00, a half-
hour late. Some people won't show up at all. If you make arrangements
to meet at your place of business, your home, or wherever it's convenient for you before going to the rental unit together, if you do have to
wait, you can do so in a place that suits your convenience.

While you are waiting, you can spend more time on your investigation, check references, or get a credit report, especially if you're not
ready to make a commitment. If you show the apartment before completing your investigation, tell the potential tenant that you'll get back
to him or her. If a prospective tenant doesn't check out in all respects,
you don't want him or her. If you don't want a particular person, then
don't call that person back.

Never close a rental agreement or take an advertisement out of the
paper until you've received the rent deposit and the first month's rent.
Here are some other necessary stall techniques to be used. To keep from
making a commitment over the phone, tell callers that you're taking
names, will put them on the list, and will get back to them once you've
made a decision. You can also tell them that the apartment isn't ready to

show yet or that someone else is ahead of them on the list, or you can ask for references and tell them you'll get back to them as soon as you've checked them out.

Remember, you have a right to rent your apartment to anyone you wish. Any potential tenant, once having seen the apartment, can turn you down in a minute; conversely, you can turn any applicant down (as long as you don't discriminate on the basis of color, race, religion, sex, or creed). You may or may not want to rent to certain people for various reasons. That's the main reason you 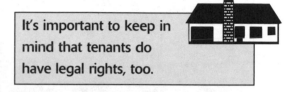 want to screen during the time of the interview. For example, you don't want to rent to anyone who doesn't pay his or her bills.

It's important to keep in mind that tenants do have legal rights, too.

I have a friend who owns several rental units. He won't rent to transients—job jumpers and seasonal workers. He seems to think, and rightly so, that they'll be in the area only for a short time, and frequent tenant changes cause stress on the property. Some of the transients leave in the middle of the night without giving notice and without paying their rent. Those are headaches and problems investors can do without.

I can tell you one thing. The large corporate apartment and real estate firms go through a thorough investigation and screening process before making a commitment. They don't take chances, and they don't ask for trouble, nor should you.

High-Risk Tenants

Government-Subsidy Recipients

The government, through HUD and FHA, has subsidized apartment owners who have agreed to take the poor and underprivileged as their tenants. You, as a taxpayer, help pay for this subsidization (Figure 15-1). If, in your interview process, you find someone who is in need, refer him or her to any of the low-rent, government-subsidized apartment units.

Figure 15-1. This is an example of government-subsidized housing. Multiunit apartment buildings are sometimes owned and operated privately, with the subsidy coming from a local housing authority to a private owner. In other cases, the government itself owns and manages the building.

Pet Owners

A tenant who owns pets, especially cats and dogs, can mean trouble. The trouble is that the tenant will say such things as "Oh, my pet's well trained" or "You don't have to worry about my dog." Invariably the pets aren't as well managed as the tenant says. Cats urinate, and when they urinate on carpet it's virtually impossible to get rid of the smell. Dogs leave a big mess in the yard and bark and bite. You, the apartment owner, are usually left to clean up. My advice is to have a no-pet policy, and stick with it. On the other hand, if you own several apartment buildings, it might be a good idea to set one building aside for pet owners only. I'm sure you can charge pet owners more rent.

Students

I have a number of friends who own real estate rental units in college towns. Here's what one said: "Those college parties are wild and go on all hours of the night. There's loud music, screaming girls, boisterous boys, and plenty of beer to keep up the high pitch." He goes on to say, "If and when you take college students in as tenants, it's not a matter of whether there's going to be a party, it's just a matter of when." He told me, and I concur, that party-going and hell-raising tenants, college students or others, can and usually do create a lot of headaches for owners in the rental business.

I have another friend who owns a fourplex near a college campus. She told me that she's done pretty well over the years with students. She did indicate, however, that she has rented to upperclassmen and graduate students and that this has worked out well. However, one year she decided to rent to younger college students on a first-come, first-serve basis. She later said, "That turned out to be my first mistake. They turned out to be real hell-raisers. It seemed like some of them had just left home, after having been nagged and suppressed for 17 or 18 years, and now, by God, they were going to take it out on someone or something." Well, they did. They took it out on her apartments, and the damage included things like fists through the walls, sinks pulled off the wall, broken windows, beer bottles strewn throughout the premises, and a generally unkempt apartment complex. Maybe that's why the colleges insist that freshmen stay in the dormitories.

Here's another student horror story that happened to another friend of mine. He rented a three-bedroom apartment to college students. About the middle of the cold winter quarter of school, they decided it was time to have a beach party. Well, you know what a beach party means: sand and water. They laid down a plastic covering over the living room floor, hauled in loads of sand, and then filled the area (living room floor) with water. You can imagine how that ended up: water running downstairs, a ruined floor, and other costly expenses for the owner, who's still trying to collect for damages. And headaches.

Here's one more experience to give you an idea of what to expect from students. An owner rented out two units, side by side, to students. Before the first quarter was over, the students decided that it would be easier to communicate and to go from apartment to apartment if they knocked out the wall in between. So they did. My friend didn't find out until the school year was over. He hadn't collected enough rent deposits from them, so he ended up spending his own money to fix the damage. And headaches.

Summer-school students are usually temporary renters, and they need housing only while the dormitories are closed. They move in in June and out in September. These short-term rentals are not a good proposition unless the apartments would be vacant anyway. Again, it costs money whenever tenants move in and out.

On the other hand, there are some excellent student tenants. It's like any other category, however, and they have to be thoroughly checked out. With careful screening, you can usually prevent major problems.

Low-Risk Tenants

About now you're probably saying, "Who's left?" Let me assure you that there are a lot of outstanding tenants out there. As a matter of fact; only about 20 percent of the tenants cause all the problems. You want to look for and rent to the other 80 percent. Let's see who they are.

> Keep in mind that the rental business, like every other business, is competitive. Consider this when marketing yourself and your property to potential tenants.

Single and Married Retirees

These people are on the top of my list of outstanding tenants. Here's a list of things they're looking for:

- a clean, safe, and habitable building and unit
- a clean and respectable neighborhood and surroundings
- reasonable rental agreement terms

- a quiet and enjoyable home without outside intrusion
- privacy

If you can provide them with these basic essentials, you can count on retired people to live in your rental unit for years. For the most part they take care of the unit as if it were their own home, often better than the owner of the property. They're not demanding if their basic needs are met, and they are always right on time with their rent. From my experience, they are some of the best tenants there are and receive a four-star rating in my book of recommendations.

Professionals and Semiprofessionals

This category of potential tenants includes schoolteachers, nurses, college faculty, dental assistants, secretaries, bank clerks, office workers, and assistant managers. Most of these people are sophisticated and reliable, take care of their apartment, pay their rent on time, and, in general, are fair and understanding. I highly recommend this group. Remember, your apartment is *their* home. It's a possession that they want to take pride in, even though it may be only temporary.

Married Couples

A young married couple has the same qualities and traits as the young professionals, and most of the time they are one and the same. However, the young married couple will eventually be looking for a larger apartment or a home, so they are temporary tenants. Another factor to consider when dealing with young married couples is that eventually they're going to have children. Children and retired people living near each other can often create conflicts.

Serious Students

College juniors and seniors and postgraduate students all make good tenants. They usually take their schooling seriously, in general are more mature, and have gotten over the teeny-bopper, beer-drinking stages of their lives.

There are many others who make good tenants. The preceding list is only a guide to some owner-tenant relationships that have worked.

Maintaining Good Relationships with Tenants

One last note about tenants: when you get good tenants, take good care of them. Keep them happy and satisfied. It's not only to your financial benefit but it's also good for your peace of mind. And let me tell you that peace of mind, along with good tenants, eliminates a lot of

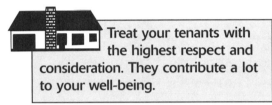 headaches. Ninety-five percent of the time, this business is void of bad experiences. In fact, most bad experiences are self-inflicted through faulty management practices.

Treat your tenants with the highest respect and consideration. They contribute a lot to your well-being.

Rent Deposits

Rent deposits in this business are a must. They are, in fact, your insurance protection. These deposits can protect you against property damage, breakage, cleanup, garbage removal, and past-due rents. When tenants move, they'll attempt all sorts of money-saving schemes. If they're not held responsible for the cleanup, they'll leave the premises dirty. Without the rent deposit as your security, you'd end up paying for the cleanup.

When you receive a rent deposit, put the money in a savings account. Those rent deposits have to be returned to the tenant, less any costs for breakage and cleanup, plus interest. However, you should not return rent deposit money until you have made a thorough inspection of the premises.

Some "hard-nosed" owners make it a real battle before returning deposits to tenants. In fact, some landlords make a business of keeping as much of the rent deposit as they can; it's a side business. The tenants are almost helpless once they move out. But there is one way tenants can resolve this problem: they can report it to their local office of consumer affairs. They may not get their money back, but at least they have the satisfaction of blemishing the record of the landlord who has held back part of their rent deposit.

Leases

A lease is basically a contract between the landlord and the tenant. In general, anything can be put in a lease, from the amount of the rent to who's responsible for garbage. Often leases aren't that effective. If a person's going to move out, he or she is going to move out. However, the lease can offer the owner some protection.

An entire book could be written on the various types of leases. Standard forms are available, and Figure 15-2 is a sample copy of a commonly used landlord-tenant lease consisting of a rental lease, agreement/contract, and rental application. These documents are shown to give you an idea of how thorough they can be. However, it is my feeling that a lease as comprehensive as this one isn't all that necessary.

More important than the lease is screening the potential tenant. Once you are satisfied with someone's qualifications, then a simple lease to protect yourself is all that's necessary. Incidentally, an important item you might consider including in a lease is a stipulation that, should it become necessary to hire an attorney to resolve any problem, the tenant will pay the attorney fees. It may not be allowed in a court of law, but the clause might deter any problems from escalating unnecessarily.

Some Final Tips About Tenant-Landlord Relationships

1. Knowing what tenants are looking for in an apartment—cleanliness, safety, quiet, and privacy—helps in setting up a real estate rental business. Having good tenants and having good apartments usually mean you can expect a zero vacancy factor in the rental business, which will translate into a profitable venture.

2. When negotiating with a potential tenant, be ready to deal with any

Agreement or Contract

THIS AGREEMENT is made between ONE STOP HOME RENTAL COMPANY, owners or representatives for _____ and
TENANTS:_____
_____
_____
For the rental of real property known as _____
_____

TENANTS AGREE to pay rent for the property on a month-to-month basis starting: Date:
_____. The agreed monthly rental rate shall be: $ _____
per month and shall be due and payable in advance on the _____ day of every calendar
month. (Rent due date.)

TENANTS AGREE to pay last months rent of $_____ in advance, to be used only for
last month of tenancy and only after tenants give owner thirty (30) days written
notice to vacate property. Tenants further agree to rent property for a minimum
of six (6) months.

TENANTS AGREE to pay an advance cleaning/security deposit which is refundable if property is left clean and undamaged and if 30 day written notice to vacate property is
given. Advance cleaning/security deposit for this property is: $ _____. Owners
will refund deposits within fourteen (14) days after all keys to property have been
returned. If any deposit funds are withheld, Owners will provide an itemized statement showing their disposition. Tenants agree to forfeit all advance deposits if
tenancy is less than six (6) months unless otherwise specified under Special
Agreements, below.

TENANTS AGREE to pay a late charge of $20.00 in addition to rent due if rent is not
paid within five (5) days of rent due date. Example: If rent due date is on 1st -
a late charge is due if rent is paid on 6th.

TENANTS AGREE to pay a $20.00 additional service charge on all returned checks
(Bounced).

IT IS FURTHER UNDERSTOOD that TENANTS are responsible for any losses to their
personal property while living at this rental location. It is agreed between the
parties, Owners/Tenants that all Tenants' personal property shall be the responsibility of the Tenant only - Owners are not in any way obligated to protect or
guarantee losses of Tenants' personal property. This is agreed by the undersigned
parties to this Agreement.

It is agreed that only the following people or pets may live on this property:_____
_____
_____

TENANTS AGREE TO ABIDE BY AND COMPLY WITH THE FOLLOWING REGULATIONS:

A. To keep property in good condition - to keep yards clean.
B. To keep noise levels reasonable so as to not disturb other tenants.
C. To not alter dwelling or property without prior written permission of Owners.
    (Includes painting.)
D. Not to make auto repairs on property if such repairs take longer than a single
    day. (1 day) Repairs may be made inside enclosed garage areas. (Out of sight.)
E. To pay for all repairs from any damages caused by Tenants or their children.
F. Tenants agree to allow Owners/Representatives to inspect unit - show to prospec-
    tive Tenants, at reasonable time, if a 24-hour notice is given.
G. Tenants agree to allow no other person/persons to live in unit or on property
    without approval of Owner/Representative.
H. Tenants agree to pay all rents or deposits on agreed times and will pay late
    charges, if applicable.
I. Special Agreements:_____
Violation of any part of this Agreement or non-payment of rent when due shall be
cause for eviction under appropriate sections of the State Code, and Tenants shall be
liable for the Court costs and reasonable Attorneys' fees involved.

Each Tenant hereby acknowledges that he/she has read this AGREEMENT, understands it,
agrees to it, and has been given a copy.

OWNER/REPRESENTATIVE _____ DATE   TENANT _____ DATE

ONE STOP HOME RENTAL COMPANY
Mailing Address: TENANT _____ DATE
P.O. Box 493039
Redding, CA 96049-3939   TENANT _____ DATE

Figure 15-2.

ONE STOP
HOME RENTAL

LANDLORD-TENANT RESPONSIBILITIES
AGREEMENT & CONTRACT BETWEEN THE PARTIES

A. LANDLORD shall be responsible for all systems such as: roofs, heating-cooling, electrical, plumbing (MAIN LINES ONLY) & the operation of same.

B. TENANTS shall be responsible for maintenance & repairs of local fixtures which are not main lines & which are operating properly: When house is leased to tenant. ITEMS INCLUDED ARE: Plugged up drains in kitchen & bathroom sinks, plugged up toilets, broken windows, damaged appliances, damaged carpets &/or window coverings & generally all leased property which becomes damaged or non-working during the term of tenancy. This provision is not intended to cover normal wear & tear to the property.

C. TENANT is responsible for keeping rental property in good condition during term if this lease. This provision includes the house or apartment & the outside yard or common area.

D. TENANT agrees to pay for all damages to property caused by occupants. (Residents or Guests) during the period of this tenancy.

INSURANCE: Owners carry insurance for fire damage to the building only. Owners DO NOT provide insurance for tenant's personal properties and furnishings. To protect yourself it is suggested all tenants obtain a tenant's insurance policy to provide for personal losses is case of a fire.

ABOUT YOUR DEPOSIT $$ MONEY

THIS FORM IS NECESSARY FOR DEPOSIT REFUND. FORM MUST BE FILLED OUT ON MOVE-IN DAY AND RETURNED TO ONE STOP RENTAL OFFICE FOR YOUR PROTECTION.

Property _____ Unit _____

Type of Unit _____ Occupant _____ Move-In Date _____

Items	Condition		COMMENTS
	Move-In	Move-Out	
Living Room and Dining Room			
Doors and Locks			
Floors and Baseboards			
Walls and Ceilings			
Windows and Drapes			
Electrical Fixtures			
Electrical Switches, Outlets			
Closets			
Kitchen			
Doors and Locks			
Floors and Baseboards			
Walls and Ceilings			
Electrical Fixtures			
Electrical Switches, Outlets			
Range and Refrigerator			
Sink & Garbage Disposal			
Cabinets			
Windows			
Counters			
Bedroom(s) 1			
Doors and Locks			
Floors and Baseboards			
Walls and Ceilings			
Electrical Fixtures			
Electrical Switches, Outlets			
Windows and Drapes			
Closets			
Bedroom(s) 2			
Doors and Locks			
Floors and Baseboards			
Walls and Ceilings			
Electrical Fixtures			
Electrical Switches, Outlets			
Windows and Drapes			
Closets			

Figure 15-2. (Continued)

NOTICE TO TENANT:

Tenants are requested to report all damages to house or apartment to manager.

In the case of damages caused by tenants or occupants-tenants are expected to make necessary repairs or hire service repairmen to make repairs at tenant's expense. Items normally include plugged-up toilets, clogged drains, forced open locks & broken windows. These items must be kept in good repair by tenant of record - This Contract.

INSURANCE: Owners carry insurance for fire damage to the building only. Owners DO NOT provide insurance for tenant's personal properties and furnishings. To protect yourself it is suggested all tenants obtain a tenant's insurance policy to provide for personal losses is case of a fire.

| | Condition | | COMMENTS |
	Move-In	Move-Out	
Bedroom(s) 3			
Doors and Locks			
Floors and Baseboards			
Walls and Ceilings			
Electrical Fixtures			
Electrical Switches, Outlets			
Windows and Drapes			
Closets			
Bedroom(s) 4			
Doors and Locks			
Floors and Baseboards			
Walls and Ceilings			
Electrical Fixtures			
Electrical Switches, Outlets			
Windows and Drapes			
Closets			
Bathroom(s) 1			
Doors and Locks			
Floors and Baseboards			
Walls and Ceilings			
Windows and Drapes			
Shower			
Lavatory and Tub			
Faucets			
Toilet			
Electrical Fixtures			
Electrical Switches, Outlets			
Closet			
Towel Rack			
Bathroom(s) 2			
Doors and Locks			
Floors and Baseboards			
Walls and Ceilings			
Windows and Drapes			
Shower			
Lavatory and Tub			
Faucets			
Toilet			
Electrical Fixtures			
Electrical Switches, Outlets			
Closet			
Towel Rack			

Beginning Inventory Date_____ Signature of Tenant _____

Signature of Owner or Agent _____

End of Term Inspection Date _____ Signature of Tenant _____

Signature of Owner or Agent _____

Figure 15-2. (Continued)

Rental Application

ONE STOP HOME RENTAL CO.

A DiVISION OF JMK TRADERS
P.O. Box 493039
Redding, CA 96049-3039

PLEASE FILL IN ALL BLANK LINES BEST AS YOU CAN - VERIFICATION OF YOUR
CURRENT INCOME - EMPLOYMENT STATUS - WILL BE NECESSARY IN ORDER TO
PROCESS YOUR APPLICATION.

ALL HOLDING DEPOSITS PAID WILL BE REFUNDED IF THIS APPLICATION IS NOT
APPROVED. DEPOSITS FOR APPROVED APPLICANTS CANNOT BE REFUNDED.
THEY WILL APPLY TO SECURITY DEPOSIT.

PROPERTY YOU WISH TO RENT (ADDRESS)_____

NAME OF APPLICANT(S)_____

OTHER NAMES USED WITHIN LAST 3 YEARS_____

LIST NAMES OF ALL OCCUPANTS WHO WILL LIVE IN HOUSE OR APARTMENT.

_____   _____   _____

_____   _____   _____

LIST ALL PETS THAT WILL LIVE AT PROPERTY: NUMBER TYPE WEIGHT

_____

YOUR PRESENT ADDRESS_____HOW MUCH IS RENT$____

HOW LONG HAVE YOU LIVED THERE_____

HOW MUCH IS SECURITY DEPOSIT $_____

WHAT IS OWNER's (AGTS.) NAME_____TEL. NO._____

HOW MUCH SECURITY DEPOSIT WILL YOU GET BACK OR EXPECT TO GET BACK?

_____

WHAT IS YOU REASON FOR MOVING?_____

HAVE YOU EVER BEEN EVICTED? ____ YES ____ NO BY WHOM_____

IF YES - EXPLAIN WHY_____

YOUR PREVIOUS ADDRESS_____HOW MUCH RENT_____

HOW LONG DID YOU LIVE THERE (YRS.)_____SECURITY DEP.PAID $_____

WHY DID YOU MOVE?_____SECURITY DEPOSIT REFUNDED $_____

NAME OF OWNER OR AGENT_____TEL. NO._____

YOUR SOCIAL SECURITY NO._____DRIVER'S LIC.NO._____

SPOUSE SOCIAL SECURITY NO._____DRIVER'S LIC.NO._____

YOUR PRESENT EMPLOYER_____TYPE OF WORK_____

ADDRESS OF EMPLOYER_____TEL. NO._____

PERSON TO CONTACT WHO CAN VERIFY YOUR EMPLOYMENT_____

HOW MUCH DO YOU EARN FROM SALARY OR WAGES $_____ PER MONTH

   NOTE: IF INCOME IS FROM AFDC - SHOW AFDC $ AMT. AND WORKER'S
      NAME & TEL. NO.

OTHER INCOME YOU RECEIVE: SOURCE_____AMT. $_____

OTHER INCOME YOU RECEIVE: SOURCE_____AMT. $_____

Figure 15-2. (Continued)

YOUR BANK_____ ACCOUNT NO.:_____

ADDRESS OF BANK_____ TEL. NO.:_____

WHO WOULD CO-SIGN THIS APPLICATION TO HELP YOU RENT THE PROPERTY IN
THE EVENT YOUR CREDIT INFORMATION IS NOT SUFFICIENT (NAME):

_____

NAME (2) TWO CREDIT REFERENCES - STORES WHERE YOU PURCHASE ON CHARGE
ACCOUNTS:

A. NAME_____ ADDRESS_____ TEL.NO._____

B. NAME_____ ADDRESS_____ TEL.NO._____

EMPLOYMENT OF OTHER OCCUPANTS(S) OR SPOUSE WHO WILL LIVE IN HOUSEHOLD.

A. NAME OF OCCUPANT_____ EMPLOYER_____

   HOW MUCH EARNINGS PER MONTH $_____ EMPLOYER ADDRESS_____

B. NAME OF OCCUPANT_____ EMPLOYER_____

   HOW MUCH EARINGS PER MONTH $_____ EMPLOYER ADDRESS_____

LIST ALL AUTOMOBILES YOU OWN - OR VEHICLES YOU WILL BRING TO THE PROP-
PERTY. ONE STOP RENTAL MUST HAVE THIS INFORMATION TO PROVIDE PARKING
SPACES -- ALSO I.D. NUMBERS FOR YOU.

AUTO-MAKE & MODEL_____COLOR_____VEAR_____LIC.NO._____

AUTO-MAKE & MODEL_____COLOR_____YEAR_____LIC.NO._____

AUTO-MAKE & MODEL_____COLOR_____YEAR_____LIC.NO._____

WHO IS PERSON TO CONTACT IN CASE OF EMERGENCY (RELATIVE OR FRIEND):

NAME_____ RELATIONSHIP_____TEL.NO._____

STREET ADDR._____CITY OR TOWN_____ST.____ZIP_____

NAME (2) PERSONAL REFERENCES - FRIENDS, REAL ESTATE AGTS, NEIGHBORS,
PREVIOUS LANDLORDS:

1. NAME_____ ADDRESS_____ TEL.NO._____

2. NAME_____ ADDRESS_____ TEL.NO._____

HAVE YOU EVER FILED BANKRUPTCY ___YES   ___NO   WHEN_____

DO YOU HAVE PERSONAL POST OFFICE BOX TO SEND YOUR REFUND CHECKS FOR
DEPOSITS OR REIMBURSEMENT FOR CASH EXPENSES YOU MIGHT HAVE?

          _____ YES   _____ NO

SEND CHECK TO: P.O.BOX_____CITY_____ST_____ZIP_____

AUTHORIZATION TO VERIFY INFORMATION

I AUTHORIZE THE LANDLORD OR HIS AUTHORIZED AGENTS TO VERIFY THE ABOVE
INFORMATION, INCLUDING BUT NOT LIMITED TO OBTAINING A CREDIT REPORT
AND IF THIS APPLICATION IS ACCEPTED I AGREE TO EXECUTE THE RESIDENTIAL
LEASE OR RENTAL AGREEMENT WITH ONE STOP HOME RENTAL COMPANY.

DATE:_____19____   APPLICANT:_____

                           APPLICANT:_____

YOUR TEL.NO_____ONE STOP RENTAL AGENT:_____

APPROVAL DATE_____FILE NO. JMK:_____

NOTE: WE DO NOT CHARGE A FEE FOR CREDIT CHECK INFORMATION IF YOUR
APPLICATION IS DENIED. ONE STOP RENTAL CO. WILL REFUND YOU TOTAL
DEPOSIT. IF APPLICATION IS APPROVE - YOUR DEPOSIT WILL BECOME PART
OF THE SECURITY DEPOSIT AND/OR RENT.

Figure 15-2. (Continued)

personal prejudices you may have about lifestyle and morality. If you don't believe unmarried couples should be living together, you probably shouldn't be in the rental business. A high percentage of young couples who rent apartments aren't married. Don't make it your business to convert them. If you think they should change, let your minister handle it. All you're interested in is having a reliable tenant who pays the rent.

3. If you have chosen and screened your tenants carefully, you have already avoided all sorts of problems. However, in case something does happen and it appears that there might be a problem within your rental unit—whether it's a complaint about noise or about pets, or it's a tenant who hasn't paid the rent—take action to get the problem settled immediately. Don't let it fester and allow it to turn into a catastrophic situation. In my experience of handling rental properties, I have taken special pains to screen my tenants, and this has paid off. I don't think that I've had more than three or four problems that caused stress, and, for the dollars I've made in this business, I can easily handle a few problems. When interviewing potential tenants, keep in mind that there are going to be a lot of forceful "smart alecks" out there who know how to work the system. They might have been evicted from some other place, or they don't pay their rent and then move on to another apartment. Therefore, always stay ahead of these applicants in the interview so you have the opportunity to turn them down at any time.

4. Don't make fun of your good tenants, either privately or publicly. Think of it this way: if you were in a retail business and a customer came to your store or shop or professional office and spent $500 or $600 a month, every month of the year, you would cater to that customer. Tenants are the same. They are your customers, regular and steady, every month of the year. They represent an important part of your future financial well-being.

Questions and Answers About Tenants

The Landlord's Perspective

Q. *Is there an ideal tenant?*

A. Yes. Any tenant who takes care of the property and pays the rent on time is an ideal tenant. An ideal tenant will make you wealthy.

Q. *How can I tell if a prospective tenant will pay the rent?*

A. Most of the information you will need to make that determination should come out in your telephone or personal interview. You should know at the end of the interview where the person works, and that tells a lot. In addition, if you take my advice, you'll have ordered a credit report, and that too will tell a great deal. If you check past rental references, you'll know if they pay. A general rule is that a tenant should spend about 30 percent of his or her income for rent. So a person who is earning $2,000 a month can easily afford a $600-a-month apartment.

The Tenants' Perspective

Q. *We rented the downstairs of a duplex. About three weeks after we moved in, nothing had been done about the yard care, so we called the landlord. He said, "Oh, the yard and sidewalk are up to you to care for. The mower's in the garage." Can they do this?*

A. Obviously, there was a lack of communication at the time of rental. It appears that you might have two choices: move out or take care of the lawn.

Q. *I've been renting for three years. I called to see if I could paint. The landlord said he would pay for the paint if I would do the work. Is this usually how this kind of work is done?*

A. Yes. Unless there's been some arrangement made ahead of time, it's fairly standard for the landlord to propose this kind of agreement.

Q. *I signed a lease-contract for rent, and now, before the lease is up, the landlord wants to raise the rent. Can he do this?*

A. No. That lease and the conditions of the lease are binding and would be upheld in any court. You might consider contacting your local or state office of consumer affairs. Sometimes going to court is more of a problem than it's worth, so the best thing to do is work it out with the landlord.

Q. *What happens when I try to fix something in my apartment, but it turns out to be more of a problem and more costly than I had anticipated? Who has to pay if extra help is called in?*

A. Self-repair projects can often turn into major problems. Settling the cost factor is something that has to be worked out between you and the landlord. Most landlords are comparatively sympathetic and will help; however, others are "hard-nosed" and will insist that you pay. If that is the case, you probably have no choice. If the damage is done because of an act on your part, then obviously you can be held responsible.

If you take good care of your tenants and take care of your property, you'll eventually develop a reputation as a reputable landlord. This alone can attract some of the most desirable tenants.

Avoid the undesirable tenants, who add up to frustration, trouble, damage to the property, nonpayment of rent, and eviction. Sometimes you might say, "I wish I wasn't in this business." You don't need an abundance of extra anxiety in this business.

Chapter 16

Establishing a Sound Credit Policy

We've pretty well established the fact that tenants are the lifeblood of the real estate rental business. The next thing is to realize that the rent is the plasma that keeps the business alive and well. Learning how to set a credit and collection policy for the rental property business is an all-important phase of management. If you're new in the business, or even if you've been in the business for years, you need to learn everything there is to know about establishing a credit policy for your operation.

The Credit Report

That credit report can and usually will tell the story of how someone has acted with other people and other obligations. It reveals the complete paying habits of how the individual has paid his or her bills. Although, I must add, you can't depend on that report to be 100 percent reliable or that it'll ensure you don't get a bad apple. It's still necessary to interview and "eyeball" that potential tenant thoroughly.

On the basis of that credit report, however, you can usually count on eliminating or accepting a potential tenant just on the basis of how the individual has paid his or her bills. I have a friend in the real estate business who received a credit report showing legal action had been taken against an individual for drugs. You want to keep your property drug-free. If it's a substandard report and there are things you don't like, tell the potential tenant, "You don't meet our standards for rental." Don't be specific or give any reasons unless you're pressed to do so.

Setting a Credit Policy

The most basic, simplest, and best credit policy to establish is this: *the rent must be paid on time.* That means, if it's due on the first of the month, that's when it's due … not on the fifth or the 10th or 30 days later. You soon learn that tenants operate their financial lives from paycheck to paycheck. Most tenants have a car payment to make each month, along with the other living expenses. Those expenses go on, month after month. The only basic change in this pattern may occur if a tenant receives a pay raise.

Because their money is budgeted so tightly, if tenants use the rent money for other expenses and get even one month behind, it becomes difficult for them to catch up. Two months behind can mean disaster, and there's no way a small independent investor can wait two months for that rent check.

Checking a Prospective Tenant's Credit History

Let me explain something profoundly important for any real estate investor: whether I owned one rental property or one hundred, I would not rent to any tenant until I found out how he or she pays the bills.

In the first place, I don't want a poor-paying tenant in my apartment. It's nothing but grief. I've also learned over the years that poor-paying tenants are unacceptable for my apartments for other reasons. Poor-paying tenants not only abuse their financial commitment, they also abuse property. That means that, if they're evicted, the owner will have to spend a considerable amount of money cleaning up the apartment, with no financial backing.

Also, poor-paying tenants don't take care of other services. Sometimes they leave garbage in the basement, yard, or hallways, ... probably because they didn't pay for garbage service. You'll also find dilapidated cars or motorcycles parked in the yard. They simply can't afford to get them fixed and move them, so they leave them wherever they've broken down.

So, you see, that credit file or report can be a history with many tales. For anyone in this business, a credit report on prospective tenants is important. You might ask, "How will I know whether or not I'm going to get paid? How can I find out this information?"

Joining a Credit Bureau

The answers to those questions are very simple. There's a surefire way to control poor-paying tenants: join a credit bureau. There are approximately 3,400 credit bureaus throughout the United States, serving every rural and urban community. In addition, there are three national credit-reporting services—Experian, Equifax, and TransUnion. All of the reporting agencies have access to credit information.

Within a short distance from where your business is located, there's a credit bureau that can serve you. That bureau can and will provide reporting service to any and all businesses, including real estate rental property owners and managers. Most bureaus provide a number of services, including reporting, collecting on returned checks, and collecting past-due accounts. They also collect past-due rent and money for damage to properties.

The primary service you, as an investor, will need is the reporting service. Credit reports are immediately available by telephone, mail, or computer. In fact, you can rent a computer, put it in your own office, and have credit reports immediately without having to call. The credit records maintained by the bureau consist of the payment records and habits of individuals and businesses. These include local as well as national ratings. The individual file includes all credit card ratings, bank payment records on loans, department store accounts, real estate loan payment records, and student loans. The file also includes judgments and bankruptcies, as well as accounts for collection turned over to the credit bureau. Incidentally, only a credit bureau can record and report accounts for collection on an individual.

Feasibility of Membership

The credit bureau service is reasonably simple to join and comparatively inexpensive. Most bureaus charge an annual membership fee of anywhere from $60 to $120. Then there's a per-report charge of $1.50 to $2.50. Check the business directory of the telephone book to find the listing of the credit bureau serving you. Call the manager, introduce yourself, and explain your business and the type of service you need. In turn, they'll give you all the information about their membership, including the services available and the costs.

Think of it this way. If you get a credit report on one bad risk, one poor-paying tenant, that you don't have to rent to, you'll have paid your entire membership dues for at least a year, ... or more. Furthermore, if you know your tenant pays bills promptly, then you know you'll get your monthly rent on time, and you'll be able to operate your business with more peace of mind, and that's worth a lot.

I'm not saying that you can depend 100 percent on the reliability of the credit report, so it's also important to conduct a personal interview and "eyeball" that potential tenant. But in general I can say that you can usually count on eliminating or accepting potential tenants just on the basis of how they pay their bills.

I have a friend who's in the rental business. He checks with his credit bureau on every potential tenant. He tells me that when he's ready to reject a tenant on the basis of the credit report he simply tells them, "You don't meet our standards for rental." He said from that point on he doesn't reveal anything specific unless he's pressed to do so.

I also know there are some credit bureaus that keep police records in their files. When you join your credit bureau ask if it's their policy to do so. If so, it'll reveal a great deal about an individual, especially if you want to keep your apartment or rental unit drug-free.

Using Credit History Information

It is good to have information on prospective tenants, but the next important step is to use that information. If potential tenants have a history of not paying credit obligations, whether it's a drugstore bill, doctor, hardware store, or whatever, the odds are good that they will be slow to pay or won't pay their rent.

I know landlords who think they've got a certain charisma when dealing with people, and, despite the fact that a person has an appalling credit record, they still believe they will get paid, even if others do not. That's not the way to do business. Then there's the landlord who wants to fill a vacancy, no matter what. Even though the applicant for the apartment may have a bad credit record, the landlord, Mr. Nice Guy, thinks he will get paid because that tenant may cheat other people, "but not me." Also, some operators in this business let greed and impatience get in the way of commonsense management. They get the negative information, but they just don't want to believe it, so they rent anyway.

These are the kinds of experiences that get investors into financial difficulty. Most of the past-due accounts end up with a collection agency or are charged off to bad debt. The best practice, then, is to get the information, use it, and reject those tenants who don't pay their bills. You'll be much further ahead and make more money.

Enforcing Your Rent Policy

Establishing and enforcing a rent-credit policy isn't all that difficult. It's important to let the tenant know you appreciate his or her business, but you also have to let that tenant know that there are bills to be paid. If you've set a policy that the rent is due on the first of the month and the tenant doesn't pay on time, there's nothing wrong with calling and asking for your money. This request, for what's rightfully yours, can certainly be done, at least the first time, on a friendly and businesslike basis.

Having been in this business for many years, I can tell you that, at one time or another, you're going to have a tenant come to you and ask, "I'm short this money and I cannot pay the rent. Can you wait?" Or "I had to make a car payment, and I don't have the money right now." Or "My daughter went to the dentist, I had to pay the bill, and now don't have enough for rent." If you're dealing with a divorced tenant, you may hear something like this: "My children came to visit me, and I had to pay their transportation so I don't have the rent money."

These are usually all well-rehearsed stalling tactics. It's a time in this business that, as an owner, you've got to be assertive and take a stand. My theory about dealing with these kinds of situations is this: tenants' concerns should be food first, lodging or rent second, utilities third, and everything else after that … including the car payment. If a tenant tries to pull one of the stall tricks, present these priorities to him or her. At the same time let the tenant know you're not in the loan business.

When confronted with a stalling tactic, I let tenants know that I don't have any obligation to them other than to provide the housing we agreed on. If they're looking for and need financial help, that's a personal and family responsibility, not mine. This is a business, a business of renting apartments. You expect to be paid when the rent comes due. You're not in the business of playing second fiddle to a car payment or any other excuse. Tell tenants to seek help from a relative, friend, or anyone else … but not you. I have no qualms about letting tenants know that there's a monthly mortgage payment due and that payment depends totally on getting the money in to make that payment. The bank won't wait. Being assertive usually gets results, and, once you set the tone and let tenants know you mean business, it usually doesn't happen again.

Using Instinct Alone to Identify a Credit Risk

I know people in this business who can't turn down a tenant. They say, "He sure looks good to me, and I know I'm going to get paid." So, on that basis they'll take the tenant—by looks, without any credit information. It's what's called "eyeball decision making." If prospective tenants look good, they must be good. Credit managers who make decisions this way usually end up with credit losses and accounts for collection. There's only one sure way of protecting yourself from credit losses, and that's to check on an applicant's history.

There are real estate investors who'll approve a tenant on the spot and go back to the office and call for a credit report. This system is about as reliable as "eyeballing," and it doesn't work either. The collection departments of credit bureaus are filled with accounts on people who don't look like poor risks.

Let's say you have a tenant in one of your apartments who is not paying rent. Obviously, you're losing money. It's as bad or worse than having a vacancy. The first step is to correct this situation before it gets out of hand. It's a case of either getting paid or getting rid of the tenant. You're not obligated to provide free housing to anyone, and not being paid rent is "free" housing.

The last thing in the world you need, especially as a beginning investor, is an occupied apartment that isn't earning any money. The mortgage has to be paid, the expenses don't wait, so the rent has to be there. Therefore, make up your mind that you're in the real estate business for one thing, and that is to make a profit, not to make friends. Making a profit takes money. The only way to get the money is to collect the rent, on time. The way to get paid on time is to rent to people you can be certain pay their bills.

Chapter 17

No-Nonsense
Leases

There are a number of leases and various contracts you'll want to use for your real estate rental business. Most of the forms and examples I'll provide in this chapter are just that, examples. You can make up your own to fit your particular needs. I'll give you the basic outline and you can use what you want. As we go, the comments in parentheses are explanations and reasons for most of the information that you'll request.

The Rental Application

Let's start with the rental contract. The rental contract starts before you've made any commitment to that potential tenant about renting an apartment. This will give you enough preliminary information to let you know if you want to proceed with the application.

First, put the name of your firm or your personal name at the top of the form, then list the location of the property and the apartment or unit number. Next, be sure to add the number of people that will occupy the location. (I suggest this because, if you have a one- or two-bedroom apartment and an applicant has several children, you'll know ahead of time and can eliminate the tenant by simply telling him or her that the apartment isn't large enough for the family.)

As you create your rental application, there are specific kinds of information you want applicants to provide. I suggest you create blanks (of the appropriate length) for the following items of information:

1. the applicant's name

2. the applicant's Social Security number (You'll want the Social Security number because you need it to get a credit report. I'll have more to say about the credit report as we go.)

3. date of birth (You'll want to know if the applicant is a teenager or mature adult.)

4. the applicant's current address and a permanent home address (If the applicant is a student, you'll want to know their permanent address in case you have to get in touch with a family member.)

5. the make, model, and year of the applicant's vehicle

6. the license number and state of the vehicle (You may also want to ask if the car is insured and the name of the carrier.)

7. the applicant's driver's license number

8. for the applicant's source(s) of income, the employer's name, and the company's phone number

9. the applicant's job title (and possibly his or her supervisor's name)

10. how long the individual has been with that company

11. the applicant's income (by either the month or the year)

    (Employment information is important because it provides financial facts about applicants.)

12. the name of the applicant's bank, its address and phone number, and the type of accounts the applicant has (checking, savings)

13. the person's current landlord, his or her phone number, the address of the rented property, amount of monthly rent, length of tenancy, and his or her reason for moving (You may want to ask for one

other previous landlord and request the same information about that landlord.)

14. a couple of personal references (names, addresses, phone numbers, and relationship to the applicant)

(You'll want to have this information in case you want to get in touch with the tenant at some point in the future.)

The last item should be the following statement:

In compliance with all the provisions of the Fair Credit Reporting Act, I certify that I understand the permissible purposes for obtaining my credit report and give notice that the above-named firm or individual may request a credit report for rental purposes. I have read and understand this contract.

With this signed authorization you can proceed to your local credit bureau to get a credit report on the individual. If the credit report is good and everything else looks good, you can be assured you'll get your rent paid. On the other hand, if the applicant doesn't have a good credit report, you don't want the individual as a tenant. The credit report protects you either way.

At the end of the form, provide a line for the applicant to sign and date the document. At the bottom of the page, include the following three words, preferably in bold print:

EQUAL HOUSING OPPORTUNITY

That completes your application form. After you've selected someone you think will be a good tenant, you'll need a lease.

Lease and Contractual Agreement

Once you've completed your investigation, including a credit report, and you've approved the tenant, the next step is having a binding lease.

At the top of your form put **RESIDENTIAL LEASE.** Immediately following this title I recommend including the following statement:

The (name your state) Attorney General's Office has certified that this lease complies with the (name your state) Plain Language Contract Act.

On a residential lease, start with the name of the resident applicant, the individual responsible for paying the rent. Provide space for the applicant to list all the people, who will be living in the unit and their dates of birth. Next put your company name, the location of the premises, and apartment number. Then put in the duration of the lease and state whether it's a month-to-month contract for a specific number of months. Put in the starting date of the contract and when the lease ends, if applicable. At this point, put in the notice period, that is, whether it's a contract from the first to the first of each month or whatever date is applicable.

Next, specify the amount of the monthly rent and any other charges, for example, the utilities, if the tenant is responsible for them. At this point, you can also include an amount for a service charge. (I'll explain below how this applies.) Name the authorized manager, most likely yourself, or an agent or apartment management service you've assigned to oversee the apartment, and include an address and phone number in case the tenant needs to contact the manager.

Provide spaces for at least two signatures, one for the authorized manager or owner, and the other for the residents, or you may want to provide space for several signatures here, especially if you're renting to college students. (You want to make sure all of them are responsible for the apartment and the rent.) Then, in bold letters, state the terms of the contract:

Terms and Conditions

Financial Agreement

Payment: Resident will pay management the full monthly rent before midnight on the first day of each month (or whatever you've agreed on) while this lease is in effect and during any extensions or renewals of this lease.

Obligation for rent: Each resident is individually responsible for paying the full amount of rent and any other money owed to the management.

Payment of rent after eviction: If resident is evicted for having violated any term of this lease, resident must still pay the full monthly rent until the apartment is re-rented, or the date this lease ends, or, if the lease is on a month-to-month basis, the next notice period ends. If the apartment or unit is re-rented for less than the rent due under the lease, resident will be responsible for the difference until the date this lease ends or, if the lease is month-to-month, until the end of the next notice period.

Service charge for late rent and returned check: Resident will pay the service charge if the full monthly rent is not paid by the fifth of the month. Resident will also pay a fee of (put in here the amount of whatever your state law allows; most states allow $30) for each returned check.

Use of Apartment

Occupancy and lease terms: Only the persons listed above as residents may live in the apartment or rental unit. Persons not listed as residents may live in the unit only with the prior written consent of the management. Residents may use the apartment and utilities for normal residential purposes only.

If the management (you) is unable to provide the apartment to the occupant at the start of the lease, the lessor cannot sue the management for any resulting damages, but the lessor will not pay rent until he or she occupies the apartment.

If the tenant moves out before the end of the lease, that resident is responsible for all rent and any losses incurred, including court and attorney's fees.

If the occupant decides to move out on the date the lease ends, the occupant must give the owner prior written notice.

When the lease ends, the management and occupant can mutually agree on a month-to-month lease.

If the lessor violates any terms of the lease, he or she can be evicted immediately and without prior notice. Any illegal substance, including drugs, constitutes unlawful possession and is grounds for automatic eviction.

Subletting: Resident may not lease the apartment to other persons (sublet), assign this lease, or sell this lease without the prior written consent of management.

Resident promises:

1. To avoid any and all acts of loud, boisterous, unruly, or thoughtless actions that interfere with the rights of the other residents to peace and quiet, and to prevent his or her guests from doing so;

2. To use the apartment only as a private residence and not in any way that is illegal or dangerous or which would cause a cancellation, restriction, or increase in premium in management's insurance;

3. Not to use or store in or near the apartment any flammable or explosive substance;

4. Not to interfere in the management and operation of the apartment building;

5. That the common areas, or area surrounding the building, will not be used by the resident without the consent of management;

6. That any member of the resident's household or any guest of the resident or anyone acting under his or her control will not manufacture, sell, give away, barter, deliver, exchange, distribute, possess, or use any illegal drugs, or to engage in prostitution or any prostitution-related activity, or to unlawfully use or possess any firearm, or to allow any stolen property on the premises;

7. That the resident will not keep a waterbed or other water-filled furniture in the apartment without the prior written consent of management;

8. That the resident and any guest will not keep any animals or pets of any kind in the apartment without the written consent of manage-

ment. Resident will be given a three-day eviction notice if pets are found on the premises.

Condition of Apartment

Management promises:

To keep the apartment or unit and all common areas fit for use as a residential premises;

To keep the apartment in reasonable repair and make necessary repairs within a reasonable time after written notice by resident, except when damage is caused by the intentional or negligent conduct of the resident or his or her guests;

To maintain the apartment in compliance with applicable health and safety codes, except when a violation of the health and safety codes has been caused by the intentional or negligent conduct of the resident or his or her guests;

To keep the common areas clean and in good condition.

Conditions of keeping premises livable: The tenant is not to damage or misuse the apartment or waste the utilities provided by management or allow his or her guests to do so, or paint or wallpaper the apartment, or make any structural changes in the apartment with the prior written consent of management. The tenant agrees to maintain a clean premises, give written notice to management of any necessary repairs to be made, notify management immediately of any conditions in the apartment that are dangerous to human health or safety, or that may damage the apartment or waste utilities provided by management. Further, the tenant agrees that when he or she moves out, the apartment or unit will be left in good condition, except for ordinary wear and tear, will not remove any fixtures or furnishings supplied by management without prior written consent of management; that, if the apartment or unit is damaged so that it's not fit to live in, the management may cancel this lease. If the unit is not damaged by the tenant and is found unlivable, the management will refund, on a prorated basis, rent paid up to the date of such condition. The tenant agrees to cooperate with management's efforts at pest control. This may include, among other things, resident's emptying and cleaning cabinets, drawers, and closets, pulling furniture away from walls and allowing exterminator to enter and treat the apartment.

Security deposit: The management may keep any and all of the deposit for damage to the apartment, beyond normal wear and tear, and for rent owed to management.

If management brings legal action against the resident, that resident must pay attorney's fees, court costs, or other legal fees and expenses, including fees paid to a collection agency, even if the rent is paid after the legal action is started.

The owner of the premises has a right to enter the apartment at any reasonable time to inspect or maintain or do necessary repair work and to show the unit to a prospective new tenant.

If there is a foreclosure notice on the building, the mortgage or contract for deed holder has preferential agreement and can terminate all leases.

Liability

The property owner/management is not responsible for any damage or injury that happens to the resident or guests, or any damages, injury, or harm caused by a third party, such as intruders or trespassers or other tenants.

Management has the right to collect for any property damage or repair caused by negligence or improper use by the tenant.

Management/owner is not responsible for any property damage to the tenant's own property or guest's property that was caused by the owner, nor is the owner responsible for damages or injuries caused by third parties such as guests, intruders, and trespassers. It is recommended that the resident obtain proper insurance to cover injuries and property damage.

The tenant will reimburse the owner/management the cost of repair or service caused by negligence or improper use, including damage caused by his or her family or guests, including plumbing problems, broken windows, windows being left open, abandonment of the unit, furniture and appliances left after vacancy; this includes paying any court costs and attorney's fees incurred by the owner/management.

If the tenant makes false or misleading statements, this is a violation of the lease and a cause for eviction.

Guide to Moving In

(You may wish to use this form because it indicates what you expect from your tenant.)

Rent is due on the first of the month.

All utility, cable television, lawn care, electrical, and gas bills will be paid.

No pets.

Use sewing needles to display pictures or posters. Do not use tape or tape-on products.

Do not flush sanitary napkins down the toilet. Seventy-five percent of clogged toilets are caused by these products.

Check smoke detector once a month.

Do not install a waterbed without permission of the management/ owner.

Be sure to have renter's insurance.

Moving Out Guidelines

(You may want to post this information in the kitchen cupboard in the unit.)

The following can assist you when you prepare to move out:

Contact phone, cable, utilities, and post office to terminate services.

Clean stove, refrigerator, cabinets, sink, floors, bathroom, windows, and closets.

Remove all garbage.

Turn in keys.

Leave a forwarding address. Your refund will be mailed to you within three weeks following your last month's tenancy (or check your state's laws about how soon a refund must be returned).

Crime-Free Housing

Crime-free housing benefits the owners, the tenants, the neighborhood, and the police. In some communities there are special laws covering crime-free housing. Therefore, as you invest in your community, establish good communication with the police department. They can be helpful. However, it's best to know your local rental laws.

For example, I have a friend who bought a fourplex near a college campus. After the building had been purchased, the city council and mayor passed a law that, if there's a complaint reported against a tenant in that fourplex, the police have the right to contact the apartment owner, who must then deal with the problem. If it's a major problem, such as drugs or weapons or the like, the owner must appear before the city council and answer the complaint, not the tenant. This happened to these owners after the police continued receiving complaints, mostly from neighbors. To show you how ridiculous this can be, one call came from a rejected girlfriend who wanted to get back at her boyfriend and the complaint had to be answered. Most of the complaints were about loud beer parties, too many cars parked on the street, and junk and beer bottles strewn all over the yard. There's no doubt they were legitimate complaints, but the police contacted my friend, the owner, who had to appear before the city council and answer the complaint. He then had to contact the tenants.

This turned out to be a miserable situation for everyone. This went on for a while until the college students who were living in the rental unit got tired of the constant complaints and threats. They got together and elected a 21-year-old student as mayor and another student, who defeated an incumbent on the city council. It did awaken the community somewhat, but in the long run the bureaucracy didn't change the law. My friend, who didn't have the time or energy to deal with this, didn't want anything more to do with the community. He sold the rental property and got out of town.

Crime-Free Housing Lease Agreement

If you're in a community that has an abundance of crime, it's a good idea to cover yourself and your property. It can be done in your lease.

A Lease Addendum

The following lease addendum is an option for you to consider:

> The tenant, resident, or any member of the household, including guests or other persons, shall not engage in illegal activity, including drug-related illegal activity, on or near the said premises. Drug-related activity includes the manufacture, sale, distribution, purchase, use, or possession of a controlled substance with intent to manufacture, sell, distribute, or use, or possession of drug paraphernalia.

> The tenant will not permit the dwelling to be used for, or to facilitate, illegal activity, including drug-related activity, regardless of whether the individual engaging in such activity is a member of the household.

> The tenant or resident will not engage in the manufacture, sale, or distribution of illegal drugs at any location, whether on or near the dwelling unit premises or otherwise.

> The tenant or resident shall not engage in acts of violence or threats of violence, including but not limited to the unlawful discharge of firearms, street gang activity, intimidation, or any other breach of the rental agreement that otherwise jeopardizes the health, safety, or welfare of the owner, his agents, or tenants.

The tenant agrees that any violation of the provisions of this lease shall be a violation of the lease and cause for termination of tenancy.

This lease addendum is incorporated in the lease and the provisions of this addendum shall govern.

(Dated and signed by management and tenant.)

It's important, once you're established in the rental business, and especially if you're a landlord living in a different community, to establish yourself and communicate with your local police department. Usually they'll want to cooperate with you.

Chapter 18

Dealing with Tenant Complaints

Here's something to think about when considering the benefits of real estate investing. Up to this point, the only investment anyone has had to make in establishing this dynamic, ready-made business is a small down payment for the property. The seller or banker has financed the property, and the tenant's rent is paying off the mortgage each month. So far all the investor has had to contribute is management. If the rent money continues to flow, and there's no reason that it shouldn't, then the investor's contribution, that of managing the tenants and the property, should be a small contribution to enhance this tremendous savings and security account. Once you realize how this wealth builds, this part should come easily.

Good management practices can and will help you avoid a lot of problems. If you're serious about investing in real estate and you want to make a financially independent future for yourself, then take the time to learn how to take care of the property and the tenants. Without management, the investment could become a financial disaster.

A good example of the dire consequences of lax management is the story I told earlier about the investor who bought 10 rental units. He did a great job for the first four or five years, but then became careless about taking care of the property. He let things get run down, didn't bother to mow lawns, didn't paint, and neglected the tenants' complaints. Eventually the good tenants moved out, the money quit flowing, and an avalanche of trouble began. As the problems mounted, he lost interest in his investment and began treating the property with disdain. Gradually the properties began turning into slums. There were persistent vacancies, and the tenants living there didn't pay their rent. The entire operation got out of hand, and, the last I heard, he was going to let the property go back on foreclosure.

Working with Your Tenants

Always remember that your tenants expect to have desirable living conditions and expect the owner of the property to care for their unit properly. Part of your commitment involves making a special effort to be an attentive landlord. Your consistent efforts can and will pay off in many ways. One of the best payoffs, for example, is that you will develop a good reputation, and that will enhance your ability to choose and select the best tenants. In fact, the good tenants will seek you out.

Being a good landlord and manager doesn't mean you have to cater to every whim and wish of every tenant. What it does mean, however, is that you take care of legitimate problems. For the sake of the property, as well as the tenants, don't let irritating little things get out of hand. Fix the leaky faucet, clean out the clogged drain, or replace the torn carpet. Let the tenants know that you're concerned about their unit and about them as individuals and that you really do care about their standard of living. Remember, that apartment is *their* home and they want to keep it as comfortable and trouble-free as possible.

When confronted by a tenant regarding a problem, avoid arguments. Arguments only create ill feelings, establish a barrier between you and the tenant, and ultimately lead to more serious problems. These you can do without. Work out tenants' complaints with them, but don't let them take advantage of you. If you do, they'll chase you to death with their complaints and requests.

If you've developed a good reputation in the business and if you've done a good job of screening your tenants, you should be getting the best. If they are the best, they should have your respect and consideration.

Taking Advantage of Complaints

It's not difficult to use tenants' complaints for positive actions. Resolving problems provides you with good opportunities to communicate directly with your tenants. If you give them reliable service, they'll go away feeling good, and chances are they'll remain devoted and loyal as tenants and speak well of you. This is how you can develop a "good landlord" reputation. Incidentally, good experiences and communications with your tenants will also make you feel good.

Service adds that special touch. It's that extra effort, or it's doing something that's totally unexpected. Service doesn't take a lot of time, very little effort, and practically no money. Service is something that is positive, and the returns are usually manifold, especially if the word gets out that you're a service-oriented landlord. The word will get out, and this word of mouth, the best telegram system in the world, will add to your ability to get and keep the best tenants.

Solving Tenants' Problems

No matter how many units you own, one or one hundred, no matter how new and well kept the apartments are, there will be minor problems that consistently need attention. Here's a list of things that occur off and on during any period of time, and about which you can expect to get calls:

- a lost key to an apartment
- hall or basement lights burned out
- plugged sewer
- leaky roof
- door won't open or close

- window won't open or close
- a broken door lock
- a leaky faucet or shower
- a washing machine or dryer out of order
- no heat
- water leaking through ceiling
- freezer defrosting when it shouldn't
- stove burner doesn't heat
- garbage disposal clogged
- carpet is dirty
- apartment needs painting
- sewer backed up in basement
- refrigerator doesn't cool
- bathtub doesn't drain
- kitchen sink won't drain

These complaints fall into three categories, and each category requires a different response:

1. *Catastrophes.* This category includes a backed-up sewer, water in the basement, leaky roof, water leaking into the ceiling, heating system out of order, broken windows, and other exterior deterioration. These complaints and/or problems call for *immediate attention.*

2. *Money-Savers.* This category covers a leaky faucet, coin-operated washer or dryer not working, hall lights too bright, and broken windows that cause heat loss. These problems don't call for immediate attention, but they should be taken care of as soon as possible.

3. *All Others.* Painting, carpet cleaning, cleaning premises, excessive materials collected in basement, and so on, are things that can be done at any time: over weekends, during vacations…. There's no urgency.

The most important advice I can give you regarding tenant complaints is to take care of them as soon as possible so that a small problem doesn't turn into a catastrophe.

The Art of Eliminating Complaints

Eliminating irritating complaints from tenants makes this business much more pleasurable, and, fortunately, there are some steps you can take to reduce the number of complaints. First, consider hiring (by giving a rent reduction) one of the tenants. Let the tenant look after the building and the grounds. Be certain there's an understanding that the pay comes in the form of rent reduction so you don't have to set up a payroll. An in-house manager can handle all the minor complaints so that you, the owner, get called only in case of an emergency.

Here is a second method of eliminating complaints. Oftentimes, you'll be dealing with persistent complainers. Let them know, in a firm and assertive manner, that you can't be running all the time to solve petty, nonemergency problems. Once you show complaining tenants that you mean business, eventually they'll quit calling. Some of these tenants will finally decide that it's a lot easier to solve the problem themselves rather than going through the hassle of dealing with an assertive manager.

If you reach the point that a tenant's frequent calls do not seem to be letting up, propose to him or her that maybe he or she would be happier and better off in another apartment or renting from someone else. That usually ends the problem. The tenant either stops complaining or moves out. Either way, you're better off and have fewer headaches. Remember, this is a headache-elimination book.

Chapter 19

Raising
the Rent

Rents: Commonsense Rent Control

The name of this business, the real estate business, is to charge the most rent possible to make the property profitable. Rent is your road to financial security.

There is no prescribed way to determine rents. Rents generally are based on whatever the traffic will bear. This concept, in our free-enterprise system, is better known as *supply and demand*. As an investor, you must have each apartment and rental unit contribute to an overall sound economic program for financing the property; otherwise, why bother to invest in real estate? If you're not willing to charge enough rent, your equity will suffer. You might as well put the money in CDs.

Your best approach is knowing the rental market. For instance, if there are very few vacancies in your particular investment community, then take advantage of the good market. Buy investment property and charge rents accordingly. On the other hand, if there are a lot of vacancies, you should reconsider the amount of rent you charge. You may need to drop the amount for each apartment. In general, it's a lot better to charge $10 or $25 a month less for rent than to have a vacancy for a month or two.

Here's something to think about when you consider how much to charge for your apartments or rental units. Ask yourself: "If I rented and lived here, how much would I be willing to pay?" Another way to determine how much rent to charge is to check with neighbors, especially in large apartment complexes. Once you know what prices they charge, and you know what kind of apartment or property they have, then you can pretty well determine your rents accordingly. Incidentally, when you see large apartment complex owners raising their rents, it's a good time to analyze your rents. Also, visit with fellow investors, especially the small, independent, part-time operators. Keep in touch with them, and find out how much they charge. That should give you an idea of what your apartments are worth.

Raising Rents

You are justified, and smart, to raise rents at certain times. For example, government employees and Social Security recipients receive annual cost-of-living increases. This *cost of living* means housing. It's a time to consider rent increases. Also, inflation is an ongoing economic condition, and taxes are always increasing. Both cases call for increased rents.

The easiest and most convenient time to raise rents is at a time of vacancy or in between tenants. If the market will bear it, increase the rent each time a tenant moves out.

Charging Rents That Are Too Low

Sometimes small, independent investors become personally involved with their tenants and let their emotions overcome common business sense. They lose sight of why they are in the business. This is especially true when it comes to charging rents. Many times I've heard landlords say, "Oh, they're such a nice couple—I hate to raise their rent." Or "She's such a nice old lady, never demands anything, lives on Social Security—I just don't feel right charging any more rent." All that's well and good, quite considerate, and shows great compassion. But remember, you're not in the rental business to make friends, to be a nice guy, or to be the community benevolent society. If you feel the need to be a do-gooder, be a Scout leader or collect for the United Way in your community, but don't do it with your real estate business. You're in this business to make a profit and build a secure financial future *for yourself.*

Charging too little rent and not raising rents when they should be raised is futile and foolhardy. It might be considered nice, but it certainly doesn't make business sense, and it won't add a penny to your bank account. And, as far as the retired couple and the nice old lady who rent from you is concerned, the odds are pretty good that most of these people have a pretty hefty savings account. I'd be willing to bet that, once they leave the apartment, Joe Nice Guy Landlord will be quickly forgotten. You might have thought you were really doing a good deed or that you might be in line when the estate is settled, but in reality it is highly unlikely that the heirs are going to sit there in the attorney's office settling the estate, and say, "Oh, that wonderful Joe Nice Guy Landlord was so good, and he took such good care of my mother. I think we should let him in on some of the inheritance."

If you feel compelled to give your money away, don't give it to a stranger by not charging sufficient rent. Charge the proper rent, and then give your extra money to your family. I'm not advocating being obnoxious; it's just a matter of using common sense and charging the proper rent for the apartment, not the person. As a matter of fact, it's just as easy to be a nice guy and charge the correct rent too.

Having a lackadaisical attitude about charging proper rents means you're probably not making sound business and financial judgments and decisions. Sometimes we have a tendency to overlook the obvious. For instance, I don't think anyone would stand on a street corner handing out dollar bills. Not charging enough rent is just like giving money away, ... giving it to your tenants. If an apartment can bring in $500 a month rent and you're charging $450, you are giving that tenant a gift of $50 every month.

Assessing the Proper Amount of Rent

I knew a real estate investor who had the greatest reputation with his tenants. He never raised his rents. For this reason his tenants thought he was a great guy, and they said nice, flattering things about him. I would too if I were getting a gravy deal. I told him he couldn't put those nice words in the bank.

Dispelling the Cadillac Image with Your Tenants

I don't think it's a good idea to drive up to your apartments, in front of your tenants, in a big "status-symbol" car. If you do, I think you're asking for trouble because you're going to get a negative reaction. For example, one of the tenants might say, "This guy's making big bucks if he can afford that kind of car. He must be charging too much rent and ripping us off." Or a tenant might say, "If he can afford that kind of car, he can afford to fix up or paint my apartment."

I recommend tending to your apartments wearing casual clothing and driving an older car so that you look like you are "one of them" and can't afford anything better. After all, these people are probably living in apartments because they can't afford a house. In addition, do your own work to give the tenants the impression that you can't afford to pay to have it done.

Tenant Leases

I've thoroughly discussed leases in the previous chapter, but there's one more thing you should know. For the most part, a lease doesn't hold a lot of water. For instance, if tenants are going to move out in the middle of a lease, they're moving because they have to. However, the lease can protect you against past-due rent and cleanup and repair expenses. An entire book could be written on drawing up leases. I recommend that you check with an attorney or find a lease form you can use. (These can usually be found in stationery stores.)

Some Final Tips on Property Management

Management is an extremely important, indeed, crucial, part of a successful real estate investment … if you want to make a profit. And, let there be no doubt about it, management means work, as it does in any other business. But, remember, this is your business, and any profits your successful business earns because of your work is money you keep.

Some of the promoters who hold real estate seminars give the impression that all you have to do is buy the property, and, overnight, without any work or effort, it turns to gold. That isn't the real world of real estate. The work you put into your business will secure your self-employed status. What a great feeling it is not to have to go through a boss or through a committee to make decisions. It's true that you are out there on your own, but the experience is exhilarating. And the odds are pretty good that, if you have learned the business of real estate investing and you know what you're doing, those decisions you make will be correct. But, even if you do make a mistake, so what? That too is a learning experience, and it will eventually pay off.

Real estate investing is an exciting business!

Chapter 20

No-Nonsense
Evictions

The Problem of Occupied Apartments Not Earning Rent

T here are several ways to address the problem of having an occupied apartment that's not earning money, in other words, a tenant who is not paying rent. Of course, the best advice is hindsight advice: "This should never have happened in the first place." If there has been a concerted effort to check on tenants before they move in, there should be no such thing as an apartment not earning its keep.

But let's say we have a case when the tenant was checked out and the record was good, but after some time his or her record started turning bad, and he or she quit paying the rent. The first thing to do is analyze the situation. Find out if the tenant is working full time. Does it look like the tenant is spending money on things rather than paying the rent?

The next thing to do is confront the tenant *assertively* about what's going on and to ask for the rent money directly. If it appears that it's just a matter of getting the tenant's priorities straightened out, then it's a matter of setting up an agreement and making sure the agreement is followed. That agreement means getting the rent paid on time and you getting your money. Let the tenant know that you're not going to be the "low man on the totem pole" and that the rent comes first.

When dealing with a tenant during these crucial times, it's important to remain assertive. It's not a time to listen to any excuses. Additional stalls mean no money and more problems. Insist that the tenant pay you the rent money every month if he or she intends to stay in the apartment. Whether the tenant has to beg, borrow, or steal, whatever it takes, the rent must be paid.

If all this doesn't work and the tenant doesn't get the money and makes more excuses, then the next step is eviction. Eviction is truly one of the real headaches of this business. However, it doesn't happen that often, especially if the tenant is checked out thoroughly before entering into the lease agreement.

Evictions

Let's say you have a tenant who isn't paying. I don't mean that the individual is behind 15 or 30 days. I mean he or she has settled into the apartment, and there's been no rent paid for 30 to 60 days. What's next? This is a time when it takes some *strong and assertive action.* If you don't act now, this kind of problem can cause a financial crisis for you.

There's only one way to get that apartment or rental unit back in the profit picture, and that's by eliminating the problem: the nonpaying tenant. Getting rid of that nonpaying tenant is called *eviction.* There are many legal ramifications of evicting a tenant. Each state has specific laws that spell out how this can be done. But it appears that the only way, the legal way, and the one that will work best, is hiring an attorney. Don't try to evict someone without getting legal advice.

Before taking this drastic step, there are some other methods worth trying. I've told you several times that I've been in this business for 35 years. During that time, I've had to evict tenants, not that many, but some. The tenants I've had to evict were *not* paying rent. Here's what I've done. First of all, 99 percent of the time that tenant knows he or she is in the wrong, that he or she is behind on the rent, and that money is owed. It's impossible to hide the raw truth. Most of the time that tenant is going to be embarrassed about this experience. The truth is that he or she doesn't want this brought out in public. So, have a confrontation and present the complaint and the problem.

Next, by being extremely assertive, let that tenant know you want him or her out, and out *right now!* At this stage of the game you're going to know whether or not you've gotten the tenant's attention. Usually, when that individual is confronted with the truth and knows he or she is in the wrong, he or she won't put up much of a fight, if any at all. The tenant often becomes meek and humble, gives in, and knows it's a no-win situation.

Sometimes there can be tears. In this case, don't give in, and don't back down. Don't change your mind if you see tears. If you give in and allow that tenant to stay, with shallow promises of payment, you're going to prolong the problem, and, in a month or two, it will be the same story all over again. If you become wishy-washy, you'll end up being the loser, and the tenant will take advantage of you and walk all over you. The tenant doesn't have much to lose.

Second, there's one other way to eliminate tenants without going through a protracted legal eviction: buy the person out. Let's say a tenant is two months past due on the rent, and there's no indication that he or she will get caught up. Go to the tenant and offer to buy him or her out. Offer to release him or her from the obligation of paying the past-due rent plus $200 cash to leave the premises within 24 hours. It's costly, but consider your alternative. If you proceed with eviction, you have to hire and pay an attorney. It also means the tenant can stay in the apartment and possibly get more months' "free" rent. This too is costly. In the long run, buying out can be cheaper, and you'll get the apartment cleaned up and back in use immediately.

Let's take a look at some of the reasons that tenants can be evicted:

- property damage
- poor housekeeping

- loud parties
- uncontrolled drinking
- violence
- abusive language
- tenants' and neighbors' complaints
- late hours
- unkempt premises
- loud and/or dangerous pets
- fights and rowdiness
- nonpayment of rent

Protecting Yourself Against Legal Action

When dealing with an eviction, or any problem with a tenant for that matter, *never* enter the apartment without authority. *Do not* lock the tenant out of the apartment, and do not confiscate the tenant's property in lieu of past-due rent. Do not forcefully enter a tenant's premises without legal authority to do so.

When confronted with any legal situations involving a tenant and your property, always contract with and get the advice of an attorney and keep precise and detailed records of all events. That means keep a daily log or diary, right from the first communication, and record all the following information:

- time, date, and communication at time of confrontation
- reasons, in writing, for the confrontation
- chronological order of events, including dates and times
- all conversations involving the dispute
- names of others involved in the dispute

Good records are a valuable asset in all real estate transactions and can prepare you for any unusual or unforeseen circumstances.

I can assure you that, if you do end up in court over any legal dispute having to do with your property, those well-kept records will speak louder than words. The landlord sometimes has a tough time dealing with the court system. Some judges think all people who own apartments or rental properties are "rich and selfish." In a lot of cases judges will look at the case of the "rich landlord" versus the "poor persecuted tenant." If you've ever been to court, you know that precise, well-prepared records will win. Usually the defendant will end up being caught in a lie. When you have accurate records with the dates, times, and the various conversations that have taken place, the judge knows you're not trying to pull one over on the tenant or the judge.

Whatever you do, don't get angry, don't use threats, don't be abusive, don't use foul language, and don't do anything illegal.

Maybe something like this will never happen to you, and the odds are good that it won't, but in case it does, be prepared.

Collecting Past-Due Rent

Despite all of our well-laid plans, and although we've done everything possible to protect ourselves from having tenants who don't pay their rent, we can, on occasion, get stuck. When this happens, it calls for immediate action. Here's why:

- $100 paid on time is worth $100.
- $100 past due 60 days is worth $90.
- $100 past due six months is worth $67.
- $100 past due one year is worth $45.
- $100 past due 60 days, six months, or a year is also a lot of anxiety, something real estate investors can do without.

There's nothing worse than having to write off a bad debt. It's something that makes most of us boil. Therefore, if you end up with a bad debt, do something about it, and take every conceivable action necessary to get your money. Being nice isn't going to get a penny. In fact, being nice only leads to more trouble, more loss, and more anxiety.

Start your collection efforts by contacting the tenant who owes the money, and tell him or her, again assertively, "My accountant [or banker, or wife, or anyone] told me I have to get this money collected because if I don't, I'm past due on my mortgage payment." You can even say, "If I don't get the money, I'm in trouble, and I've been ordered to collect or else."

Be aggressive and assertive. Let the tenant know you mean business. Keep the pressure on for the payment. Call frequently and demand payment. If you don't get action and can't get the job done on your own, the next step is to use a bill collector, and don't wait. Tell the tenant he or she has 30 days to pay, or that the bill will go to a collection agency. Then do it.

Bill Collectors

Get this debt out of your hands so you can get on with positive things happening with your real estate. Work with the good tenants and your good property. Don't waste time and effort, get burned out with an overdose of anxiety, and then get sick and tired of the whole operation. Turn the bad debt over to a credit bureau of your choice for collection. If you use a credit bureau, that account for collection will appear in the tenant's file. At least you'll have some satisfaction of knowing that bill will have an effect on his or her credit rating.

If the credit bureau is good and if the tenant is working, the bureau will get your money. The credit bureau will charge a fee, from 33 to 50 percent. You'll have to take this in stride, but 50 to 67 percent of something is better than a lot of nothing.

Attorneys

You can, of course, use an attorney and take legal measures to collect the past-due account. However, I've found that most attorneys don't like to handle these small accounts.

If your debtor has contacted an attorney to represent him or her, it's my understanding that you have to cease all communications with the debtor and communicate only through your attorney or the debtor's attorney. However, don't take any abuse from the debtor's attorney if you're in the right, and don't accept a settlement.

Another method of taking legal action on your own is by using the conciliation court or small-claims court.

Here's the way that works. Conciliation court was established so that anyone could file a complaint without having an attorney involved. You pay a fee to file in the court, and the hearing is held before a judge. He or she rules that you're right or the debtor is right. If you're right, you get a judgment. That's the end of the action in a conciliation court because the court doesn't collect the money. Therefore, you have to follow through once the judgment is issued, and there are some legal ramifications involved. In fact, it's usually more trouble than it's worth.

The best bet is to use a credit bureau because it will do all the court work.

Part Four

Moneymaking Strategies

Chapter 21

The Fixer-Upper: The Smart Way to Real Estate Profits

There's no doubt in my mind that one of the best potential profit makers in the real estate investment business is the *fixer-upper*, that is, the renovatable property. This is especially so for the ambitious, smart, independent starter investor who really wants to dig in and do some work. Renovatable houses, duplexes, and apartment buildings are moneymakers and produce great financial rewards for a number of reasons.

First and foremost, of course, is the fact that most of these properties that need work can be purchased at a reasonable price. For instance, I know of properties that were sold with no down payment. (This, of course, doesn't qualify as a nothing-down deal because, in the end, it takes capital to make the improvements on the property.) I also know of one property that was bought by paying the back taxes. In fact, you'll see this property and read all about it later in this chapter.

Second, almost from the time the first project within the property is completed, there's a substantial increase in its value. In fact, sometimes it takes no more than a general cleanup of the premises or a simple paint job. I can't give you any concrete proof of this other than to tell you simply that that's the way real estate works.

The third financial benefit of renovating properties, whether an apartment, a duplex, or a single-family home, is the fact that, once the renovation is completed, rents can be increased. Consequently, the increase in income eventually will pay for the improvements. Once the improvements are completed and paid for, the next step is to invest the profit back into additional renovation, which will increase the value of the property, which will again justify an increase in the rents. This entire series of events becomes a perpetual money machine.

The fourth financial benefit is the fact that the money spent on renovating property is tax-deductible. Thus, the investor receives the increased value of the property while still deducting depreciation. Not only is the expense deductible and charged against the property, but any losses from the improvement can be deducted from the investor's personal income.

The final benefit, but not the least, is that the increase in value from the improvement of the property adds equity. Equity means borrowing power. For instance, let's say the property is purchased for $50,000 and the cost of renovations is $5,000. In all probability the property value will increase to $65,000. That means there's $10,000 equity from the original purchase price, and all that's involved is the $5,000 cost plus time and work.

I once bought a run-down sixplex for $60,000 (not in New York, Los Angeles, or San Francisco). Over five years I spent my time and some money in renovating the apartments. There was no major work that needed to be done, but I upgraded some of the kitchens and bathrooms, replaced worn-out carpeting, and did some cleaning and general repair work. When the work was completed at the end of five years, the apartment building was appraised at $110,000.

Benefits of Renovating Property

Obviously, the financial gains, which are indisputable, are worth the time, work, and effort. However, there are other benefits in investing in these kinds of properties, especially in today's market when you consider prices of the traditional A-1 investment properties. (Remember, though, there's certainly nothing wrong with buying A-1 properties. For the small, independent, part-time investor, however, I figure there's much more to gain in buying renovatable properties.)

One of the benefits, although not financial, is that the investor has complete control over the location, the neighborhood, and the specific property itself. That is, by waiting and checking, sometimes the right property comes along that has the potential of making money. Always remember that there's no reason you have to buy the first property you look at or the first property that comes along. Take your time. When you start searching for investment property, and especially renovatable property, pick a good, stable, growing community. Avoid slums. Don't invest in locations that have deteriorating circumstances, freeways, industrial developments, and decaying neighborhoods.

Getting Ready for the Renovation

Renovating isn't easy, but it can be an enjoyable experience. The best advice I can give to anyone contemplating this kind of investment is to get in and remain in a good frame of mind. If you think optimistically, your project will be more enjoyable as well as more profitable. The next step is to get your family enthusiastically involved. They can be important. Then, once the property has been acquired, set out your plans. Know just what you're going to do to improve the property and set up a budget so you have some idea of how much money is involved. Know ahead of time if you have to borrow to pay for the renovation.

There are a number of things that can be done to the property that don't cost money, such as cleaning the yard and premises, trimming trees and shrubs, eliminating debris and junk, making general repairs, and cleaning halls, basement, stairways, and the general premises. Attending to these details can make a difference in the kinds of tenants who are attracted to the property. The better the property, the better the tenant, the more rent, and, ultimately, the higher the value of the property.

To be a general renovator doesn't take any special talent. It helps to be a jack-of-all-trades, but more importantly it takes ambition and determination. Doing any sort of physical work takes a great deal of emotional and physical energy. Don't take on more than you can handle. Work with your family. Don't get into a state of getting tired of the project and then wanting to quit or thinking you might have made a mistake. All projects will work themselves out.

Finding Good Help

An important component of renovating property is having capable, reliable, and inexpensive help, which includes you, the investor. In fact, your work on the project will be very important. You're going to have to do the work of supervisor, contractor, carpenter, carpenter's helper, painter, and general laborer.

If you get into a major renovation project, such as moving walls, building cupboards, plastering, or wiring, you'll need professional help. What I've found to work out best is finding within my neighborhood, community, or from my friends a retired carpenter—retired, yet active. Retired carpenters are often looking for small part-time jobs. The one I found worked for a reasonable wage, and his expertise saved me considerable time and expense. With him, I was able to sit down and go over the project so that I knew ahead of time how much time and money would be involved. In addition, having been in this business for many years, he had accumulated all the tools necessary to do the work.

Another source of good help that I have found was my hometown lumberyard manager. Lumberyard managers deal with contractors and carpenters every day, so they are knowledgeable about fixing, repairing, and renovating. When I renovated my properties, I bought all my products from one lumberyard. From this I received several benefits. First and foremost, I was given a contractor's discount, but I also received a considerable amount of free advice regarding construction problems I encountered. And, oftentimes when I got into trouble, the manager of the lumberyard would go right out to the site and help. This service was invaluable and inexpensive.

I also found, and you will too as you get into this business, that tenants can be available and helpful in doing various tasks. You can usually count on some tenants to paint, some will help in doing cleaning work, and some will fix leaky faucets and plugged drains. I had one tenant who wanted a shower rather than a tub. I could see he could handle this project, gave him the go-ahead, paid for all the materials, and ended up with a much more valuable bathroom.

Financing the Project

Be prepared ahead of time with all the financial plans for renovation work. Contact your banker for short-term (60 to 120 days) financing, then agree to refinance the property once the project is completed. Don't overspend and don't overrenovate. Don't make so many improvements that you'll never get your money back. Remember, you're a renovater, not a remodeling contractor. The difference is that the renovator is a fixer-upper. A remodeling contractor doesn't just fix up, he or she rebuilds. When you fix up and need new products, to save money remember that it's not necessary to put in the best of everything. Watch for hardware store and lumberyard sales. Buy products and fixtures that are stable, adequate, and inexpensive. Another money-saver: spend your time, effort, and money on inside improvements. For the outside it's important to keep the premises clean and neat, but it's not important to have a rock garden or expensive shrubbery. Tenants are going to rent on the basis of what's inside that apartment, not what's in the yard.

Finding the Right Property

A fixer-upper is not an abandoned property, nor is it a dilapidated or shelled-out building. A fixer-upper in a slum area is not a good long-term investment. A fixer-upper is a property that has been neglected by the current owner. It's a property that hasn't been cared for and needs some general maintenance. Look for owners who have paid off the mortgage, used up their depreciation so there's no longer a tax write-off, and now want to sell. Or look for owners who no longer want to take the time or spend the money to maintain their property. Some of the best buys I've found are those owned by absentee owners.

Here's a list of sources who could direct you to available properties:

- other apartment owners and investors
- an apartment owners' association
- building supply firms and carpenters
- newspaper advertisements
- lawn signs
- real estate agents

Ask wherever you go. A lot, in fact, most, of these kinds of properties aren't listed, so don't rely on real estate agents. It's necessary to become involved in the real estate investors' subculture world. The good news about buying directly from an owner is that there are no realtor's fees to pay.

Negotiating the Terms

When it comes to fixer-upper properties, there's not a great deal of competition out there. A lot of investors don't want to invest the time and effort required to make these projects work. Usually this kind of property can be bought at a bargain price. This puts you, the buyer, in the driver's seat when it comes to making terms.

Start by knowing and setting your own limits. This goes for money, as well as your work time. Know ahead how much money you can use as a down payment or for closing costs. Here you might consider negotiating your time, work, and labor as the down payment. Then, let the seller know how much money you can pay for the property. Also let the seller-financer know how much interest you can pay, as well as other details of the terms of the purchase. You'll find that some of these properties are owned by lending institutions and they've gotten them back on foreclosure. Those would be the most depleted properties, however, and it takes some extra work, money, and skills to get into some of these projects.

As you negotiate the terms with the seller, point out every negative aspect there is about the property. Describe all its defects, and then emphasize how much work, time, and money would be involved to get the property back in shape again. Also look at the history of the property. Ask the owner to show the records of how much rent was taken in and how much it cost to operate the property. If the property is losing money, let the seller know. Point this important fact out so that the seller knows that you know.

Whatever you do, don't, under any circumstances, take the word of the real estate agent about the finances of the property. The agent is going to tell you everything is profitable and doing well. In fact, realtors will tell you almost anything because they're out to make the sale.

Ask the owner for the vacancy record of the property. All investors keep a precise record of how their property is doing, showing the tenants' names, the total income, the expenses, and the vacancies. The number of vacancies tells a lot about a property. If the number is high, it means there's something wrong with the property. Ask to see all of the records, analyze them, consider whether you can turn the property around, and then negotiate.

Adding to Property Value Through Renovation

Keep in mind, as you analyze the property, that a few simple projects can make a difference. For instance, a potential tenant who sees a cluttered yard, a "dead" motorcycle or car sitting in the driveway, a junk-filled basement, dirt throughout the hallways and entryway, or worn-out carpeting is not going to be too enthusiastic about moving in. Indeed, any people interested in the apartments in such poor condition may only add to the "junk," and they are not the kind of tenant you want anyway. The point is that taking care of these simple things will enhance the property and will attract a better class of tenants—and a better class of tenants is advantageous for many obvious reasons.

The Simple Paint Job

Probably the least expensive of all renovation projects, the one with the best return for the dollar invested, and the one that can and will enhance a property the most is a simple paint job. The good thing about painting is that expenses are limited to the paint and equipment. The profit comes from doing the work yourself or with family members. The fact is, painting can be done by anyone at any time—over weekends, during vacations, or in your spare time.

Some people like to paint; some don't. It's not what one would call a favorite pastime. For most people, it's a matter of determination: making up their mind that they're going to have to do it and then doing it. It doesn't take an expert or professional, and painting is where the money is.

I can't take the displeasure out of painting, but I can give you some tips to save yourself money.

Exterior Painting

Use white. There are several reasons for this. First of all, when you're finished painting, invariably there's paint left over. If all the leftovers are white, they can be combined and used in the future. When the job is done, find a five-gallon paint pail with a good cover, pour the leftover paint into it, and save it for a future job. Obviously, if you use a different color for each property, you'll end up with partially used paint pails. Another reason for using white is the fact that colored paint fades quickly, which means the property has to be painted more frequently. Finally, when you use white paint, you can "spot-paint" an area so that it's not noticeable; that is, if there's a small amount of paint peeling, you can scrape and paint the spot without painting the entire building. My advice for you as an investor is, then, to stay away from colors.

Interior Painting

All the years I've been in the apartment business, I've used only two colors for interior painting: white, for kitchens and bathrooms, and an off-white, water-based paint. I use this color in every apartment and house and in every room. The reason for using this one color is the same as the reason for using white for all exterior painting: when there are leftovers, they can be consolidated into one can and used for the next paint job. When tenants ask to paint their apartment, I tell them that I will approve the work if they'll do the painting. I then furnish the paint, starting with the leftovers. Incidentally, I use a semigloss, water-based paint for the kitchen and bathrooms and a flat water-based paint for the other rooms. I don't use any oil-based paint.

Vinyl Siding

Of all the improvements I've made in renovating older properties, none has been more advantageous than covering the exterior with vinyl siding (Figure 21-1). The first and foremost reason I say this is that vinyl siding eliminates all, and I mean all, exterior maintenance. I've put vinyl siding on many of my properties, and, since doing so, I haven't had to spend a penny on paint jobs. I had one hail-damage loss on one of the buildings, but the particular siding I had used had a lifetime guarantee, so the siding company put on all new siding.

In addition to vinyl siding's being a money-saver, it enhances the looks and the value of the property substantially. Furthermore, it can be washed, won't chip or peel, won't dent or rust (extreme hail can damage vinyl but hail can also damage wood, aluminum, metal siding, and paint), muffles outside noises, and won't interfere with TV reception (some metal siding can obstruct some TV reception [Figures 21-2 and 21-3]).

Vinyl siding can be purchased in different widths of four, five, or eight inches, and each piece is easily replaceable one at a time. A new piece can be installed in minutes. Unlike paint, vinyl siding always looks new. That means five, 10, or even 15 years down the line (and I've had vinyl siding on some of my properties for over 15 years), the property will still have the same original appearance. There's no depreciation. All

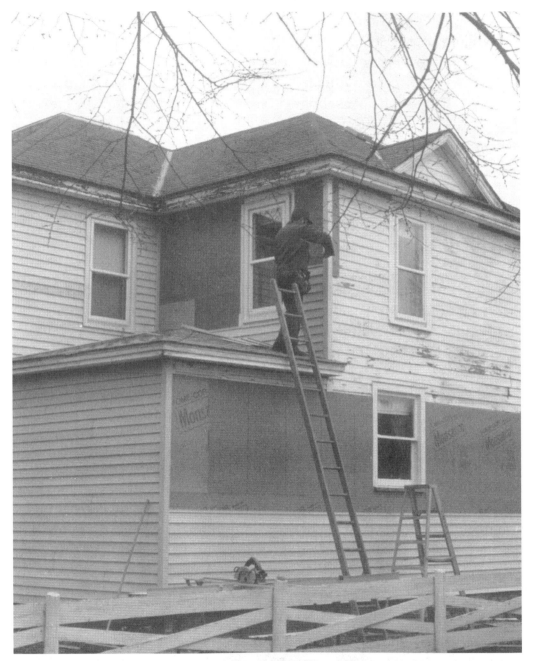

Figure 21-1. As you can see, vinyl siding covers all wood scars, blemishes, and paint chips. The installer here is putting on a layer of Monsanto insulation in addition to the siding, which is an option. Aluminum is put around the soffit and fascia, which eliminates all exterior maintenance.

Figure 21-2. Before: This one-family home is located in a desirable middle-class residential area. The property was in need of improvements, the most conspicuous of which was a paint job. This property, for an investor-renovator, has great potential for improvement and upgrading, and with each improvement will come profit from the added value.

of these features, of course, contribute to the appreciation of your property, which is how money is made in the real estate business.

Is vinyl siding a good investment for your property? It is more expensive than painting; however, once the siding is in place, the exterior will no longer need to be painted. However, here are some other factors to think about:

- Is there a considerable amount of damaged wood siding that needs to be replaced?
- Are there areas of wood rot?

Figure 21-3. After: Here is the same house shown in Figure 21-2 after improvements. The vinyl siding has covered all the scars and blemishes. This now is a first-rate property. Vinyl siding has added thousands of dollars to the value.

By answering these questions, you'll get a better idea of whether siding is a good investment for your property.

Something else to consider is that, if the building is covered with siding—vinyl, aluminum, or metal—it's not necessary to replace any broken or warped pieces of the original siding, nor is it necessary to sand, scrape, clean, or paint. When completed, all defects are covered and covered permanently. Also, vinyl siding is an excellent insulator because it seals all cracks and crevices and becomes an excellent windbreaker. Incidentally, other insulation can be added prior to putting on the siding, as you can see in Figure 21-1.

A good idea when installing siding is to also cover the soffit and fascia with aluminum. This usually can be done by the same contractor. This, of course, eliminates any maintenance, and it is permanent and indestructible coverage (Figure 21-4).

Figure 21-4. In this photograph, vinyl siding is being installed on an apartment building, which, again, eliminates outside maintenance.

Finding Renovation Properties

For the most part, properties that need repair and fixing up are those that have been abandoned, have had poor management and upkeep, or have been foreclosed. These kinds of properties can be found almost anywhere, and they can be single-family homes, duplexes, fourplexes, or apartment buildings. For example, the property in Figure 21-5 has been converted into a threeplex, and that shown in Figure 21-6 has been owned by an investor for many years. He's collected rents, paid off the mortgage, and taken the tax write-off. However, as you can see, the original investor hasn't spent much time or money on upkeep and maintenance. For these reasons, it is a prime example of the kind of property that a new investor can take on and make some money with. A simple exterior upgrading and paint job will add substantially to its value. Sometimes the original investors just don't want to do some of the work—that means that, for the "go-getter" investor, it's time to move.

Figure 21-5. This is a large older home, probably built back in the 1920s as a one-family home. It's been converted into a threeplex and is an example of an affordable property for the small independent investor because of its age.

There are some important aspects of this kind of investment to watch out for. For instance, a key to making the most profit is to find a *low-priced property in a high-priced neighborhood.* Don't, and I repeat, *don't buy a low-priced property in a deteriorating neighborhood.* The reasons, of course, are obvious. Low-priced properties in a deteriorating neighborhood can be losers. As I've said before, there's no sense in buying a $60,000 property, investing $20,000 in renovation, and ending up with a $65,000 property. You want the neighborhood to upgrade the property, not depreciate it.

For example, Figure 21-7 shows a single-family home being renovated. What makes this a good potential investment is that it's located in a decent residential area. In this case, the home adjacent to the investment

Figure 21-6. This property is a fourplex, located in a mixed apartment-residential area, across the street from a church. That church adds to the location in that it increases the property's rentability and enhances its value.

property is in good condition, and, of course, the surrounding properties will upgrade the value of the investment. With some work and effort, this property has the potential for profit, not only from the actual renovation itself but also from the appreciation in value because of the renovation.

A good place to look for renovatable property, as I pointed in Chapter 4, is in viable rural communities. Usually there aren't slums and decaying neighborhoods in smaller communities as there are in urban areas. Figure 21-8 is a good example of an apartment building that needs renovation. There's nothing here that can't be handled by any investor (Figures 21-9 and 21-10). Most of the work is cosmetic, that is, painting and fixing up. Once the new investor acquired clear title to the property, he started renovation. This included exterior and interior work, painting, repairing, new windows, stoves, refrigerators, air conditioners, new carpet, new bathrooms and kitchens, and labor (Figures 21-

Figure 21-7. This single-family home is in the process of being renovated. As you can see, the porch has already been removed. A deteriorating porch can detract from the value of any property and, more often than not, doesn't really add any value. The house is obviously in need of general cleanup and a paint job.

11 and 21-12). Once the renovation was completed, the bank approved a $90,000 loan, which covered the cost of renovation. The total cost of the property came to $96,000. Now there's sufficient income from rental to pay the upkeep, utilities, maintenance, and mortgage payment. Because everything is new, there will be only minimal building maintenance costs for several years. The value of the property, in today's market, is $96,000, and this value will increase with time. All in all, this is a good real estate investment with a bright future.

Figure 21-8. Here is a picture of a property before renovation. This building was built in 1917. It has structurally held up over the years and, as a starter renovation project, was in fairly good condition. The main reason it has held up is because it was built on a solid, stable foundation and basement. The basement, in fact, is free of any defects, is leak-proof, and solid. The three stories of exterior stucco siding are free of any cracks or defects, so it wouldn't be necessary to spend a great deal of money to renovate.

Upgrading to a First-Class Property

Figure 21-13 shows a first-class renovatable property. I say "first-class" because this property, a duplex, is located in a solid middle- to upper-middle-class residential area. In other words, here was a low-priced property in a high-priced neighborhood. In this setting, the only thing that could happen to this property, even with the slightest bit of renovation work, was that it would increase in value; conversely, it would never decrease.

Figure 21-9. This is a rear view of the apartment complex in Figure 21-.8. The old wooden back porches have been removed. The exterior stucco is in good condition, despite its age.

What made this a good investment? This property was built as a three-bedroom duplex back in the 1940s, and the original owner lived in it until his death. During that time there was very little maintenance, as the overgrown evergreen trees illustrate. The owner kept the original cupboards, fixtures, furnace, and electrical service; in fact, nothing was ever remodeled. In truth, remodeling wasn't all that necessary because, you see, there were schoolteachers living in the rentable side so there was very little if any abuse. The property wasn't decaying in any way, nor was it run down. It was simply old and in need of attention and care. For a renovation investor this property (in a community of 15,000) presented an ideal investment.

Figure 21-10. This is an example of the interior rooms in the apartment building shown in Figure 21-8, obviously before renovation. As you can see, nothing has been remodeled in years.

When the owner died, the property went into an estate. The heirs, all living in distant communities, were anxious to get the estate settled so they could get their money. These circumstances meant it was a good time to buy. As it turned out, two brothers, who were contractors, bought the property for $68,000. When the purchase was finalized, they proceeded with renovation. After the renovation, there's no doubt the property will have a value of over $100,000. Figure 21-14 shows the finished exterior of the property in Figure 21-13. Sometimes it doesn't take much to enhance the looks of property. Eliminating the overgrown trees added tremendously to the looks, and the value. It's not difficult to see how much brighter the interior of each room must be since removing the trees. They covered the entire building and detracted from its appearance. Since this is an example of a prime investment property, let me tell you more about it.

Figure 21-11. Here is the property shown in Figure 21-9 after complete renovation. One of the first (and best) conversions in the project was installing gabled roofs. Flat roofs are losers. No matter where you live, flat roofs will eventually leak from the forces of wind, hail, rain, snow, and freezing, and they demand constant repair and replacement.

First, this is a three-bedroom duplex, and three-bedroom rental units are hard to come by. Second, over the years the property did not have hard use; on the other hand, few improvements were made on it during this time. The older kitchens had the original cupboards, and the floors were covered by the original linoleum. Both units still had fuses rather than circuit breakers (Figures 21-15 and 21-16). Although everything was old, I have to tell you it was in A-1 condition. Third, the price of the property, which sold for $68,000, was right. This price was attractive to the contractors because they could do the renovations themselves. As investors, they would gain in two ways: they wouldn't need much capital to make the necessary improvements, and the value would rise quickly since it was on the low end of the scale to begin with. Fourth, and very importantly, the property is located in a middle- to upper-middle class residential neighborhood, with many $150,000-plus homes in the area.

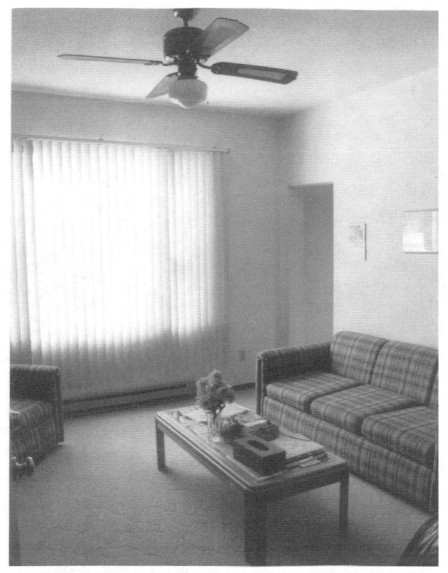

Figure 21-12. These are the same rooms shown in Figure 21-10 after renovation. As you can see, the unit has become very rentable.

Finally, the work that had to be done on the property wasn't extremely expensive: cupboards, new wiring, some new plumbing, interior painting, and carpeting (see Figures 21-17 and 21-18). Once these things were done, each unit could bring in at least $600 per month income. Each unit

Figure 21-13. This is a picture of an investment property before renovation.

is self-sufficient, and each tenant will have to pay his or her own utilities. The only cost to the owner will be taxes and insurance.

Once the improvements were made, the property increased dramatically in value because of its location. This was a gem.

Rejuvenate, Renovate, or Reject

Some properties aren't worth the time and money necessary for renovations. A full-scale renovation can be expensive and time-consuming, so getting involved with a loser can be a costly proposition. If a renovation project becomes a financial loser, it's not only a loser as far as the money and time are concerned, but it's also a loser in that an investor can and will lose interest in real estate investing. That's very important because real estate is just too good a deal to pass up.

And, while I'm on the subject of burnout: it's important for you, as an investor, to know your limitations, both in your work ability and your finances. Before starting a renovation project, have a good idea of

Figure 21-14. This is the finished exterior of the property shown in Figure 21-13.

what repairs are needed and what they'll cost. Ask advice from others. Take a carpenter or a lumberyard manager to the property and have him or her analyze whether it can be a profitable investment.

Advanced Renovation

Some projects take more time, effort, and money than others. Advanced renovation also takes more skills. Therefore, it's a good idea for any investor in real estate to become a jack-of-all-trades. Most entrepreneurs I know who have come up the ladder the hard way have automatically been forced into becoming a jack-of-all-trades. At any rate, what this means is that, as an owner-investor, you can cut costs tremendously by being able to do some of the repair and carpentry work.

Some things that can be done to improve the exterior of the property aren't all that costly. For instance, shutters can add to the looks of

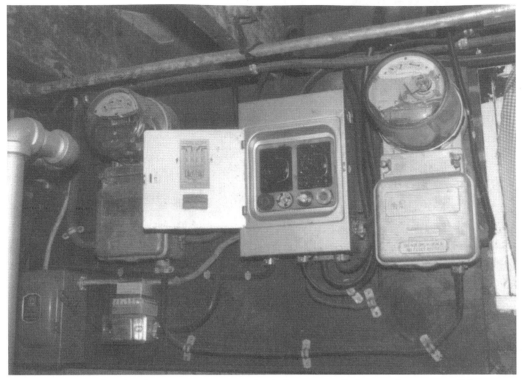

Figure 21-15. The duplex in Figure 21-13 had the original electrical circuitry. It's important to call to your attention, at this point, that in the process of appraising an older building for renovation, a prime concern should be the electrical service. Most of these older buildings still have the old fuses rather than circuit breakers. The conversion process to circuit breakers is of concern because of unforeseen costs. First, it is necessary to have an electrician do the conversion work, and electricians are costly. Second, and this is important to know ahead of time, there's a possibility, when installing a circuit breaker system, that the particular building code may require that the entire building be rewired. This can be so costly that it is not worth the investment.

some buildings. They are comparatively inexpensive and give the property an added touch. However, don't overdo them. Too many can be an added expense and can make the building look gaudy. Don't use wooden shutters; they need constant maintenance and painting. As they weather, they begin to look dingy and depreciate, rather than appreciate, the looks of the property. Vinyl shutters are reasonably priced, don't have to be painted, and can be installed by anyone. Also, most older buildings need window glazing and some window replac-

Figure 21-16. Here is a conversion to circuit breakers in the duplex in Figure 21-13. Fortunately for the investor, it wasn't necessary to rewire the entire building.

ing. A novice can do this work.

Back in the 1950s slate siding was sold to property owners by the carload. The problem with this kind of siding is that it cracks and breaks. This has a tremendous effect on the value of some of these older buildings. As a potential buyer, you can use it as a negotiating factor. Brittle slate siding is virtually impossible to replace or repair. If you already own a property with this siding, don't paint it. It takes gallons of paint, and, once painted, it fades quickly and easily.

Some Final Advice

Listen, in any work you do on your property, it's all right to make a mistake or two. Mistakes are learning experiences, and those are worth a lot when it comes to knowing the real estate business. As you become more

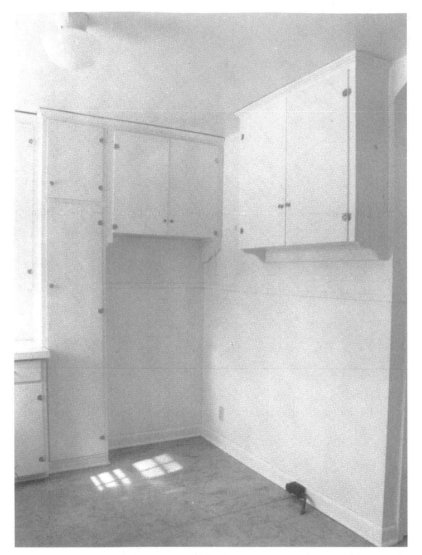

Figure 21-17. There is nothing more appealing to a potential tenant than a clean, neat, well-kept kitchen. That's where the center of life is focused for a lot of people. When there's company, they congregate in the kitchen for their visit. What that means for any apartment owner is that the kitchen should have a good appearance. In this picture of the original kitchen in the property shown in Figure 21-13, you can see a clean, painted, and well-kept area. Obviously, it's not going to be shut down by the city health department. Its overall good appearance can be largely attributed to having had good tenants in the apartment for many years. (They were schoolteachers.) But then, for the renovator, if you look closely, you'll find that the kitchen still has the original inexpensive linoleum floor and that the cupboards, although in good shape, have an old-time look about them.

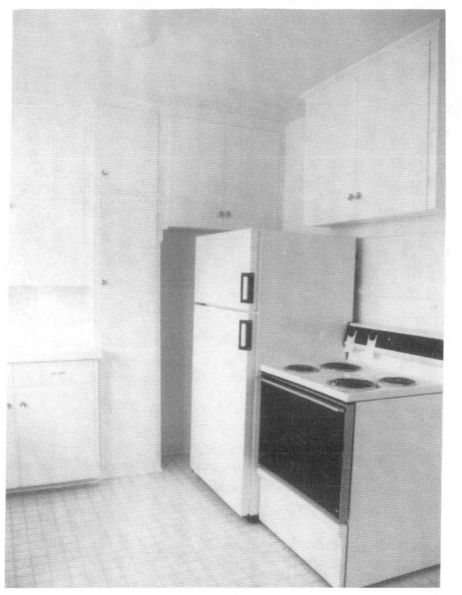

Figure 21-18. This is the finished, renovated kitchen in the property shown in Figure 21-13. Renovation consisted of simple, comparatively inexpensive remodeling: a new floor, new handles on the cupboards, and painting, which has upgraded the rentability of the apartment and the value of the property.

Figure 21-19. This is another complete renovation project. You'll note in the series of pictures (Figures 21-19 through 21-21) how the first picture shows a somewhat run-down complex that obviously was in need of work. The main problem with these buildings was flat roofs. If flat roofs leak, and they usually do, they become a deterio-rating factor of a property unless they are replaced.

successful in the business and the money starts flowing in, then you can sit back, buy more property, hire someone else to do the work, work less yourself, and make more money.

Full-Scale Renovation

Becoming a full-scale (not full-time) renovator can be, and is, a very profitable real estate venture if managed diligently and properly. The secret to the success of the renovation business—and this is advice I usually pass on to the small independent investor—is to know that this is a time-consuming business and that it takes a lot of effort and deter-mination to make it pay. But, as with any other real estate investment, there's no reason that anyone can't do renovating. Figures 21-19 through

Figure 21-20. In this picture, you can see that the owner has started the renovation of the buildings in Figure 21-19. The first job was general cleanup. This alone made a major difference in the look of the property, the value, and its rentability.

21-21 illustrate an average-ordinary-people project. Figure 21-19 shows a sixplex that was run down almost to the point of no return. However, the investor-renovator, who, by the way, is a full-time barber by trade, took on the project on a part-time basis, on weekends, vacations, and days off. Most of the work was done by hired help rather than a contractor. This help cut down on the costs substantially, but the investor had to have everything well planned and coordinated.

What made this property so attractive was the initial purchase price. Here's what happened. In the first place, the apartment building was closed down by the fire marshal. From that point on, everything went downhill. The original investor, an insurance agent, decided to quit making the payments so the bank foreclosed on the property. This took near-

Figure 21-21. The final stages of the renovation of the building in Figure 21-19 consisted of eliminating the flat roofs. The owner also painted the buildings, added a couple of sets of shutters here and there, and generally enhanced the property. As you can see, there's a dramatic difference, which, again, has increased the value of the property as well as its rentability.

ly one year. Next, the bank tried, in vain, to recover some of their losses by selling the property "as is." No one was interested. As bankers, they were not the most astute real estate managers and they couldn't sell the building, so it sat empty for two years. Over that time the taxes kept accumulating, with no rental income, so the bank got further in debt.

Finally, after the year of foreclosure and two years of vacancy, the barber-investor offered to buy the property on these conditions: first, that the bank would finance the renovation and, second, that he would pay all the back taxes. The bank agreed to these terms. The full purchase price for the property was approximately $6,000, the total of the back taxes. The bank, of course, was forced to write off their mortgage loss from the original investor.

Chapter 22

Inexpensive Renovation Projects to Consider

Good Housekeeping

The least expensive improvement, and the most beneficial for any property, is maintaining a junk-free yard and premises. Simple chores such as eliminating weeds, keeping the yard mowed, and trimming the shrubbery can add to the appearance and value of any property.

Interior cleaning is equally important: be sure the hallways, basements, and storage rooms are clean. Most of us have a tendency to overlook some of the clutter. On the other hand, prospective tenants notice this right away. The appearance of the inside of an apartment is very important. Good tenants—the kind you want—are very observant and are quickly turned off by poor housekeeping. All interior housekeeping pays off in a stable and/or appreciating property value, and good clean premises attract good clean tenants. This also applies to front entryways and doors. The first thing new tenants see is the front entry.

Basements often become a catch-all. Tenants come and go and oftentimes leave various items in the basement. Use this space for added profits. First of all, install laundry equipment if it isn't there. This service is very good because tenants don't like to go to a laundromat. Coin-operated equipment is available new and used. The used equipment, which I've bought off and on, serves the purpose. If you're not in a position to lay out the money to buy new equipment, an option is to contact a washer-dryer vendor that will install coin-operated equipment; the usual split is 50/50.

Keeping the Property in Good Condition

Sometimes we go about our business and ignore some of the small repairs that need to be made, thinking nobody else notices them. Yet, some of these things, like a greasy kitchen stove, can turn a prospective tenant off immediately. Once they see this dirt and are turned off, they're gone—there's no second chance. You definitely don't want to lose a good tenant over a small item that can be simply handled.

It's not only important to keep the premises clean and in good repair for prospective tenants, but cleanliness has an overall effect on the value of the property. Here's a case in point. I was contacted by a real estate agent about a sixplex that was listed for sale. When I first looked at the property, I thought it was hopeless. Weeds were growing in the yard, the front entry needed painting, the walls in the hallway had chipped paint, the carpet hadn't been cleaned for years, the mailboxes were dented, and the basement was filled with old mattresses, luggage, cans, and other debris tenants had left. It was about to enter into the slum category.

After looking the property over, I came to the conclusion that, with some cosmetic work, like cleaning up the yard and the building, along with a small amount of painting, the building had the potential to become a good investment. Because of the appearance, the price was comparatively reasonable. As a matter of fact, I'm convinced that if the sellers had taken the time to fix up a few things, the property could have sold for several thousand dollars more than they were asking. At any rate, I did buy the property and since have cleaned, painted, and fixed it up, and it's turned out to be an excellent investment. The point of this story is this: take good care of your property on a regular basis; don't let things accumulate until they get out of hand and it's too late.

Tenants like to have a secure place to live, so keep working locks on the doors and windows. (Incidentally, it's a good idea to keep one apartment key for yourself. Periodically, tenants will call and say they've locked their keys in their apartment.)

To squeeze more profits out of the property, make sure that the building, the windows and doors, and the attic are well insulated and don't leak. Simple things like stripping doors and windows against air leaks are inexpensive. Most weather-stripping can be installed by a novice, and it doesn't take too much skill to rent a blower and add attic insulation.

Cutting the Cost of Painting

I've purposely left painting for last as one of the sweat equity benefits. Painting can and will add immeasurably to the overall appearance of the property, both inside and out. More importantly, a paint job can increase the value of a property significantly, probably more than any other individual upgrading project, and painting is one of the least expensive methods of upgrading real estate. Not only is painting inexpensive, it's a job that anyone can do, which means that family members can pitch in and help.

Most people don't like to paint; however, it's something a conservative or, let's say, a cheapskate, investor can do to increase profits. This is a simple fact of life for the real estate investor who wants to make money and get ahead.

Here's how to save time, work, and energy when it comes to painting. First of all, get the tenants to do the work if it's an inside job. Offer to buy the materials if they do the work, and they usually will. I find that tenants are happy to paint because they can see how nice the apartment looks once the job is done. I also find tenants will do other work once they see the benefits. I've had tenants shampoo carpet, clean hallways, and do some minor remodeling. I had one tenant who was so good at keeping up his apartment I gave him the OK to put in a small workshop in the basement where he kept his tools and equipment. It didn't take long until he was fixing things for other tenants, as well as doing minor repair work around the building. I think he did it because he was treated with the best of consideration, and I certainly let him know how much I appreciated what he was doing. He never once asked for money.

Now, getting back to painting. If the tenant won't do the work, hire family members. Avoid hiring professional painters if possible, to save money. Next, as a money-saver, go to your local paint store and offer to do all of your business there. Then ask for a discount. Painting contractors get a discount—there's no reason that you shouldn't have the same. In fact, shop around, and you'll find a paint store that will give you a discount. Finally, take good care of your brushes, pans, rollers, and other equipment. If you don't, you'll be buying new materials every time you paint.

Regarding the paint itself, I've found that it's best to avoid colors. I use only white for exterior painting as well as for the kitchens and bathrooms. For everything else in the apartments, all of them, I use an off-white color. If you paint every building white, and use only off-white for all interior rooms, you can store what's left over and use it again on the next job. Then there's no waste. In addition, white doesn't fade as colors do.

I save all the leftovers of off-white and use them for filling nail holes as well as for spot-painting in places such as behind a sofa or in places where the paint has been chipped away. Another benefit of using only one color, an off-white, is that, when an apartment has to be repainted, it requires only one coat.

I've always been convinced that a bad paint job is one of the best bargaining points for a buyer. Therefore, if you plan to show your property, it pays to paint it first.

An Ongoing Process

It's a good idea to upgrade apartments and properties on an ongoing basis. Don't let things slide; pretty soon they can become overwhelming and out of control. Set aside time periodically to check the properties and do the work that needs to be done.

Once a renovation project has been completed on a property, the next step is to start the process all over again. If the property is producing a net profit and you don't need the money for living expenses, my advice is to put it back into the property. In so doing, the new renovation adds more value to the property and rents can be raised, and this then becomes an ongoing process. For example, let's say an apartment has an older bathroom that needs upgrading. Or maybe the kitchen needs remodeling. Either of these can be done on a part-time basis without a lot of capital. The odds are pretty good that a dollar invested in renovation will earn at least two dollars in property value.

There are some projects that anyone can do that will enhance the appearance as well as the value of properties. I have discussed some of these before, but let's take another look.

Exterior Cleanup

The yard and premises can be rejuvenated at no cost simply by cleaning out trash, junk, and weeds and by growing grass, eliminating sucker trees in the yard or around the foundation, and starting inexpensive shrubbery.

Interior Cleanup

Housekeeping is important to rental property. Clean, well-lighted hallways, basements, and storage rooms are not hard to maintain. I know some managers, including myself, who let things go for a period of time and pretty soon there's such an accumulation of junk that it becomes a chore. We all seem to get accustomed to looking at a cluttered mess and doing nothing about it. It's carelessness, and it's poor housekeeping. I know this: a potential tenant looking at the property will notice it immediately and will be turned off.

Refuse

Garbage-collection areas and garbage cans can give a bad impression if left without care. This can diminish the overall appearance of the property and depreciate its value. Keeping the area clean, neat, and in good shape is neither expensive nor time-consuming, and a new garbage can periodically is not an expensive item either.

Front Entry and Doors

One of the first impressions a potential tenant gets of a property is the front entry. Make sure it's clean, well kept, and well lighted. Paint whenever necessary to make the entry more attractive. Have a clean and adequate mailbox for each tenant.

Basement

Basements become catch-alls in apartment buildings. Tenants come and go, and, as they do, they leave various items, from boxes and cans to mattresses and davenports.

Inside Apartment Cleanup

A dirty, grimy kitchen and bathroom can be a real turnoff to a potential tenant. It takes very little effort and time, and practically no money, to keep these areas in good shape. Here's a list of things to keep clean:

- kitchen cupboards
- corners
- sinks, tubs, and toilets
- floors
- stoves and refrigerators
- carpets

   Remodeling a kitchen can be inexpensive and adds to the attractiveness and rentability of an apartment. Consider replacing older, wooden kitchen cupboards with metal ones. Also think about replacing the old cast-iron sink with a stainless steel sink. With each added improvement, there's the potential of increasing the rent.

The bathroom is another room that can be inexpensively upgraded. A new toilet seat can make a world of difference in the general appearance and attractiveness of a bathroom. Like the kitchen, it should be kept clean, especially at the time of a tenant turnover.

Locks and Security

People like to have a secure home, so it makes sense to have good working locks on the doors and windows.

Insulation and Energy-Saving Devices

Simple energy-saving steps, like stripping doors and windows against air leaks, are inexpensive. Most weather-stripping can be installed by a novice. It's also possible for an amateur to install attic insulation by renting an insulation blower, available at your lumberyard.

Chapter 23

Self-Management
and Sweat Equity

By now you should be well aware of the fact that you're entering into, or are already involved in, a dynamic and exciting business that can have a dramatic impact on your future. For this reason, you should consider real estate a business, whether it's part-time or full-time, not a hobby.

When I first went into the business, I more or less treated it rather casually. I figured it was something I could do at my leisure on weekends, holidays, and vacations. This concept of part-time involvement is partially true because most of the work can be done on a part-time basis. Still, it must be treated with a serious business sense and attitude. (Not so serious, however, that you get anxiety attacks or ulcers.) At any rate, keep attitude toward your real estate on a business basis, but don't let it interfere with your personal life. Better yet, let the family become involved with you.

As I got established in the business and started to accumulate more property, it didn't take long to realize that the real estate represented quite an investment. The equity began building, along with appreciation, and that represented wealth and money, considerably more than I had before. I quickly discovered that my net worth, at least on paper, was increasing dramatically, almost on a monthly basis, every time I made a payment on the mortgages. I then decided these investments weren't by any means a hobby but instead a viable and substantial business that represented savings and security. For that reason I became serious about it.

Since then, needless to say, I no longer treat this business casually, as a hobby, or even as a sideline. It became first and foremost in my mind.

Despite the need for a serious attitude about the business, it is a business that can be done on a part-time basis. Here's how it can work. Periodically take a day or weekend to catch up on the various demands of the property, kind of a fix-up day or weekend. Once the work is done and everything is caught up, you can sit back and relax and wait for the next list of things to do. In this way, the operation doesn't become an overwhelming burden.

Make sure you do take care of the various problems because, if you don't, your tenants will think you don't care. If they get the impression that you don't care, they won't care either.

Let's Talk About Sweat Equity

Sweat equity is free. It may take a little perspiration but you can't lose. Sweat equity simply means doing your own work and, thereby, increasing the net worth or value of the property. This means upgrading your property, fixing, painting, cleaning, or whatever it takes to improve it. Usually sweat equity doesn't take that much cash, maybe some paint or some hardware replacement or whatever, but there's no major expenditure involved.

Your Savings and Investment: Primarily Your Time and Work

As one watches the TV skits about buying real estate (the get-rich-quick shows), you get the impression that it's simply a matter of going out, buying property (some say for nothing down), and then sitting back and watching the money roll in. That's simply not the way things work. The fact is that real estate management becomes a serious business and takes work. There's no easy way out. If you want to make money in this business, you're going to have to make up your mind that it's a part of your financial career, and, like any job, you have to work at it. That's the bad news.

The good news is that this business is not a time-consuming job. All of the work can be done several ways. First, management means buying on the right terms, renting to the right tenants, and taking care of the tenants. Next, it's a matter of taking care of the property, as we said, on weekends, evenings, or holidays and vacations.

Remember something important: your only investment that has created this substantial savings account is your time and work, in addition to your down payment. Always keep in mind that, as long as the rent checks come in each month and pay off your mortgage, then your contribution to this savings, that of management, should be easy.

Good management practices can prevent a lot of problems. If you're serious about the investment business, take the time to learn the business and learn how to take care of the property. If you let small repair tasks go without attention, they will eventually become disasters, which could mean financial losses. Here's an example of what I mean.

I know an investor who bought five duplexes, all in a cluster. He did a great job for the first four to five years, but then he became lax and careless about taking care of the property. He let things get run down, didn't mow the yards, didn't paint, and neglected the tenants' complaints. Eventually the good tenants moved out, and the money quit flowing, which started an avalanche of trouble. As the problems kept piling up, he lost interest and began treating the property with disdain; in fact, he totally ignored it. Next, the properties turned into slums. Persistent vacancies occurred, and the tenants living there didn't pay their rent because he wouldn't make repairs. The entire operation got out of hand. The last I heard, he was going to let the property go back on a mortgage foreclosure. The once-successful business had become a virtual sinkhole.

Making Money by Doing the Work Yourself

I know I told you that 95 percent of your involvement would be mental and about 5 percent physical. With real estate you become involved with both kinds of work, but at least you have a choice in that you can determine just how much time, work, and effort you want to put into the business. Many types of chores must be done in managing rental properties, and whichever chores you can do yourself will save you money, and those savings can make a difference in your profit. It's called "sweat equity," but it's also called "money." Take a look at the following list to see what you're willing to do instead of hiring someone:

- collecting rents
- bookkeeping
- paying bills
- cleaning hallways and laundry room
- cleaning vacant apartments
- making minor repairs
- painting, inside and out
- mowing lawns
- shoveling snow

If we don't do the work, what's the alternative? Hired help, and hired help costs money, which eats into the profits. Now, it's nice to call someone up and ask him or her to fix this or that, but what happens sometimes is that we become complacent. In the real estate business, it's pretty easy to become "old, fat, and lazy." Pretty soon we think it's easier to hire someone to do the work.

To give you an idea of costs, real estate managerial firms charge anywhere from 5 to 15 percent of the gross income to manage properties. Not only is this costly, but hired managers rarely take care of the property as well as you would. They tend to be more lax, take a shortcut whenever they can, or just don't do whatever needs to be done. Hired managers often overlook repairs until they become real problems. They fix only what has to be fixed and let other things slide.

Then there are professional repairers. Repairers are not cheap. I've been in this business for many years and have experienced a moderate amount of success. I could easily afford to pay a repairer. However, as I look at the basic reason for my being in business, that is, to make a profit, I find that being my own manager and repairer is the best investment I could have made. To this day, I still do some of my own repair work, and I know this cost savings adds to my financial well-being. When I do the repairs, I know they're done right. When the entire operation is in good order and things are running smoothly, then I know I've made the right choice, investing in real estate. And there's no doubt in my mind that if I can do these things anyone can.

Incidentally, you can pay yourself for the work you do on your own property in the form of a payroll check and charge this expense to the business.

Getting It Fixed Right the First Time

When repairing something—whether it is a sink, a closet door, a window, or drapery rods—fix it right, and make the repair strong, durable, and long-lasting. Tenants don't take care of things the way owners do. For instance, if you're putting in a towel rack and it doesn't seem strong, take the time and effort to make it stronger. Maybe you will need larger screws, or whatever, but fix it right. In that way you're not going to have to go back later and fix it again. Returning to make the same repairs over again is costly not only in terms of money, but in time and energy. Conserving your personal energy will help you avoid burnout.

"Nuts-and-Bolts" Ideas That Save Time and Money

Don't overfix. You shouldn't install a chandelier where a simple light fixture would work. The chandelier won't add to the value of the property, nor will it enable you to increase the rent.

When remodeling or renovating, buy as many products as possible from sales, such as closeouts, crazy days, garage sales, foreclosures, church bazaars, and auctions. Always keep your eyes open for building materials. If you don't buy on sale and you use the same hardware store, appliance store, or lumberyard all the time, ask that merchant for a discount. Tell him or her that you're in the real estate investment business.

Another idea that can save you time and money is this: keep a small tackle box or toolbox filled with assorted screws, bolts, and nuts for when you have to do general maintenance work. If you're working in an apartment and you need a screw or bolt and don't have one handy, you'll have to make a trip to the store, so this little idea can be a time saver.

Another time and energy saver: if you own several apartment units, make a list of the various repairs and tasks that need attention. Then pick a day or a weekend and do them all at once. Once you get in the swing of things and start doing the work, everything seems to flow and work for you. You'll see progress being made, and you'll feel good about getting these jobs done.

Check each apartment when there's a vacancy. (It is easier to fix up an unoccupied apartment.) Also make sure the apartments are fresh and clean—places you personally would live in.

Learning Some Plumbing Skills

Probably 80 percent of all tenant service calls are for plumbing, leaks, backups, flushing, and repairs. Here's what you'll hear:

- The toilet is plugged.
- The toilet keeps leaking.
- The sewer is plugged.
- The kitchen sink or bathroom shower faucet is leaking.
- The garbage disposal doesn't work.
- There's no hot water.
- The water heater leaks.

I'm sure I don't have to tell you how expensive it is to hire help to do these types of repairs. Because of this cost, I've learned some basic plumbing skills so that I can take care of the calls on my own. It's not necessary to become a full-fledged plumber, but there are some things any handyman can do.

The National Retail Hardware Association, 5822 West 74th Street, Indianapolis, IN 46278 (www.nrha.org) has 51 "how-to" brochures on topics such as "How to Unstop Clogged Drains" and "How to Fix Toilets and Sewers." These books are comparatively inexpensive, and if you don't want to spend the money, check out the books from your local library.

The following are some "how-to" things that anyone can do.

"Roto-Rooter"

If you own several apartment units, you might want to consider buying a small Roto-Rooter. Used ones cost about $275. One service call from a professional plumber costs $40 to $90, and, maybe, in some cities more than that. Ninety percent of the time the drain is clogged because of tree roots. Simply run the Roto-Rooter through once to clean them out. Root killer costs $9.95 per jug, which is enough to unplug a drain. If the tree roots become a perpetual problem, have one of the tenants flush root killer down the drain every two weeks or so. Be sure it's done at night so there's the least amount of flushing. In that way the killer has a chance to stay in the pipes and work overnight.

The other 10 percent of the time that the drain is plugged is usually because of sanitary napkins that clog the drain. In this case, put a note in each bathroom to the tenants: do not flush sanitary napkins down toilet.

I've learned—the hard way, of course—that generic toilet paper doesn't dissolve. Because of this, it can get caught in the drainpipe, especially around tree roots. If you have a tenant using generic toilet paper, ask him or her to change to a brand name.

Leaky Faucets

Leaky faucets are common occurrences. The main cause of leaks is that the rubber gaskets wear out and have to be replaced. This job is fairly simple and can be done by anyone. Keep an assortment of gaskets in your toolbox so you don't have to run to the store every time. By the way, when making the repair, don't forget to shut off the water before disconnecting the faucet.

There are times when the entire faucet has worn out and has to be replaced. In this case, take the worn-out faucet to the hardware store so you're sure you get the right size for replacement. The job is comparatively simple and, again, can be done by anyone.

Toilet Flushers

Inside the tank there's a rubber ball cock that wears out and has to be replaced frequently, which is not a difficult job. Again, don't forget to shut off the water; then remove the worn-out stopper. It costs about $40 to have a plumber do this simple job.

Water Heaters

Water heaters can be repaired. The main cause of an electric water heater defect is a burned-out heating element. These parts can be replaced by anyone. Here's how. Shut off the water, and turn off the electricity. Take the water pressure off the tank by opening a faucet after the water's been turned off. Most tanks have a faucet at the bottom. Turn this on and drain the water out; the tank doesn't have to be drained completely. Then, with a strong wrench, take out the electrical unit and replace it. Sometimes this electrical unit is in there very tightly, so you may need a hammer and chisel to get it loose. Once the new element is in place, be sure it's tight and doesn't leak.

This is only a general overview of some of the various tasks that an owner-investor can do to save money by not having to hire high-priced help. As you get involved in the business, you'll find many more simple tasks that you can do yourself and save money. And, remember, you're in this business to make money.

Replacing Carpeting

Carpeting is one other inexpensive method of upgrading property. When carpeting is worn out and dirty, it's best to replace it. The minute potential tenants walk into an apartment, the first thing they see is the carpeting. If it's bad, they'll be turned off immediately. On the other hand, new carpeting can make the inside of an apartment, no matter how old it might be, look fresh, clean, and new. It's a sound investment.

Getting Bids

When doing any improvement on your property that represents a sizable amount of money, whether it's a major overhaul, revamping of the interior, installation of new electrical service, or general work, get more than one bid. If you don't get more than one bid, it's possible that your one and only friendly contractor will *eventually* take advantage of this friendship and start charging a little more than he or she should. Bids will keep that contractor honest, friend or not.

To sum up, sweat equity is work, but it's a moneymaker for any conscientious, serious real estate investor, and it works.

Chapter 24

Enhancing Profits Through Financial Management

I'd like to tell you how to operate a real estate business, or any other business for that matter, without bookkeeping, payroll, income-tax reports, and all the other paperwork that goes along with the operation. As we all know, however, that's not possible. That being the case, the next best thing is to find a way to keep the paperwork as simple and uncomplicated as possible. Let's start with bookkeeping.

Hiring a Bookkeeper

You can be assured that, by using an accountant or a certified public accountant (CPA), you're going to end up with an elaborate double-entry bookkeeping system, and it's going to cost money. Not only that, but it's possible that the system will be something you might not understand. Don't be bamboozled into thinking you need a high-priced and time-consuming bookkeeping system.

To avoid costly accounting services, I developed my own plan, and it has worked for years. I've used this system with one property, and I've used it with multiple properties. My plan is simple and inexpensive, and it doesn't require an accountant.

First of all, I use a checkbook. I have a 9½" x 11" three-ring bound checkbook. Each page consists of three checks. Each time I pay a bill, I enter the transaction by writing the reason for the check on the stub of the checkbook, along with the location of the property. At the end of the year, I simply add up the expenses from the stubs. I also staple the receipts right to the stub for which the check was written; thus I have a complete record of the transaction. I also record on the check stub the rental income. I keep a monthly ledger of the tenant's rent so I can cross-check and make sure each month that the rent has been received. This is a simple, uncomplicated system, but it works.

By keeping the accounting system comparatively simple and easy, I have more time to devote to profitable ventures, such as looking for ways to cut costs, finding new properties to buy, and actually caring for the properties I own. Recognize and use your own creative skills, no matter what phase of the business you are in. Everyone has the ability to build their own program, whether it's bookkeeping, managing, or buying real estate.

With all that said, if you're on a computer, that's a whole different program, and I can't help you.

Keeping Financial Records

Although I advocate keeping simple records, I also advocate keeping good, understandable, and easily available records. You need them for your own financial report and for your tax records. In case of an IRS audit, you don't want to be searching all over and not finding the records that give you the needed tax write-off. After all, that's a major part of the real estate investment business, and it's money in the bank.

I do believe that an audit is a fairly remote possibility for the small investor. If you're honest about your deductions, there's no reason to fear an audit. I was audited once, a number of years ago. The IRS found nothing at fault, and I'm convinced the reason was the fact that I had good, clear, and precise records readily available. I found that the IRS is concerned about two items when they do a real estate investment audit, other than the basic concern of honesty. One is that you have receipts proving the respective expenditures. The other concern has to do with the price you paid for the property. That price determines your depreciation, which, as I said before, is an important part of the real estate investment business. The IRS knows this, and that's why they want the proof. Remember, in that price there are three items: the cost of the land, the cost of the building, and the cost of the personal property. There's a difference in the depreciation time of the building and the personal property, and, of course, there's no depreciation allowance for the land itself.

Keeping Solid Proof of Any Questionable Expenditures

As we all know, in any business there are perquisites, or "perks." Perks are oftentimes looked at by the IRS with some mistrust, and, if they're overdone, they could call for an audit.

Here's an example of what I mean. I have a good friend in the real estate business who likes to travel. Whenever he can, he'll attend real estate seminars in Acapulco, Hawaii, St. Thomas, or any other exotic place, especially in the winter since he's a Midwesterner. He has every right in the world to attend these meetings and every right to charge the expenses to his real estate investment business if he actually did attend the meetings for his business. But if the meetings are secondary and aren't attended, and the meetings are really an excuse for a vacation, the IRS will come down hard. On the other hand, if you find yourself in need of such a conference, by all means go.

If your spouse is an officer or co-owner of your real estate business and is involved in the business, then he or she also has a right to attend with his or her expenses charged to the real estate business. But be sure your spouse does attend the meetings.

I've told you that you can go. I've also told you that you can charge the expenses of this trip to your real estate business. I also want to tell you that the IRS has some reservations about perks and these kinds of trips. Since this is the case, here are some tips to follow.

When attending these meetings, keep an accurate and precise diary of the events, which should include your complete daily activities, the meetings attended, the subject of the meetings, the names of the speakers, and the precise record of the expenses incurred each day along with the receipts of the expenditures. If by chance the IRS audits your records, you'll have positive proof of your deductions—deductions, I might add, that are justified and correct.

Make certain that you keep precise records of all other deductions, too. If you travel to and from your home to your property for work, the cost of this travel is a deduction; also any expenses incurred on the job are deductible since these are a legitimate part of your business. Take them—it's money in your pocket sanctioned by the income-tax laws.

Dealing with the Business Payroll

Because of the controversies involving various potential federal appointees, you've probably become aware that, if you hire people and put them on a payroll, you will have considerable expenses. Those expenses, such as Social Security and unemployment insurance, as well as the costs of maintaining the income-tax records, can devour the profits of the real estate business, and you will want to avoid them. In the small real estate business, there's no need to hire people as employees. It's best to hire independent contractors. Have a complete understanding with them before the job starts that they are not working on an hourly basis but on a contract basis, per job. It's not a bad idea at all to have the contract drawn up in writing so there's no misunderstanding.

Tenants as Employees

Again, you want to avoid the expenses of a payroll; however, tenants often are eager to work on their own apartments. Tenants will sometimes paint, clean, fix, and repair. Qualified tenants can also make good property managers. They can clean halls, show apartments to prospective tenants, and make sure everything is in order and operating smoothly. Again, avoid the payroll. Talk to your accountant about how this can be worked out with a deduction in their rents.

Family Members as Employees

I've given you a lot of advice here about avoiding a payroll. The next thing I'm going to do is give you advice that conflicts with what I've just said: a family payroll is a good real estate investment. Let me explain. If you have qualified family members who are school-age (high school or college) and who want to work, use them in the business. It's an excellent opportunity for them to earn college education money with pretaxed dollars. That is, if you put them on the payroll, you pay taxes only once and you get the deduction. On the other hand, if you use your personal income to pay school expenses, those expenses are not deductible.

Family members can paint, fix, clean, mow lawns, or do any of the work needed around investment properties. If they are away at college, have them work on weekends, holidays, and vacations. Not only is this a good moneymaker for your family business, but your children can receive an invaluable real estate education. I've even used my children as apartment managers, giving them decision-making positions. This experience has enhanced their real estate skills, and, sometime in the future, this experience can—and will—pay off, either in the job market or in personal and individual investments. It's a great learning experience for them.

Bean Counting

Bean counters are the shrewd business managers who know how to squeeze out profits. They don't let anything slip through the cracks. Bean counting means not paying $119 for something that costs $99. They are competent fiscal managers who know how to cut costs, scrutinize expenses, and make sure a dollar spent gets a dollar returned.

Operating as a bean counter means constantly shopping for bargains. It means chiseling the price whenever and wherever you are buying materials and equipment, labor and parts, or real estate itself. The epitome of the bean counter was a guy named Ben Franklin, who said, "A penny saved is a penny earned." Watching the expenses on small items pays off handsomely in the profit picture.

Bean Counting Insurance Costs

Insurance is a highly competitive business. There are many agents out there, and most of them would like to write a policy for your real estate business. Therefore, shop around, contact several agents, negotiate, and then get bids. There's no reason to take the first agent's offer, unless it's the best.

Also, check the deductible clause of your insurance policies. I was able to save 20 percent of the premium cost by increasing the deductible from $100 to $500. Most small, independent real estate investors, like me, fix wind-torn doors or broken windows and usually don't file the small claims. I figure the principal reason I have insurance is to cover major losses.

Monthly Premium Payments

Making insurance payments monthly, rather than yearly, doesn't save money, but doing so can certainly help the cash flow. Ask your agent to carry your premium account on a 30-day monthly pay plan. That way, there's no large premium due. However, be sure your agent will carry this type of a payment without an interest charge.

Incidentally, it's a good idea to have only one agent. That agent is apt to treat your business more fairly and with greater concern about costs.

The Financial Drain of Status Symbols

We're back to the car one more time. It's important enough to go over again. I can tell you that years ago I was a status seeker, and at the time I thought the most important thing in my life was being able to impress people with the kind of a car I drove. I wish someone had hit me over the head to wake me up to the futility of buying new cars every time I turned around. If I had bought real estate instead of all those cars, I would have been a millionaire many times over. But no, I got caught in the new-car trap and bought cars and cars and cars … ad infinitum.

The remarkable thing is that, in one year, one car wasn't enough. First I bought a new Buick Special. Then months later, that same year, I had to have a bigger 1953 Buick Roadmaster, the biggest and most expensive model. I ended up with a multitude of monthly payments and a worn-out car. The worst part of it was that the car dealer got my money and bought real estate. Today he's wealthy.

Owning new, flashy, expensive cars, like other insignificant status symbols, is part of a game some people play. If you play right along with them, it will be hard to resist the temptation to spend beyond your means, and you may end up comparatively broke. I know this: these "things" will keep you working extra hours all your life, and I can guarantee you that buying status symbols that are too expensive in relation to your income will keep you from buying investment real estate.

The next time you're in the showroom of your friendly new-car dealer, ask yourself, "Am I buying this car to impress my neighbors and peer group? Or am I buying this car because I need it? Will my family be better off after I buy the car?" When you've answered these questions to your satisfaction, then ask one more question of yourself: "If I give my money to the car dealer, how much investment property is he going to buy with my money?"

This is a how-to book. My job is to show you how to make money in the real estate business. I would also like to show you, in some way, how to manage your money. So, my advice is this: buying expensive cars is futile. If you've learned nothing more from this book than this, then I have succeeded.

I know I needed a learning experience back some years ago, or at least a lecture about how cars would drain my finances. But there was no one around and no how-to book for me to read. I was unable to see the waste in spending so much money on a horrendous, meaningless, shallow status symbol. But as I have told you from the beginning of this book, my purpose here is to instruct you on how to gain financial independence and establish a good savings account, in part by learning from my mistakes and experience. Here it is. Take a hard-learned lesson from me: don't get caught in the "car trap"; it's the height of stupidity. Remember, I said the real estate business is a brainpower business. Here's a chance to use that intelligence.

One last thing: buy real estate now as an investment, and some day you can buy, with cash, the finest luxury automobile made, and you can buy it for your own self-satisfaction, not as a status symbol. All you need to do is wait. Take your time. Real estate investing can and will pay off for you. Car buying won't. End of car lecture.

Obtaining Investment Capital

I regularly upgrade my apartments. I do this for several reasons:

- The rents can be increased as the property is improved.
- All improvements increase the value of the property for future sales.
- All improvements become a part of the tax write-off benefit.

Upgrading and improving apartments takes money, sometimes extra money, more than is brought in from the rents. For the most part, the income just covers the cost of operation, and it isn't very often, for the starter, that there's a profit at the end of the year. Actually the profit comes in the form of the appreciation, equity, and depreciation tax write-off.

Incidentally, let me point out here something that I think is important: If there is a profit after all expenses are paid, I highly recommend putting that profit right back into the business, either into new property or into improving the property you own.

So, if there is no money from the property income, where does this extra money come from to make the improvements?

Using Your Own Money for Investments

Should a small, independent, part-time real estate investor use his or her own money to renovate and repair real estate and to buy additional properties? This question is especially important if it means taking on more indebtedness. I don't have a clear and concise answer to this question. The only answer I can give you is that each person has to use his or her own judgment and consider whether or not this money spent can be used without creating family financial hardship. But there are several options to consider.

Let's take a $100,000 investment property, financed at 6.5 percent interest, amortized over 30 years. The payment is $632.07 per month. The total for the 30 years is $227,543. Now add only $200 per month to the payment, which would make it $832.07 rather than $632.07. The $200 is about what one would invest in an IRA savings account. But, with this $200-per-month additional payment on the mortgage, the property is paid off in just 16.25 years, rather than 30 years. Also, rather than paying $227,543, the total with this additional $200 payment per month is $162,138. In that 16.25 years you will have spent $39,000, but you will have saved $65,405 in interest on the original mortgage.

Another thought to consider is that, if you're a young starter investor, raising a family, it might be best to spend your money on your family needs. On the other hand, if you're a middle-aged investor buying property during your peak earning years, you might want to get the property paid off more quickly and have the rental income as personal income with no mortgage payment.

No matter how you invest the money—the bank's, the tenant's, or your own—there's no better place in the world to invest than real estate. It's secure, safe against inflation, has earning power that never ends as long as the property is taken care of, and has income that can't be taken away. And it's a business you can call your own.

The Wisdom of Assuming More Debt

Probably as tough a decision as any of us can make is whether we should take on more debt along with more monthly payments. That's especially true for those of us who've had to work hard to accumulate and build whatever security we have. But you will find, as you progress and grow in the real estate business, that there will be times when you need additional money. It may be for buying more property, renovating property, or buying new appliances and equipment. When this does happen, we are besieged with doubt and anxieties. We often think, "Where will the money come from to meet the payments?" Or we might think, "What if the tenants quit paying their rent, or they all decide to move out and then there's no income?"

Let me address this issue and allay your anxieties. If you've invested in the right location, if you've taken care of your property *and* tenants, if you've handled your finances in a proper manner and have not lived beyond your means, and if you're serious about building and accumulating wealth, then the real estate will take care of itself. It just works that way.

Most of the investors I know have never experienced a rash of vacancies. And most of the investors I know have always been able to come up with the money they need, and most of the investors I know have succeeded in this business. On the other hand, I have seen some investors who have bought property in the wrong neighborhood or community; I've seen some investors who didn't learn the business and paid too much for real estate; I've seen investors who didn't know what they were getting into; I've seen investors who were undercapitalized; and I've seen investors who have lived too extravagantly and used the real estate money for their own personal spending. Those investors have had vacancies because they didn't take care of their tenants. Ultimately, their mismanagement led to financial problems. Then they went broke.

Those investors who have used just plain old common sense have avoided most of the problems. The fact is that the good manager using common sense is always out there looking for good investments. He or she knows how to handle finances and takes debt in stride because it ultimately means more profits.

My advice is this. When you are making plans for a loan, know what you are doing. You can learn by consulting with your banker, an associate, a friend, or a family member. Go over the investment program, and know how the debt will be paid off. Ask for advice from people you respect and trust. This knowledge can be very helpful. Once you feel confident about what you're doing and you know that the plan looks good, then you're on the way. If it looks good, don't procrastinate. Procrastination only creates more anxieties and becomes an emotional sinkhole. And, while I'm at it, don't ask for advice from negative people.

Seeking Additional Investment Capital

As you start searching for investment capital, you'll soon discover that financial assets speak loudly and with power. That power, borrowing power, represents the ability to get loans. No one knows this more or better than your local banker. Your real estate represents money and borrowing power. I talked about this before, but let's go over it one more time because it is the heart of the matter and the source of building and accumulating wealth:

- *Equity.* Rents, other people's money, pay off the mortgage, which builds equity.
- *Sweat equity.* This is your own time, work, and effort invested in the property, which increases its value.
- *Appreciation.* Time, the natural ally of real estate, along with good care of the property, increases its value.
- *Inflation.* The value of real estate increases with natural inflation; there's no money involved on the part of the investor.

All of these aspects of real estate investing increase the value of the property. As the value increases, so does the net worth of the owner and subsequently his or her borrowing power. The borrowing power is what the banker needs to insure the bank loan.

Obviously, we all know that banks are in business to make a profit. That profit is based on earning interest on good loans and points. We've talked about these before. Also, as you can now see, if you have the borrowing power, you can go into a bank and demand a loan to fit your needs, with *low* interest and no points. That's the power of money.

Partnerships

One option some people have used to acquire investment capital is taking on a partner. I'm skeptical about this practice and don't recommend it. It may work in equity sharing but that's about it. Usually people go into partnerships for financial or managerial support. This support more often than not does not materialize. When the partnership starts, everything is fine. There's a camaraderie at the beginning, and all goes well. The partners get along well, and the work is equally shared. Usually in partnerships the spouses will pitch in, and everything seems to work well. The partners feel good about each other. However, as things progress, this good feeling is short-lived. One partner eventually stops doing his or her share of the work. The other partner takes notice, and pretty soon one of the spouses is saying, "Why should we do all the work and not get paid?" About then there's a breakdown in communication, and the partnership weakens. Subsequently, the moral, financial, managerial, and work structure of the partnership collapses.

The next stage of events in a partnership breakdown affects the property. The apartments and buildings are ignored by the partners and their spouses. No one takes care of the vacancies as they should be. Ultimately the property is vacated, and, as this happens, the value decreases substantially and has to be sold for little or nothing. The end result is the real estate is gone, the money is gone, and the friendship is terminated. No one gains.

There's something else to keep in mind regarding a partnership: you can be held liable for your partner's debts. This can include personal and/or business obligations and civil and criminal charges. This fact alone should discourage anyone from thinking about a partnership. Listen, if the real estate property is good enough for a partnership, it's good enough to buy on your own.

Chapter 25

Managing Real Estate Through a Crisis

It would be nice to have a 100 percent guarantee that every property was a good buy, that there would be no problems, that every investment would be a money maker, that there would be no financial setbacks, and there would never be such a thing as a tenant complaint to have to deal with. I wish I could report that every real estate deal is a bed of roses.

It would also be nice if we could inherit enough money so we could invest in mortgage-free real estate with no debt and plenty of rent to cover any financial problems. But, as you and I know, very few of us get this kind of start. Realistically, we know this isn't the way things happen, and it's not the real world of real estate. The fact is, in the real world of real estate, there are some bad buys, poor investments, and financial problems that can cause trouble. Let's take a look at some of those things that can contribute to a bad investment:

- high purchase price
- defective property
- insufficient income to cover expenses
- dramatic value decreases after purchase
- costly repairs not anticipated at the time of purchase

- unforeseen high vacancies
- overrenovating older property, causing increased debt load
- chronic repairs
- a need for refinancing
- high interest
- high monthly payment
- job change or loss of income
- leaving community and hiring expensive building management service
- insurance loss with inadequate coverage
- using reserve cash held for taxes and using it for personal expenses

The lifestyle of the owner certainly can have a dramatic effect on the outcome of the investment. For instance, there's the ever-present threat of the owner's taking the rent and buying a Maserati instead of a Ford.

Choosing a Common-Sense Road to Recovery

When most of us invest in rental properties, we experience great exhilaration once the rent money starts rolling in. It's part of the Great American Dream, being self-employed, having our own source of income, and building a financially secure future. There's all that money coming in that we hadn't had before, and it seems so spendable. The problem for some of us is that we let our spending get out of hand. We spend it on things other than paying the real estate bills. Pretty soon we're in financial trouble, and this can ultimately lead to a financial sinkhole.

Don't let this happen to your business. Make certain the rent money is put in the bank and kept there for paying the bills. Also, remember that taxes have to be paid twice a year. Have a reserve account for this money. It's important for every small, independent investor to know that, for the most part, rental property *does not* make a profit for the first three or four years. That means every penny of income taken in has to be budgeted to pay the bills.

It is very important when you acquire your first investment property that you set up a real estate budget. Make a financial analysis of the entire operation. Know what money you need and when you need it. Don't overlook any of the expenses of the operation. Here's a list you can use to determine the cost of operation:

- interest and principal on mortgage or loan payment
- insurance
- taxes
- utilities
- cleaning and maintenance
- legal and bookkeeping services
- repairs
- supplies
- labor
- fuel
- soft water
- garbage
- advertising and promotion
- dues and memberships
- refunds
- travel and vehicle expenses

Solving a Cash-Flow Problem

For rental property to operate correctly, there should be adequate *cash flow*. In other words, there must be enough income to pay all the expenses. If there is insufficient income from your property to cover the expenses, it is important to find the cause and correct it immediately. For instance, if the cost of heat or utilities is higher than you had expected, find a way to cut the costs. If you pay the heat in an apartment building, you'll find that tenants will open a window in the middle of the heating season to cool down the apartment rather than turning down the thermostat. If this is the case, contact the tenants and ask their cooperation.

Also, to save on utility bills, consider putting in lower-watt light bulbs in the halls and basement area. If you own the washer-dryer service in the building, consider increasing the cost, let's say, from $0.50 to $0.75. These small increases may seem stingy, but saving pennies here and there will add up to dollars eventually.

Another method of cutting costs to improve cash flow is to do whatever work you can on your own. Rather than calling an expensive service or repairperson, go to the apartment building and see if you can make the necessary repairs. You will be surprised at how many things can be repaired without calling expensive service people.

To increase income, consider raising rents, especially if doing so will make the difference between success and failure of the investment. If the rent isn't high enough to cover expenses, raise it. Let the tenants know why—they will usually understand. However, make sure you don't price yourself above and out of the market. In other words, you want to charge what the market will bear, but you don't want to end up so high that you lose tenants.

It's difficult to continue raising rents. Eventually the tenants will look elsewhere. At a time when the income is needed because of other financial difficulties, the last thing you need is vacancies and no income. How to determine and charge the correct amount of rent is a crucial part of real estate management, something you'll want to learn. A part of the management skill of making a successful investment is to learn not to charge too much and create vacancies. On the other hand, you must learn how to charge enough in order to have sufficient income to pay the expenses.

When you're deciding what rent to charge, you must find out what the traffic will bear. This skill is a primary concern of management. The answer lies in knowing what other apartment owners charge. The best way to learn this is to talk to other investors in your community. I own a property in a large city. Whenever I have a vacancy, I call a friend who owns a number of apartment complexes. This friend is active in the business every day, knows the market, and knows rents. I tell him about the kind of a unit I have and ask what he thinks is a fair rent for that kind of a unit. My friend doesn't think of me as a competitor, so he gives the advice I need quite freely. After all, I own a duplex, and he owns a number of apartment buildings. At any rate, I find his answers to be honest and helpful 99 percent of the time. If I'm not quite sure of his response, I'll call another investor. Eventually, after several calls, I'll get a pretty good idea of what rent to charge. Incidentally, this is an example of how much good can develop from becoming an active member of an apartment association in your city, neighborhood, or community.

In addition to this source of help and information, there's another way to determine rents, and that is to check the newspaper "for rent" ads. Call the numbers in the ads as though you were a prospective tenant and ask how much the rent is. With a little assertive investigative work, you should come up with an answer.

Another method of getting out of financial difficulties is to consider refinancing. If there's a short-term mortgage with a quick payoff, the payments may be too high. In this case, contact the banker or the seller-financer (contract-for-deed holder) and ask to renegotiate the contract. Describe the problems you're having, and say that the payments are too high. Explain that it's a matter of getting the payment down or not being able to succeed in the business.

The possibility also exists that, if there's sufficient equity, you can negotiate a second mortgage on the property. A second mortgage should be undertaken only in an emergency situation and only with a full understanding that the payments must and will be met on time.

Getting Out Quickly

If the real estate investment is a bad deal, if it's not going to work no matter how much effort you put into it, if there's insufficient income to cover the expenses and no way to increase this income, and if there's no way of getting refinancing, consider turning the property back, either on a voluntary basis through an agreement with the mortgage holder or contact an attorney and go through foreclosure.

Keep in mind that if you turn the property back, you can be held liable for some of the losses. For example, let's say that you have a contract-for-deed with a $50,000 balance and you turn the property back to the contract holder. If he can get only $40,000 on a resale, then he can come back and hold you responsible for the $10,000. If this situation should occur, be sure you have good legal representation and advice. In fact, before returning the property, under any circumstances, you should definitely have an attorney help you make the various financial decisions that have to be made. Incidentally, returning the property is a step you should take only if the situation is totally disastrous and cannot be corrected in any other way.

Obligations from Debt

Going through financial growing pains and assuming debt can be difficult for any small business, whether it's for improving property or buying additional property. Many investors have gone broke because they couldn't and didn't control debt. Debt should not be taken lightly. It must be paid back.

There's only one person in a small real estate business operation who can solve any of the financial problems, take the blame, correct the errors, and make sure the operation is running smoothly: the owner of the property.

Bankruptcy

Bankruptcy has become very easy and almost socially acceptable. It's the thing to do, like a status symbol for the deadbeat crowd. You see people being almost praised for filing bankruptcy—after all, they "beat the system."

Many people, including a multitude of attorneys, will tell you to get rid of your financial problems by filing bankruptcy. They'll tell you it's easy and inexpensive (needless to say, the attorney will get his or her fee before anyone else is paid) and that once you file bankruptcy and get rid of all your bills, you can start borrowing all over again. Some will even tell you that it will not affect your credit record. There are some scam operators out there who will promise, for a fee, that they'll get the record of bankruptcy off your credit file. The truth is that they can't and won't. That bankruptcy record will remain a permanent part of your credit file for *10* years. Not only will it have an effect on all your future credit buying but it will also definitely affect your real estate investing business.

For instance, a bankruptcy on your credit record will eliminate any possibility of being approved for an FHA or VA mortgage, and you will have great difficulty in getting a Visa, MasterCard, or American Express credit card. Most major mail-order and department stores will refuse to issue a credit card to anyone with a bankruptcy. It's something you'll fight, in the credit world, and it's not worth the problems you can and will encounter.

In all the years I've been involved in the business world, I've never once seen a legitimate bankruptcy. I say this because 99 percent of all bankruptcies can be attributed to one or more of the following contributing factors:

- greed
- squandering
- poor management
- overspending
- gross financial irresponsibility

The one percent of legitimate bankruptcies are caused because of catastrophic illnesses with extreme medical costs.

When you come right down to it, a bankruptcy is no more than a legal document to steal someone's hard-earned money. Usually it involves money from innocent victims, some of whom have worked very hard to acquire their money. Good investors and good financial managers just don't let themselves get into a position in which they have to resort to filing bankruptcy.

Competent Financial Control

Let's go back to that old saying of Benjamin Franklin: "Watch the pennies, and the dollars take care of themselves." This advice is sound. Actually, it's difficult to find words strong enough to express the importance of financial responsibility in the real estate business, or any other business.

Financial responsibility is extremely important because it is the *key* to the success or failure of the real estate business. The bankruptcy courts are filled with small business managers who have gone broke because of a lack of financial accountability and responsibility. Unfortunately, when some people experience even a modicum of success, they seem to forget the basics of commonsense fiscal management. Quick and easy money, for some people, is a new experience and one that a lot of people just can't comprehend. It's awesome.

A Financial Sinkhole

In the real estate business, that awesomeness comes from the fact that the extra money coming in at the beginning of each month accumulates pretty fast, and it looks like it's all free and clear. Sometimes, consciously or unconsciously, it's easy to ignore the cost of operation. It's also easy to say, "I'll just spend a little bit of that money and nobody will notice." Or, "I'll make up the money for the real estate taxes later." And then spend the tax money.

What happens next is that the debt increases. When it reaches a certain amount, there's a realization that it's necessary to get back on the road to recovery. It's fairly easy to make a quick trip to the bank for a loan and feel, rather deceitfully, that borrowing money will alleviate the trouble and the payment can be made with next month's rent. This is the beginning of that financial sinkhole, and eventually, if it's not controlled, it can lead to a disaster.

What occurs next is the one thing that causes more failure than anything else in the business world: personal overspending. *Personal overspending,* that is, spending beyond your means, is the most pathetic financial sinkhole you can get into. Keep yourself alert to your financial goings-on, and avoid personal overspending like the plague. If you find yourself getting into financial trouble and don't know where to turn, my advice is to not let false pride get in your way. Find someone you can communicate with about your situation. Those with whom you'll discuss these problems will most likely be compassionate, understanding, and helpful. Not only can they help you with much-needed advice, but they can be emotionally supportive when it's most needed. Just having someone to talk with can alleviate a lot of the pressures and anxieties that are brought on with the stress of financial difficulties.

If you see a crisis coming on or if you're in the middle of a crisis, don't ignore it; don't let it linger and fester. Decide what has to be done to solve it, and then do it! Ignoring it only creates more anxieties and headaches. Whatever you do, don't let problems remain unsolved and end up with sleepless nights and, ultimately, an early grave.

As I've mentioned before, seek help whenever you have a problem. That help can come from a friend, a family member, a fellow investor, or even a banker friend. The banker usually won't charge for his or her advice. On the other hand, if you need professional help, that of an accountant or attorney, expect to pay, but, regardless, seek help.

Controlling Personal Finances

It's important to consider personal overspending in relationship to real estate investing because real estate puts new investors in a position they may not have experienced before, that of having to control their own financial life. That is to say, if personal overspending becomes a problem, the tumble down from an investment program can be devastating.

I suppose if I had a guaranteed method for controlling personal overspending that worked, I would be a millionaire many times over by selling it. The truth is that I don't have a method, nor does anyone else. That method can be developed only by the individual involved—the overspender. In most cases, the overspender comes up with a workable plan only when the financial situation hurts enough that something has to be done—if it's not too late and if it's not already a financial sinkhole.

The easiest way to solve a severe financial problem, of course, is not to get into one in the first place, but that's easier said than done. I suppose, for those of us who have struggled on the way up to get where we want to be (financially speaking), when we see all those trappings, we want them, and want them right then. All caution and concern are thrown to the winds, and we buy them before we can actually afford them. One thing leads to another, and we find ourselves in a financial sinkhole.

My advice, for whatever it's worth and as simplistic as it may sound, is to be careful. Spend and live within your means. Don't try to keep up with the country club set, at least until you're ready. If you wait it out in the real estate business, you probably can buy the country club eventually.

In order to get your personal and business financial life in order, set up a budget, and then live by it. In the real estate business you know pretty much ahead of time all the bills that have to be paid. For instance, if the insurance and taxes cost $2,400 a year (and most of these big bills are due all at once), then put aside $200 a month to cover these costs. Put the money in a savings account—at least you'll earn some interest on the money, and it's kind of protected because in a savings account, it might not be quite as easy to get at as in a checking account. Whatever you do, *don't* spend the money saved for paying obligations for personal things, thinking that you'll make it up later. If you do, you're asking for financial trouble.

Operating a business shrewdly is a necessity, as is being a "cheapskate," which is how one of my friends describes me. Well, maybe it's true, but those conservative, nonspending methods work. They help to avoid financial setbacks and also help build a secure financial future. Incidentally, my friends don't see me when I'm going first class and enjoying the fruits of my labor. The reason they don't is because they didn't go into the real estate business and can't afford to get there, even coach class.

I'll guarantee that if you're patient, take your time, live within your means, spend wisely, and invest shrewdly, in good time you too will be able to go anywhere you want and go first class. Real estate can do that for you.

The "Cadillac" Image

There's no sense asking for trouble you don't need. I figure if you're driving a Cadillac and should be in a Ford or Chevrolet, you're asking for trouble. When you do drive that Cadillac and you should be in a Ford, most people know it. So you're really not fooling anyone but yourself. You're not going to impress anyone, and it seems to me that it's just too costly a status symbol. Quite frankly, if you're a beginner in the real estate investment business, you don't need things like that. Ownership of real estate itself is enough of a status symbol.

Here's how buying status symbols beyond our means can get us into trouble. I know someone who had operated a small business, including some investment property. The business did well, but his lifestyle grew faster than his money, and soon he was spending more than he was earning. Ultimately, the business failed because of his high living and personal overspending. As he rode the skids down, after all the despair of going broke, losing all the real estate and his business, Mr. Status Seeker drove from his foreclosed home to his rented apartment in a Cadillac. He just couldn't give up that false, hopeless image.

So take heed. Don't overspend or overextend your lifestyle, and don't live beyond your means. If you're in financial trouble, get control of it. Get rid of the Cadillac in your life, and get your priorities straight. Think financial security first, then think Cadillac, if that's what you need.

It's easy to look back, after the fact, and identify the reasons that people fail. This kind of judgment is known as *hindsight*. We're all experts at it. It doesn't take any intellectual whiz to look back at someone with the Cadillac image and say, "He shouldn't have done it." The truth is that knowing how to avoid serious financial problems must come from more than hindsight. It must also come from a combination of understanding the cause of these failures, learning from those who have experienced the causes, learning from those who have experienced the failure, and then using our own foresight to know how to avoid this kind of financial predicament. It's better to know the answers before the problem arises. Therein lies the key to good managerial skills. It's knowing how to manage money to avoid a financial crisis.

Time: An Ally in a Financial Setback

With real estate, most financial setbacks are temporary, unless they become overwhelming. The reason I say this is that the prices of real estate and the rents are constantly in a state of flux. Most of the time that financial movement is on an uphill swing, which means real estate all by itself, with good management, will create more value, and more income, and subsequently lessen the chance of failure.

If you should experience some minor temporary setback, don't panic. Take your time, and time will be on your side. If you can get through it, the real estate will take care of itself. Patience is a virtue you'll want to nurture if you enter the real estate business.

Chapter 26

Long-Term
Profit Strategies

We're getting close to the end now, and I don't want you to lose
sight of what this book is all about. For that reason we'll go
through a short summary of what's been said. There might be some rep-
etition, but the information and messages that are repeated are important enough that they should be said again.

The end of the chapter will look at the finishing touches and
enumerate, once again, the overwhelming benefits of investing in and
owning real estate. You'll also see how these benefits, most of which are
financial, can improve your life. This summary will be a positive review
of real estate investing, which is a positive subject in itself.

Real Estate Investors: Average, Ordinary, Common People

I can't emphasize enough the importance of this message:

*Real estate investing is one of the best ways, if not the only way, in our
free-enterprise system, where the average, ordinary, common, everyday
person, just like you and me, can build solid security and accumulate any
amount of wealth and net worth.*

Let me assure you that solid security gives a lot of peace of mind, and the accumulated wealth provides a way to enjoy the good things in life.

There's hardly any other business through which the common person can acquire this kind of wealth or build a secure future. Most of the other investments, businesses, or professions take either special education, a lot of capital, or a lifetime of work. Even with all that, there's no assurance of success.

Real Estate: A Hedge Against Inflation

Even if we could make money and save it in a business other than real estate, inflation could still dig into our savings account. Inflation, on the other hand, affects real estate in a positive manner. As a matter of fact, real estate is usually the first of all investments that increases in value during inflationary times. I don't think you need proof of this fact, but look back in recent history. Do you remember when an average home cost $18,000 to $20,000? Compare that with its worth today. There's nothing in the foreseeable future that's going to change that financial growth.

Investment Growth Through Appreciation

Appreciation is one of the greatest financial benefits of real estate investing. Without unduly sapping our time, our effort, and, in most cases, our money, it generates profit. However, we can add our own money to the appreciation that normally accrues over time in the form of improvements and renovations. Renovations to property pay well in terms of equity. In fact, it's well-known that with correct management there's a return oftentimes of two to one for every dollar invested.

Appreciation comes with time. As I've said before, time is one of the greatest benefactors in the real estate business. You can buy real estate and manage it with competence and then sit back and watch its value appreciate. As a matter of fact, real estate often increases regardless of what the owner does. This growth seems to take place in good times as well as bad. Again, I don't see anything in the foreseeable future that's going to change this aspect of the business. It's an ongoing occurrence and almost perpetual.

Establishing Real Estate Wealth

There are proven ways to establish real estate net worth. One is paying off the mortgage. That's called building equity, building an increase in your net worth. This will take some time. You'll find that, during the first years of your mortgage, most of the payment is going for interest and very little to the principal, and it's the principal that increases your net worth. So be patient.

Just as important is making sure the property is well taken care of so that it doesn't depreciate in value. This also will take some time. Be patient.

Appreciation Through Community Growth

There's no question that improving property—that is, repairing, rejuvenating, and fixing up—increases the value of property. That improvement not only increases the value but also increases the cash flow or income. As the property is improved, rents can be increased.

A stable, aggressive, and growing community will also enhance the value of real estate. There is one factor to consider when deciding whether to invest in any community, however, and that is whether it is saturated with rentals. To protect yourself in a saturated market, you need to do some investigative work. Check with other investors. Check the classified ads to find out if there are a lot of units listed for rent.

As an investor, the last thing you need is to buy in a community where the market is saturated with apartments and you end up with vacancies and no income. What I've found effective in counteracting this situation is buying small one- and two-bedroom apartment buildings in the medium-price range, especially older, well-kept buildings. "Well-kept" is important because run-down apartment buildings will not attract good tenants. The nice thing about these older apartment buildings is that the rents are less than they are in the new, high-priced apartment complexes. Consequently, there's usually a good market for these older, smaller apartments. In addition, if necessary, it's a lot easier to lower rents in the lower- to medium-priced buildings than it is in a new high-priced apartment building. (I must say, however, that in all the years I've been investing in real estate, never once have I had to lower rents.)

Investment Capital: Using Other People's Money

To invest in real estate takes little more than the money for the down payment and closing costs. From then on, to maintain and add to the investment, the investor uses other people's money: the bank's, the sellers' when they finance the property, and the tenants', because they pay their rent, which is used to pay off the mortgage. That financial arrangement is hard to find in any other business.

Real estate is one of the few businesses in which the investor can virtually borrow almost all the money and go into business immediately. In addition, with real estate, that borrowed money is comparatively easy to find and uncomplicated to get. The bank or seller provides the purchase money, and then tenants bring the monthly rent checks. These rent checks pay off the loan, which increases the investor's net worth. Not only does the rent pay off the loan but it also pays for the interest, the taxes, insurance, and general upkeep. Sometimes there's money left over, and this is called *positive cash flow—profit*. This phenomenon goes on every day, 365 days of the year. Its perpetuation merely depends on some good sound management skills on the part of the investor.

Profit Growth Through Depreciation and Tax Write-Offs

Depreciation—the amount deducted from income for wear and tear on property—is a tax write-off; more succinctly, it's pure profit for the investor. As we all know, rarely does a property actually wear out, nor is it used up, as is the case of machinery in a factory. As a matter of fact, it more likely will appreciate in value. The history of real estate over the past 100 years, other than during the Great Depression, proves this fact beyond a doubt.

This depreciation factor is truly a great financial benefit for the investor and shouldn't be overlooked or taken lightly. As far as I'm concerned, depreciation alone makes real estate as good an investment in the business world as there is. Talk to any real estate investors, and they'll tell you they don't pay income tax as other people do because they have a real estate depreciation tax write-off.

Profit Growth Through Capital Growth

Once the cash flows through the business, the investor is in a position to put profit earnings back into acquiring more property. Certainly, it might take a few years for profits to mount up, but, take my word for it, they will. Putting these profits into buying more property is like oiling a perpetual money machine. Furthermore, money invested in improvements increases the rents, which increases the value of the property, which increases the equity, which increases the borrowing power, which gives the investor the ability to buy more property or improve existing property, which starts the process all over again. Another source of capital growth is the income-tax deduction allowed for depreciation. Every dollar invested back into the property provides another tax write-off, more depreciation, and more profit.

A Personalized Investment Program

A benefit of real estate investing, unlike a lot of other businesses, is that the investor can choose the price and the amount of property that fits his or her investment program. The investor can pick any sort of property, all the way from a small, one-bedroom home to a duplex to a fourplex, on upward to match the amount of money he or she has for investment.

Also, investments in real estate can be made by anyone regardless of age, financial net worth, or any other status. It is a route by which virtually anyone can reach the Great American Dream and can live in a secure, first-class lifestyle, with ease. There's no other way to put it than this: the average person can make it in real estate, and, as far as I can see, there's hardly any other way it can be done.

Occupational Self-Determination

In addition to financial security, another reward of real estate investing is the self-satisfaction of real estate ownership. Self-employed real estate ownership is a business that provides us with freedom and independence—freedom to operate our own business, freedom to make our own choices, freedom to do as we wish, and freedom to come and go as we please.

A successful and astute manager can come and go at will. There's no time clock to punch and no boss to answer to. There's absolutely no threat of being fired or laid off when least expected. An investor can hire people to manage the property and have all the work done by others, leaving the job of depositing the money in the bank as the only work left to do. Moreover, as I've said before, anyone can invest in real estate. An investor can have and maintain a full-time occupation or profession and buy real estate as a side business. Real estate investing is the epitome of the entrepreneurial, free-enterprise methods through which any person can literally go from rags to riches.

Cashing In on Equity: Seeing Your Investment Work

We've come to a point where you can begin thinking seriously about expanding your real estate investment program. When I say, "Cashing in on equity," I'm not talking about "cashing in" to cash, but using the equity you've established for purchasing more property. Let's take a look.

Fourplex

If you're already on your way and own a duplex this means you're now an established investor, landlord, and property owner. From my experience, this should give you a good feeling. You should also begin to see some of the capital benefits if you've spent some time on your property. This should have built up some *sweat equity* in that duplex. What I mean is that you've done work on the property, which could be painting, fixing, cleaning, whatever. Also, at this point, you should have attained a real estate *net worth*. I'm sure you know what I mean: the total value of your property less the mortgage.

Now it's time to take advantage of your work and move on by using that equity as a down payment for the next property.

Begin looking for the next investment, which could be another duplex, or you may want to consider a single-family house or a fourplex. A fourplex will give you some advantages, one being that it will bring you four rental incomes. Another advantage for a part-time investor is that a fourplex is easily manageable, along with the duplex. One more advantage is that it can be more affordable and more easily financed. When you go to your banker for financing, you'll have the equity of the duplex as security in addition to the income from the new investment to make the payment.

There's a good chance the banker will request that you refinance the duplex along with your new acquisition. The banker, of course, will take into consideration your future purchase, a fourplex or another duplex or a single-family property, whichever you choose. The two properties represents good security for acquiring a bank loan ... and believe me, bankers want security.

A Single-Family House

I mention, one more time, that if there's a good buy out there, don't overlook a single-family house as an investment property. However, keep in mind that this is an investment property, not your personal home, so you get all the advantages of investment property.

More Readily Available. It's an obvious fact that there are a lot more single-family houses available than multi-housing units.

More Affordable. Of course, a banker will also consider a single-family house as good security because it will sell more easily than a multi-unit building.

Availability of Seller Financing. At this point you'll want to take plenty of time. Thoroughly investigate the purchase of your next property. You'll have all sorts of choices. It's been said before, but it's a good idea: you may want to look at one hundred properties before you make the final decision. And if you miss one, there'll be many more thereafter.

This would be a good time to consider looking for and experimenting with a seller who could or would finance his or her property on a contract-for-deed purchase. (All the details dealing with a contract-for-deed were covered in Chapter 14.) With the duplex you'll have established a good track record, if you've taken care of the property and made the payments on the loan. It means that, whoever is going to finance the new investment, the information you provide about your first property will verify that you're a serious and interested investor. Showing that you're a serious investor and make your payments as agreed will be very important when you start negotiating a contract-for-deed or with a banker.

It's a well-known fact, among real estate investors, that sellers sell because they want to close out a property. Therefore, it's essential that the payment on that contract-for-deed be made according to terms. Contract holders don't want a buyer or investor who will run down the property and then renege on the contract, and they don't want the property back. The point is, always be a serious businessperson and investor.

More Rentable. Once more, as a reminder about the single-family house, keep in mind that there are always people looking for single-family homes to rent. Obviously, for the owner-investor, it's a lot easier to rent one unit than two, three, or four. One last word: don't think this means you have to buy a single-family house. I've discussed it because it's an option.

More Potential for Financial Growth

Success, equity, and a net worth should start coming easy for you now. You should begin to realize financial growth in your investment program, especially if you've accomplished growth through sweat equity, doing the work on your property instead of paying someone else to do it. You'll find complete coverage on "sweat equity" in Chapter 23.

You can begin to add up the values of your properties, deduct the mortgage payments, and realize the progress you're making. Part of that, realizing your financial progress, is one of the thrills of investing.

Real Estate: A Secure Investment

Rarely will an investor lose money. Even with a loser, there's always something that can be recovered. The secret to avoiding a loss is to keep the property in good condition, fully occupied with good tenants, and well managed. Then the property becomes almost a guaranteed investment.

Pride in a Job Well Done

One other feature of owning rental property is the satisfaction and fulfillment in doing a job and doing it well. This fulfillment is especially true for the small, independent investor who has bought properties, improved and renovated them, and built them into a successful business, who can then look back on his or her accomplishment with pride. That's a big part and major enjoyment of owning real estate. We can look at what we've done and say with pride, "I own that real estate. It's all mine." Quite frankly, that has a prestigious ring, so if you're looking for status among your peers, this is one way to do it. There's admiration for anyone who's acquired real estate.

The Goose That Laid the Golden Egg

We've talked throughout the book about the financial rewards from real estate. There comes a time, and it can happen more quickly with real estate than any other business, when we can spend the check from the goose that laid the golden egg. That real estate check comes from any one of three sources:

- monthly rental income
- contract-for-deed monthly payments
- cash from the bank for sold property

Once the mortgages are paid, there's a steady cash flow coming from the perpetual money machine. It's money that's 100 percent spendable for the good things in life. This income, the wealth, and the net worth represent the ultimate security I've talked about throughout this book.

Peace of Mind from Investing in Real Estate

The ultimate goal for most of us is to enjoy the good things in life that are truly worthwhile. For those of us who have come up the hard way, I've found that real estate, and real estate alone, can and will provide those things and a way of life that is secure and peaceful.

Remember when I told you to watch the pennies. By now those pennies should represent dollars. And, if you've done the right thing—that is, invested prudently—with your real estate, there should be plenty of dollars. In fact, probably more than you anticipated or realized, maybe even more than you can handle.

There's no greater fulfillment than counting the dollars you have earned and then using them for improving the quality of your life. I don't want to end this book sounding like a hedonist. I'm not. But I have found more freedom, independence, and, yes, religion with the money earned from real estate than anyone can possibly measure.

There might be evil methods of making money in real estate, for example, being a slum landlord or gouging the tenants, but these methods of making money are a waste of time and are unacceptable. Money in itself is certainly not evil, and it can, and will, increase your feelings of self-esteem and well-being. We can talk all we want about the importance of faith, hope, charity, and love, but when it comes right down to it, it is money itself that enables us to be charitable. It is money that gives us peace of mind.

Financial security can bring good things to our lives. Real estate investing is the road to that financial security.

Index

Richard H. Jorgensen is an author, entrepreneur, and real estate developer who has successfully bought and managed properties for more than 35 years. In addition to the earlier version of this book, his articles have appeared in many real estate and business magazines. Mr. Jorgensen has served on the Minnesota Governor's Commission on Higher Education and as treasurer of the Minnesota State University Board of Directors. He is based in Marshall, Minnesota.